The

Ethical, Legal, and Multicultural Foundations of Teaching

WCB Brown & Benchmark
P U B L I S H E R S

Madison,Wisconsin•Indianapolis,Indiana
Melbourne,Australia•Oxford,England

Book Team

Editor *Paul L. Tavenner*
Production Coordinator *Deborah Donner*

A Division of Wm. C. Brown Communications, Inc.

Vice President and General Manager *Thomas E. Doran*
Executive Managing Editor *Ed Bartell*
Executive Editor *Edgar J. Laube*
Director of Marketing *Kathy Law Laube*
National Sales Manager *Eric Ziegler*
Marketing Manager *Pamela Cooper*
Advertising Manager *Jodi Rymer*
Managing Editor, Production *Colleen A. Yonda*
Manager of Visuals and Design *Faye M. Schilling*

Production Editorial Manager *Vickie Putman Caughron*
Publishing Services Manager *Karen J. Slaght*
Permissions/Records Manager *Connie Allendorf*

Wm. C. Brown Communications, Inc.

Chairman Emeritus *Wm. C. Brown*
Chairman and Chief Executive Officer *Mark C. Falb*
President and Chief Operating Officer *G. Franklin Lewis*
Corporate Vice President, Operations *Beverly Kolz*
Corporate Vice President, President of WCB Manufacturing *Roger Meyer*

Cover and interior design by Ophelia M. Chambliss-Jones

Copyedited by Judy Peacock

Library of Congress Catalog Card Number: 91–77587

ISBN 0–697–12841–5

Printed in the United States of America by Wm. C. Brown Communications, Inc.,
2460 Kerper Boulevard, Dubuque, IA 52001

10 9 8 7 6 5 4 3 2 1

Contents

Preface

This book is about the awesome responsibility of teaching. The job has never been an easy one, and recent public criticism, social pressure, and demands for more teacher accountability have not made this charge any less demanding. If anything, the responsibilities are now even greater; yet teaching is still one of the most rewarding professions.

Perhaps because of the increased responsibility placed on teachers, fewer people are choosing teaching as a profession. In the past the teaching profession relied on women to fill its ranks. This is no longer the case as college-educated women now have opportunities in almost every type of job or profession and are no longer "trapped" by familial, social, and economic restrictions. For this and many other reasons discussed in this book, shortages of educators are projected at all levels in almost every state for the next two decades.

Why would someone want to be a teacher in this day and age? The answers to that question are not easy ones. The pay is still relatively low compared with that of other professions. Furthermore, the lockstep approach in career ladders, the increase in paperwork, and the spillover of social ills into the schools have not made teaching seem all that appealing. All things considered, a teacher's job is more complicated and demanding than it was even ten years ago. In the past the public focused on the problems of American education. It is time now for teachers to focus on solutions.

A new century challenges America to prepare its citizens better than ever before. Teachers face new challenges not only in the academic realm, but also specifically in the moral, legal, and cultural realms. The cause of this renewed challenge is simple. We are a new America. The cultural and ethnic makeup of the nation is different. So-called minority children are becoming the majority. As in all professions, teachers have been asked to do more with those who will inherit the world. The need for teachers to be moral models has never been greater.

The authors realize that prospective and in-service teachers are not looking for any easy answers to today's educational dilemmas. There just aren't any. Despite the sense of alienation and lack of participation they sometimes feel, teachers applaud the requirements by state education agencies that *all* be morally responsible, legally aware of their rights and accountabilities, and able to teach in a multicultural environment. This book is designed to help those going into and staying in the profession of teaching, with special guidelines for the resolution of moral questions that teachers face every day. It is not enough to say that teachers should be examples to the students by being even-handed in such duties as evaluation, punishment, and reward/encouragement. Teachers are also exemplary of moral life while in the classroom. That is not an easy role to assume. The legal cases used in this work are designed to show the relationship between teachers and their social responsibility. The multicultural element in the book integrates the moral and legal responsibilities with a transcultural perspective.

Sometimes in a book written by more than one author, it is easy to determine priority of authorship. In other cases it is not. The present volume is an instance of the latter type. While each author began working on an equal number of chapters with only the last chapter targeted for full collaboration, we each contributed so frequently in the work of the other that the final product is truly the indistinguishable effort of us both. To reflect the truly joint authorship of this project, we have arranged to alternate authorship on each edition of this volume. For the first edition we have chosen the most conventional route of listing the authors alphabetically.

For those with an incurable desire to sort out the guiding interest of authors, let us share our sense of the relevant special interests we each brought to this project. Professor Kierstead's work in educational futures research and the sociology and history of education is well known. What many do not know is that he has a considerable background in comparative education and multicultural education. Professor Wagner's research interests have been almost exclusively limited to philosophy with three subareas of special interests guiding his research, namely, ethics, legal philosophy, and cognitive science.

To bring this project to a successful conclusion, we each had to learn much about the other's areas of specialization. Together we hope we have prepared for the reader accessible and responsible accounts of issues that *should* be intimately related to one another in the literature of educational theory, but seldom are.

Fred D. Kierstead
Paul A. Wagner
Spring 1992

Acknowledgements

We both owe a debt to our colleague Dr. Andrea Bermudez. Largely through her efforts we learned to see the relatedness of the issues discussed herein. Each of us owes special mentors who helped us learn to think about subtle aspects of the social world that all too often go unnoticed. Professor Wagner's debts are principally to Israel Scheffler for his insights into the educational relevance of the philosophy of human potential, to Lawrence Kohlberg for his sensitivity to the maturing dimension of human moral experience, and to Christopher J. Lucas for his insistence that analytical skills be laid aside from time to time in order to appreciate the larger issues confronting education today. Dr. Wagner also owes much to his former law professors, Frederick Davis in torts, Jieseph Covington in contracts, and Donald Mitchell in constitutional law. Finally, Michael Martin's book on the legal philosophy of H. L. A. Hart served to clarify many issues in the philosophy of law that had arisen from reading the masters Hart, Lon Fuller, Patrick Devlin, Ronald Dworkin, and Charles Fried.

Professor Kierstead recognizes Mario Benitez for his encouragement to write this multifaceted work and James A. Banks for his insight into the problem of multiethnic teaching. Banks's *Multiethnic Education* and William Damon's *The Moral Child*, were inspirational, although the inspiration may have come, at times, from disagreement with these authors rather than from total agreement. Numerous other colleagues' encouragement, criticism, and suggestions appear in this work, without deserved recognition, but they are nonetheless appreciated.

Children Eric, Jason, and Nicole Wagner served to keep the attention of both authors clearly focused on the issues young ones *feel* they are confronting in our evolving multicultural society. Finally, Nancy Wagner's encouragement of Professor Wagner's efforts has been unrelenting and most appreciated. Fred Kierstead, Sr., and Hermione Kierstead are two people whose names do not appear in these pages, but they are there nonetheless. Our students over the years have also given us much to think about and rethink in our efforts to prepare them as teachers. Many of the words within these pages reflect their concerns to do the right thing as professionals. Paul Tavenner, our editor, deserves our thanks for being open to this book's concept and scope. Finally, Vera Fluker, Marlene Lewis, and Betty Ann Brott deserve special recognition for their secretarial support during the entire process.

Introduction

Any theory of education is, in simple terms, a theory of culture. More specifically, for a society or an individual to adopt a theory of education is to adopt a way of life. A theory of education, therefore, is at its very roots a philosophical matter. It is not just a bag of instructional tricks or a set of curriculum objectives. Nor is educational theory an irrelevant abstraction as some would have us believe. It is a worthwhile effort to make sense of the world and judge what knowledge our society needs.

Any theory of education has implicit within it a notion of what constitutes a "good" and "learned" person. These ideas of what constitutes goodness or full human development reveal the depth of philosophical commitment a society makes for its future. Once an image of a "good" or "educated" person is articulated, objectives can be formed for producing such persons *in part* through the schools. These objectives will be constrained, developed, and even prioritized by commitment already formed to particular political and social arrangements. Schooling practices in authoritarian states, for example, nullify practices favoring the individual over the state. Similarly, educational practices in early nineteenth-century America recognized the central importance of the family as a social institution and avoided offending the most deeply entrenched religions in each locale. Early twentieth-century education in America adapted the worker to an industrial society and utilitarian goals, rather than to tradition and previous enlightenment goals of a more humanistic sort. The result has been the most technically advanced and adaptable society the world has ever known. As with these examples in America's history, once a theory of education is in place, it becomes a matter of implementation (through the use of consistent principles of educational psychology) to determine how best to move individuals to appropriate roles within the grand scheme of things.

To attempt the construction of a complete theory of education in a single book would be an overly ambitious task. Universities and colleges preparing teachers in America have found it extremely difficult to equip students with even a rudimentary foundation of educational theory, though the students come to teacher education with a modest background in the social sciences, the humanities, and the sciences. The curriculum of prospective teachers includes from three to twelve or more education courses, but even this seems inadequate. Recent criticism of teacher preparation programs suggests that education courses teach too little or that student preparation in related subjects is too minimal. The problem facing colleges of education is to equip a student with a theory of life, as well as an understanding of good teaching practice. It is a matter of answering the question, What makes life worthwhile to an individual? What community structures best serve the interest of the participants? What can schools do to make answers to the previous questions a reality in the lives of the public they are educating?

No baccalaureate program in any academic or professional area has been shown to be sufficiently comprehensive to accomplish all that a teacher needs to know. Still, this is the task that challenges the wits of those trying to prepare teachers today. To this end the following chapters seek to make a small contribution.

Before cynics anticipate the suggestion that this book will provide a complete theory of education, the limits of the book's contribution must be quickly detailed. The contents of most "foundations" courses offered to prospective teachers throughout the country can be divided into two categories. First, there are courses with specifically psychological content. These courses deal with things such as motivation, learning theory, developmental theory, dysfunctional learning environments, test construction, and test measurement. Second, the other educational foundations courses deal with topics such as professional ethics; educational law, history and philosophy; multicultural studies; and political, economic, and social theory. The distinction between the two types of foundations courses is not always as apparent as the foregoing taxonomy suggests, and this is as it should be. Each foundation area contributes to what is to become for the student a body of knowledge and skills that function as an organic whole. The student's theory or definition of education includes all areas of study as outlined in these two types of courses. Consequently, not only will there be some integration of the two foundation areas but also there will be an integration of each foundation area and instructional methodology. Curriculum design and educational technology, for example, blur such distinctions and encourage students to construct highly interactive conceptual apparatus that they will subsequently use to govern actual teaching practice.

A book addressing the nonpsychological foundations of education without showing its practical application to teachers could quickly become laborious and ineffective as a tool in teacher education. Yet to be truly comprehensive in education theory and practice, teachers need much more than this one volume. This book can, however, start teachers in the right direction. Since the goal here is to assist prospective teachers to ready themselves for the classroom, the book focuses on the concepts and concerns most immediately pressing on the mind and conscience of the beginning teacher. In short, this book addresses the legal responsibility and professional ethics affecting teachers working in a pluralistic or multicultural environment.

It is hoped that as a prospective teacher you will find answers to the following questions: As a teacher, what do I owe to the student, the discipline, my colleagues, students, parents, and the state? What constraints does the law place on my activity as a teacher? What should I do when my sense of professional ethics and the constraints of the law conflict? How *do* multicultural influences affect the ethics and legal obligations of teachers? How *should* multicultural influences affect the ethics and practice of teaching?

The answers to such questions cannot be determined by references to observable fact or the construction of mathematical proofs. Still, no one really wants to say such concerns are simply a matter of personal preference—how a person was brought up or what a person happens to value. Rather, unlike decisions pertaining to an individual's favorite flavor of ice cream or choice of baseball teams (which are a matter of personal choice and social influence, respectively), decisions about whether or not it is right to be a bigot or prejudiced toward others because of race, creed, or ethnic heritage merit serious, sustained, and collective attention.

We cannot afford to be tolerant toward the bigot, but how can we defend such intolerance on our own part? How can we recognize when such intolerance becomes excessive? How can teachers make an environment for learning that provides equal opportunity? What kinds of punishment should a teacher inflict when students misbehave? These questions and concerns cannot be left to chance or the personal preference of individuals. Rather, they require reflective study of the nature of morality, law, and culture. Such study should include not only philosophical analysis of the concepts involved but also historical study of the facts that most immediately and forcefully led to things as they are.

Finally, students must not be shown "the right" answers to such matters, but how to recognize all the subtleties involved when reflecting on them. How can we construct rigorous and responsible arguments when confronting such issues? How can we discern "relevant" from "irrelevant" observations and assumptions in such matters? It is to these issues that we now turn. In addition to the content of each chapter, the recommendations for further reading will be informative and helpful. More importantly, working through the assignments and case studies presented in chapter 7 will be a way to learn how to utilize the concepts presented in the earlier chapters.

Chapter One

The Nature of Morality

OBJECTIVES

After studying this chapter you will be able to:

1. Distinguish among moral absolutes, moral universals, and moral conventions.
2. Discuss what counts as an advance in the moral domain of human experience.
3. Explain how pluralistic cultural values affect individual moral behavior.
4. Explain why a society committed to pluralism needs to seek agreement on a few moral universals.
5. Understand why teaching is essentially a moralistic undertaking.

I. Forming American Morality

A. Three Forces Molding Public Opinion

Three major forces currently shape public opinion in America: schools, advertisers, and nonprint media. Of these three, only Madison Avenue has consistently and forthrightly claimed that it sets out to shape public opinion. Public schools and nonprint media, which include television newscasters and commentators, music groups, and movie stars, typically claim, or naively assume, that their efforts are a value-free re-flection of social mores already present in society. As many recent studies have indi-cated, however, society is becoming more and more a pale reflection of a "reality" created in film and videotape.

Public school education also continues to have an impact on the evolution of American society. For example, nearly all of the great social movements of the 1960s trace their roots to political ideologies, morals, parables, and other prescriptive lessons originating in the public school curricula of the 1950s. When Martin Luther King, Jr., led his followers on the historic march to Selma, Alabama, they were accompanied by thou-sands of clean-cut, middle-class, white college students from the Midwest and Northeast. The students had learned from their public school teachers that America was supposed to be a land of political equality and equal opportunity. In college, they learned that many states had laws and social practices standing in the way of these ideals. The students acted to make things right, and the media covered their progress.[1]

The power of the media was also vividly evident from that time on. Public demon-strations, with sufficient media coverage, could provoke massive public reaction. The nonprint media were just beginning to recognize what Marshall McLuhan had written: The medium itself was the message. Since that time the media have been accused of orchestrating events to enhance public appeal, of acquiescing to the ex-ploitative efforts of select politicians, of promoting a fast-track lifestyle, and ridiculing so-called 1950s social mores. The accuracy of these criticisms is yet to be determined. One thing is clear, however; the power of the nonprint media to influence public opinion is enormous.

B. Product: Promise of Good

If these three major forces affecting public opinion are altruistic, then the country will successfully proceed in its moral development. If, on the other hand, these forces are counterproductive, progress will be impeded. Worse yet, if one, two, or all three successfully advocate oppressive, dehumanizing, or otherwise immoral ideals and prac-tices, then the moral development of the country will degenerate.

Since, collectively, teachers constitute one of the most potent forces affecting fu-ture generations, they must think carefully about the social mores they encourage and discourage. In this regard, teachers represent an important provision in a system of moral checks and balances. If teachers abdicate their social responsibility and merely mirror the message of other sources of social influence, they work against this system of checks and balances. In such a scenario, the contribution of the teaching profes-sion becomes nothing more than an echo of Madison Avenue and/or the nonprint media generally. Thus, every teacher has an obligation to reflect carefully about mat-ters of morality. Furthermore, teachers must conscientiously engineer the moral edu-cation of their students appropriately. Moral education cannot be left to Madison Avenue, to Hollywood, to Nashville, or to chance. Teachers must take responsibility for its development. All this is not to denigrate the importance of religion as a social force in American life. It is important, but religious advocates vary so much from one another that an issue (such as abortion) rarely unites and mobilizes large numbers of religious communities. In any event, the religions themselves have all lamented the impotency of their influence when compared to the influence of schools, advertisers, and nonprint media.

These ideas are not particularly new or controversial. If anything, they seem slow at arriving. Shortly after the turn of the century America's most famous educator, John Dewey, anticipated the need for education to take the lead in directing the course of the nation. In his famous work *Democracy and Education*, Dewey declared that American culture needed restructuring to meet the needs of the future. At a dinner held in his honor in 1929, Dewey elaborated, "The principle challenge for America is the moral, not the physical!" Dewey meant that the reconstruction of America requires not technical advance but moral progress. In *Democracy and Education* Dewey asserted that philosophy articulates the nature of moral advance and education makes progress possible. With this in mind, Dewey concluded, "Philosophy is the general theory of education." It is in this vein we now proceed.

II. Ethical Relativism and Intersubjective Agreement

A. Who Can Say What Is Right?

If teachers are timid, afraid to endorse a position that may, on further reflection, turn out to be immoral or at least immoral in the eyes of a certain group or a certain person, then the de facto position they are likely to project is one of *ethical relativism*. If ethical relativism is the absolutely right approach to matters of morality, then there is no problem with this posture. If ethical relativism is in some sense morally deficient (or, worse yet, wrong), then teachers must avoid endorsing it. For example, since relativists make no distinction between right or wrong, they must tolerate bigotry and prejudice toward minorities and women. If this is discomforting, then careful thought should be given to each type of relativism to avoid advocating an offensive position.

Four Favorite Brands
Ethical relativism has essentially four forms: ethical egotism, ethical egoism, ethical nihilism, and cultural relativism. Ethical *egoism* maintains that what may be right for one person *may not be right for anyone else*.

Ethical *egotism*, by contrast, asserts that right is a function of what a given person reconciles himself or herself to and that *all nonbelievers are wrong*. The Roman emperor Caligula, who thought himself a god, was an ethical egotist. B. F. Skinner's behaviorism similarly forced him to admit to an egotistic position.

Thirdly, ethical *nihilism* declares that there is *no meaning* to moral concepts. All pronouncements of right or wrong are just idiosyncratic preferences. The German philosopher Friedrich Nietzsche, for example, believed that moral rules are just something created by the weak to protect them from the strong. Nietzsche's truly strong people see no need or reason to ever be bound by these rules—or any rules. They just act on the basis of their wants—which is how it should be, so Nietzsche claimed.

Finally, there is cultural *relativism*. This position asserts that right and wrong are contingent matters *determined by the culture* in which an individual is raised. If friends and neighbors or the majority of the community believe that a given practice, policy, or idea is wrong, then the individual typically does, and should, acquiesce in their decision. People are a product of how they were raised. Selection of appropriate morals is a matter beyond their control. The influences of the community are so strong that individuals cannot do anything more than give in to the community will. And, even if they could resist the community will, they could never produce a good moral reason for doing so, since by definition none exists. That, in the cultural relativism sense, is how it is and how it should be.

The problem with all forms of ethical relativism is that they diminish the importance of moral discourse. Each makes social accord difficult to achieve. Each provokes volatile social interactions among people. Each treats moral development as a sort of fantasy. Notions of right or wrong are conceived as having no function other than to reflect the tendency of one or more individuals' approval or disapproval of a given act, policy, or procedure. Moral utterances become grunts and groans through which people express approval or disapproval. Murder, rape, and prejudice are neither right nor wrong to ethical relativists. Such acts are extolled or disfavored by individuals not because of any moral merit, or lack thereof, but simply as a matter of taste. Relativists conclude that some people find such deeds reinforcing, while others do not. Can moral matters really be this simple? Relying on personal taste alone as grounds for endorsing a moral practice leaves too much to chance. It does not reflect the possibility that people do often achieve *intersubjective agreement* on matters of morality.

Approaching "Truth"

Intersubjective agreement means recognizing a degree of individuality in each observer's perception, while also noting grounds for shared empathy. For example, if someone asked you to name your favorite flavor of ice cream, you would think it amusing, perhaps even shocking, if the questioner announced that your answer was wrong. "How can I be wrong about such a thing?" you might exclaim to yourself. "Only I know how something tastes to me!" And in this you are surely right. This kind of preference does not have an element of intersubjective agreement. Only you have access to your personal tastes. Your judgment in such matters is unimpeachable.

Contrast this situation with judgments regarding the issue of corporal punishment. Nobody supposes that such judgments reflect mere personal taste. No one is astonished that teachers go to great length to persuade colleagues to agree with them on how corporal punishment should be handled. No one thinks teachers recommend corporal punishment because they like the thought of children being hurt. No one condemns corporal punishment because it is "uninteresting" or merely "unappealing." Discussions of corporal punishment are taken seriously *because teachers sense their conclusions can be right or wrong.* An issue such as corporal punishment is resolvable through intersubjective agreement because most can agree that the topic should be addressed and a decision can be reached. All agree the topic is important because the future well-being of students is at stake. Since all involved believe, implicitly at least, that the duty of educators is to secure the well-being of students, no professional teacher is likely to dismiss the matter as trivial or merely a matter of personal preference.

Consider another more general example, slavery. And notice again how intersubjective agreement can be achieved by ever larger groups of people. Currently no country in the world openly advocates the buying and selling of human beings. The fact that such practices no longer exist leads to two important implications. First, it is possible to achieve cross-cultural agreement on the moral appropriateness or moral inappropriateness of the most obvious crimes or the most applaudable deeds. Second, knowledge of morality does advance just as does understanding of science. Nearly every society today at one time endorsed slavery. Nevertheless, neither tradition nor the advantage slavery affords those in power was sufficient to sustain the institution. Slavery is now regarded universally as wrong, morally wrong.

In the United States today, the moral wrongness of bigotry and prejudice is accepted by nearly everyone—even those willing to confess a certain predisposition toward these attitudes. If individuals are so candid as to admit to gender, racial, or ethnic prejudices, they are usually prompt with an excuse explaining why they adopted such an offensive attitude in the first place. Even today's American bigots feel uneasy defending their bigotry. This is an important advance for the moral credibility of the American people. Where there was once slavery, there now is none. Where there were once numerous bigots, there are now self-conscious apologists.

III. Thinking About Morals and Moral Thinking

A. Truth in Morality

The philosopher and educator Michael Scriven points out that there may well be no moral *absolutes*. To be absolutely certain about such matters, however, would require a person capable of recognizing and distinguishing absolute truths from those that may be species bound, time bound, culture bound, and so forth. Certainly no human today has such capabilities. On the other hand, it is possible for social scientists to track the existence of alleged moral *universals.*[2]

Moral universals are prohibitions and prescriptions regarded as right-minded by nearly all human beings at this time. The existence of such universals and the equally universal abhorrence of people against specific acts of malicious and random brutality suggest that there are grounds from which to begin moral reflection—a set of "givens," as it were, from which inferences can be drawn regarding the appropriate handling of other less obvious difficulties in the future. Thus, while few sane people are likely to endorse random brutality against widows and children, sane, bright, and morally conscientious people may debate at length the merits of such topics as abortion, euthanasia, capital punishment, bilingual education, and corporal punishment and dress codes in the schools. This suggests that some acts are universally uncontroversial regarding their moral merit, while others are far more controversial. Since the wrongness or rightness of some acts has universal appeal, there may be some underlying principle that, when revealed, may render appropriate solutions to controversial problems. Thus, if it is agreed that torturing healthy young babies is universally wrong, and acting in a "Mother Teresa" fashion is universally right, then a more universal principle that accounts for this distinction may illuminate solutions to more subtle problems regarding social policy and current schooling practices.

B. Moral Thinking: A Taxonomy

The educational philosophers Kenneth Strike and Jonas Soltis in their monograph *The Ethics of Teaching* suggest a useful tripartite taxonomy for identifying all constructive approaches to human moral experience. Strike and Soltis collect all positive approaches to moral-dilemma resolution under the following three terms: *consequentialism, nonconsequentialism,* and *reflective equilibrium.*[3] Using a slightly modified version of the Strike/Soltis taxonomy will provide an efficient conceptual apparatus for addressing the moral domain of teachers working in today's pluralistic society.

Consequentialism

Consequentialists assert that the moral rightness of an act depends on the degree to which it produces an excess of good consequences. For example, hedonists believe personal pleasure is the ultimate good. Therefore, those courses of action that create the greatest amount of personal pleasure should be pursued. Utilitarians are also consequentialists. They, too, believe pleasure is the ultimate good, but add that pleasure in toto (and not merely personal pleasure) is the ultimate good. They recommend that before embarking on a course of action, a morally right-minded person should calculate the total amount of pleasure produced, minus any allowance for associated suffering or displeasure. The decision to go ahead with the proposed action can only be justified (shown to be morally right-minded) if the result of the calculation exceeds that of any proposed alternative.

A different brand of consequentialist thinking is evident in the calculations of those trying to buy their way into the favor of a higher being. For example, imagine the members of a religious sect who believe that an omnipotent and omnipresent being maintains a sort of celestial ledger in which are recorded each believer's good deeds and bad deeds. Should a credit be due when the final accounting is made, the believer is rewarded. Should a debit be due, then the believer will be punished. For these religiously motivated moralists, goodness is determined by what they believe to be the higher being's directives, and not human pleasure. Nevertheless, their thinking is as consequentialist as is the thinking of the utilitarians and other hedonists.

There are many other versions of consequentialism. The point to remember is that any and all moral systems that make the acquisition of good consequences the point of moral deliberation are consequentialist systems. In this country today matters of public policy are most often decided on the basis of a utilitarian ethic. Consequently, the merit of utilitarianism needs to be discussed at some length.

Consider the following dilemma. You are a first-year teacher who has been reprimanded several times for letting your class get out of control. The principal herself has told you that no one in your class will learn anything if you let a few "bad apples" continue to create turmoil. You have been told further that if you do not control your class more effectively you will not be given a contract to return next year. You have every reason to believe that, except for a few discipline problems, you are an excellent teacher. You also get along well with your colleagues.

One day you are using the blackboard to help explain the lesson. Someone throws a piece of chalk up against the blackboard while your back is turned. As you look around to see who did it, the entire class breaks out in laughter, all except for Brenda. Brenda is your best student. She is still diligently writing down the notes you put on the board a moment ago. You are absolutely sure she had nothing to do with the chalk-throwing incident, has no idea who did, and, in fact, is oblivious to the entire disruption. As you look around, you spot Tommy—the class clown. Tommy is giggling and looking around with a mischievous glint in his eye. There is also Ralph, the biggest, strongest boy in the class. He is sitting upright in his chair almost glaring at you and trying to muffle a laugh.

To your surprise the principal is standing in the hallway and looking in at you. You remember her saying that in a situation such as this, it is very effective to punish the entire class for the misdeeds of one unknown transgressor. You remember she explained to you that when you cannot identify the perpetrator of a misdeed, and the other students refuse to "squeal," you should punish the whole class. "Most of the children," she had explained, "will know who did it. They should tell. If they don't, they are guilty too. Each of them is, in a sense, an accomplice. Making the whole class stay after school will ensure that the guilty party is ostracized by the other students. This strategy will restore your control over the class for a long time to come." You believe the principal is right about the effectiveness of this strategy.

The bell rings. Children are still laughing. What should you do? Ralph is just the sort of boy who would throw the chalk. And, he's sitting there looking so smug. Tommy could have done it too. Nothing happens in that classroom without Tommy's knowing something about it. But what about Brenda? She is now looking up and clearly has no idea why people are laughing. "If I make the whole class stay after, I will be punishing Brenda too," you think to yourself. "And," you groan, "I know that she is entirely without blame!" What about the other twenty-three students? Surely there must be at least one other person innocent of any wrongdoing. If you make the whole class stay after school, you will be punishing at least one innocent person unfairly and probably others. Is it proper and just to knowingly punish an innocent person for the wrong of one or more others?

The utilitarian response to this dilemma is to add up the pleasure you get from saving your job, the contentment of the principal when seeing how you have come around to her position, and the long-term pleasure of the students who will learn more in an orderly environment. Against this you must weigh the consequences to people like Brenda who learn well in any environment and who have nothing to do with the present disruption. You have mixed feelings about staying after school with the class knowing that you will unfairly punish at least one child and maybe more. Assume your deliberations show that more total pleasure is produced by punishing the entire class than by following any other course of action. As a utilitarian consequentialist, you are morally obliged to act in accord with that calculation, and that calculation alone. Consider now whether or not this course of action is right. Is there a different way the pleasure and displeasure created by the proposed alternatives should be assessed? Is there something fundamentally wrong with the consequentialist approach? What would you do? What would be the reasons for your decision in this case?

Critics of utilitarianism and all other consequentialist positions argue that there is a universal prohibition against the unfair treatment of any individual under any circumstances.[4] There is something fundamentally wrong, they say, with a moral system that allows for the punishment of innocent people—regardless of what further good might be achieved by such punishment. Defenders of utilitarianism retort that sometimes the welfare of the few must be sacrificed for the benefit of the many. Is this true? Is this what morality requires? Is there a different way to solve moral problems?

A description of nonconsequentialism may be helpful in arriving at a conclusion to the last question.

Nonconsequentialism

Nonconsequentialists believe that the morality of a practice, policy, or deed is determined by the intentions of the agent. If people intend good by their actions and decisions, then no one can justly criticize the morality of their actions. Nonconsequentialists reason that since the consequences of any action can never be fully known, individuals can only be held responsible for what they intend. For example, orthodox followers of Immanuel Kant believe that as long as their actions reflect an intention to treat every person equally as an object of highest respect *and*, with that in mind, they make the most reasonable decision, they can never be justly judged immoral. Similarly, some religious zealots believe that if their intention is to do the will of God and they have genuinely placed themselves in God's hands, their actions and decisions can never be regarded as immoral. Since Kantianism is the most prominent nonconsequentialist position, the Kantian position will be discussed at length to illustrate some of the strengths and weaknesses of nonconsequentialism generally.

Not only do Kantians believe that morality is a matter of having the right intention but also, as noted, they believe that the right intention is to regard every individual with absolute respect. Recognizing that nothing merits greater respect than human life, the moral agent plots a course of action in which no person is treated as a means to some other person's or group's goals. Thus, in the classroom situation described earlier, the Kantians argue that since the utilitarian position allows you as the teacher to subvert Brenda's interests to the greater good of restoring order to the classroom, it violates a universal moral intuition against punishing the innocent. The Kantian may sympathize with your plight but still insist that there is no excuse—ever—for abusing even one person to gain a supposedly greater good. You may lose your contract renewal. The students may be disruptive for several days because you did not exercise sufficient power to regain control of the class. But no amount of reward or pain can ever excuse the deliberate, unjust treatment of an individual. (America's founders were sensitive to this when writing the Bill of Rights. The first five amendments protect the individual from being mistreated by a self-seeking government representing, presumably, the majority. Sustained national attention to these matters is further evident in the Fourteenth Amendment, the 1964 Civil Rights Act, and numerous federal and Supreme Court decisions based on these doctrines.)

Critics of orthodox Kantianism charge that when too much emphasis is placed on an actor's intention, much harm can result because nobody is paying enough attention to outcomes.[5] The critics insist that any moral theory that neglects the consequences of pursuing certain actions—no matter how well meaning the intention of the actors—is defective. Consider the following scenario.

At one time simulation games were all the rage. They were said to help students learn about prejudice and bigotry. So, for example, a zealous young teacher might propose the following exercise for her students:

"I want us to learn what it's like to be left out for no other reason than our skin color or last name. Now, I want all of you who have blond hair and blue eyes to raise your hands. (Imagine four students out of twenty-seven do so.) Today at recess, lunch, and any other time you have a moment to visit, I want the rest of you to avoid these four people. If they speak to you, be polite, but don't be friendly. Under no circumstances are you to be with or play with these people."

At the end of the day the teacher asks the four students how they felt being ostracized from their classmates. The teacher expects the students will conclude that the experience felt bad. Moreover, she expects they will conclude that being shunned by their friends for a reason as arbitrary as hair and eye color hurts and offends. On the other hand, the students may also decide that if a person is the "right" color and has the "right" name, then participating in a society that gives unfair advantage to some at the expense of others is a good deal. In short, the students may conclude that prejudice is great if they are an oppressor and not one of the oppressed.

Fortunately, this is not usually the outcome of these simulation games. Students generally admit to bad feelings and bemoan the fact that they live in a society where prejudice continues to occur. Often, the ostracized students declare that they now know what it is like to be black, Asian, or Hispanic in a society dominated by white interests. Children often express astonishment at how lonely, angry, or confused they become in focusing attention on prejudicial behaviors. For others, no words can properly express their feelings. A few children admit to strange, aberrant feelings, feelings that are hostile or curiously nondescript. However, one thing nearly all claim is that they now understand a social experience to which they had previously been oblivious. Each of these responses seems commensurate with the teacher's presumed objectives. The likelihood of reinforcing racist attitudes seems minimal, even nonexistent.

We can easily imagine, then, the teacher's surprise if the parents of the one black child in class come in to complain. The irate parents exclaim, "How could you treat our child's life as a game!" The teacher would no doubt respond by saying something such as, "I was only trying to promote understanding on the part of my white students for the minority experience. And, it worked! Many of the kids involved told the class how much they learned of the black experience as a result of participating in the game." Angered further by these remarks, the black parents retort,

"You don't 'understand' the black experience in America by playing 'pretend' for a day. Our child does not have the option of walking out of his skin at the end of the day. Our child should not be made to feel it is relieving to his white peers to know they can, at the end of the day, walk out of a role in which he lives. Things may be tough at times for our son because he is black, but you don't make him feel better by showing him that white classmates pity the challenges faced by minorities, or are relieved by the fact they are not black. Our son is proud of being black!

Instead of misleading children into thinking they can understand the lifestyle of another subculture merely by playing pretend for a day, students are better served by seeing that their moral obligation is to respect every human above all other things! Instead of encouraging children to feel pity for a classmate because of his race, spend your time teaching all children the importance of acquiring self-respect and respect for others!"

At this, we can easily imagine the teacher's becoming angry. After all, she is the teacher! Who do these parents think they are, telling the teacher how to do her job! Also in the deepest recesses of her heart and mind, the teacher knows that her intention was to do a kindly act. She may even find herself indignant at the parents' scolding and blurt out defensively, "I was just trying to help you people!" At this point what more can be said about the chasm that exists between the disputants? Their attempts to understand one another are destined to fall far short of the mark.

What about the teacher's professionalism? Nonconsequentialists, given nothing more than the facts at hand, would have to commend the teacher since she was motivated solely by good intentions. (This hypothetical case postulates that the teacher judged the risk of ill consequences to be negligible or nonexistent.) Furthermore, even a Kantian might be forced to admit that in her attempts to produce feelings of empathetic understanding on the part of white children for their black counterparts, she was trying to produce a feeling of mutual respect. Thus, she was motivated by good intentions, and, from the Kantian perspective, she was motivated by intentions that were right-minded as well. So, are there any grounds for criticism? Are the parents of the one black child in class unnecessarily overwrought? If you were the teacher, would you feel any guilt for what you have done? Should you feel guilty? Why would anyone be offended at someone else's attempt to help "my kind of people"? Why would a parent want the school to teach respect for everyone rather than sympathy for the downtrodden? What are the "right" moral intentions? Is there some reason to believe that having the "right" moral intentions is not sufficient for a person to be moral?

The consequentialist, in criticism of the nonconsequentialist, insists that cases such as this underscore the flaws in nonconsequentialist approaches to morality. Here the teacher runs around trying to make a better world but clumsily wreaks havoc every way she turns. A theory of morality, consequentialists claim, must ensure that moral agents are attentive to the consequences of their actions. Moral agents may not remain introspective, dwelling solely on their own reasoning and thereby giving license to whatever dastardly deed their actions may effect. Moral acts should be realized as "goods in themselves" and this, critics charge, nonconsequentialists fail to do.

Rule Utilitarianism

A third position, which advocates claim includes the best features of both utilitarianism and Kantianism, is referred to as rule utilitarianism,[6] neo-Kantianism, or—as Strike and Soltis call it—reflective equilibrium.[7] This position begins by asserting that respect for individual human beings is the highest value anyone can know. Hence, respect serves as a nonnegotiable variable in any proper attempt at moral reflection. Individuals must not use another person for the purpose of their own improvement. Profound respect for human dignity is a universal requirement for rule utilitarianism. That "universal" is borrowed from the orthodox Kantian branch of nonconsequentialism. Humans must be valued as ends and not as means to an end.

The term *value* is used here in the decision theorist's sense. That is, it does not refer to a thought or stimulation that creates within the individual a "warm and fuzzy" feeling. Rather it is a discrete and objectively held variable to be applied in an algorithm or a moral calculus. No other variables, even in their entirety, can negate or mitigate in the least the value of a person. No good or set of goods or circumstances can ever be "preferred" to the autonomous enjoyment of life of any person. In short, there is never a justification for treating one person as a means, as a mere tool, in some other person's attempt to achieve an objective. We can never intend to seek our own happiness at the expense of someone else. We can never victimize another in the pursuit of further benefit, no matter how grand that benefit may seem. (See fig. 1.1.)

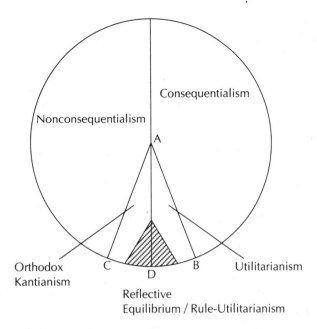

Figure 1.1 The Phyla and Species of Moral

Consequentialism (phyla) is a taxonomic device naming any approach to moral problem solving that focuses on the accumulation of good effects. Utilitarianism (species under phyla) seeks to maximize pleasure while at the same time minimizing suffering. Utilitarianism is one type of consequentialism. The triangle ABD represents utilitarianism, as opposed to all other consequentialist approaches we might imagine.

Similarly, orthodox Kantianism is one type of nonconsequentialism (phyla). Orthodox Kantianism (species) not only argues for right-minded intention but also cites two intentions for their foundational importance. (Kant claims these are two sides of the same coin: a coin he calls "the Categorical Imperative.") The first is that people should respect all people as means and never as ends. The second is that people should try to universalize their moral considerations (be willing for all humankind to act on the rules they devise). Kant believes that a third intention is equivalent to the others: people should strive to be as reasonable as possible in moral matters. While this last is of great importance to students of Kant, here it is subsumed under much else that has been said. Orthodox Kantianism can be represented by the triangle ACD.

To understand rule utilitarianism, neo-Kantianism, or reflective equilibrium, imagine an interface between consequentialism's utilitarian approach to morality and nonconsequentialism's orthodox Kantian approach. This is represented by the triangle ABC. With the interface between utilitarianism and orthodox Kantianism in mind, extract from the Kantian position the idea that no moral rule could ever be adopted that victimizes another person. Add to that concern the utilitarian position that in general moral activities should optimize the amount of pleasure available in the world, and the result is the small shaded area within ABC. This represents the specific amalgamation of the utilitarian and the orthodox Kantian position that constitutes rule utilitarianism reflective equilibrium.

A further alleged benefit of this position, in contrast to the strict nonconsequentialist position, is that it makes moral reflection something that can be objectively analyzed. If moral action rests on nothing more than a sincere desire to do good, then there would be no grounds on which to challenge the appropriateness of a given action. For example, if the teacher in the game-simulation story were, in fact, harming the self-concept of the one black child and creating undesirable pity in the minds of several of the white children, then the teacher should rethink her assumptions. However, for the nonconsequentialist there is no reason to rethink anything if the teacher expressed the right intention. That alone is good enough. Neo-Kantians, rule utilitarians, and reflective equilibriumists insist that actions ought to do more than belie the right intention. The moral appropriateness of an action should, they claim, be measured in part by the good consequences it produces, and also by the fact that it requires every person be treated with equal respect. (See fig. 1.2 for comparison.)

This last proviso comes close to reflecting the concern of the parents in the game-simulation scenario when they challenged the teacher to teach her students about respect. Respect, unlike intentions, is a mind-set that can be held dispassionately. This means that respect is an *intellectual disposition* that can be learned. An intellectual disposition is something a person can work to maintain throughout moral deliberations. An intention, by contrast, is a *feeling* in response to someone or something else. We can learn *about* intentions, but, properly speaking, we never learn intentions. We may even learn *that* on certain occasions we ought to have certain intentions, but again, that is something quite different from learning the intention itself. If a child's intention is to be respectful toward his elders, he has a feeling about the importance of such matters. On the other hand, he can be respectful toward his elders, as evidenced by his actions, without the benefit of any twinge of feeling. In the game-simulation story, if all the white children did in fact learn to be more respectful of blacks and intolerant of bigotry, then this bodes well for the simulation exercise as an appropriate curricular technique. On the other hand, if the white children learned respect and tolerance, but only at the expense of the one black child's being humiliated, then the practice must be abandoned. It must be abandoned because while achieving good ends, it did so at the expense of another person, namely, the one black child. (See fig. 1.3.)

Advocates of rule utilitarianism pride themselves on the fact that they draw attention to the tangible consequences of an action and prohibit any consequence that might victimize another person. Is this what morality should be about? Is it possible to act in such a way that no one is treated as a means to someone else's end? Does this position ensure the protection of individuals and minorities while at the same time promoting the well-being of society at large?

C. Moral Universals

Are the moral directives arising from each of these three approaches more likely to be *True* or universal than some other moral directives? Truth, as designated by the capital *T*, suggests that moral absolutes can be identified. However, until there are people with minds so grand that they can distinguish genuine absolutes from less meritorious claims of truth, intellectual responsibility demands silence in response to such questions. Moreover, since we do, in fact, live in a pluralistic society, claims regarding *Truth*, infallibility, or absolute knowledge in matters of morals are likely to provoke

Consequentialist	Nonconsequentialist	Rule Utilitarian
A. The consequences of actions determine morality.	A. There are universals of morality that must be obeyed regardless of consequences.	A. There are long-standing imperatives for morality, determined in part by weighing the consequences of the situation.
B. Concerned with the proper behavioral response to a situation.	B. Concerned that all responses reflect the right intent.	B. Concerned with intentions, consequences, and the search for consistent moral principles.
C. Decisions may be made in the best interest of the group and to the detriment of the individual.	C. Individuals and groups are not responsible for the consequences of their actions (intention alone counts).	C. Both the individual and the group must be considered. The individual must never be victimized.
D. The teacher provides problem-solving situations. The student must learn that consequences and appropriateness of rules, laws, and morals will change.	D. The teacher must teach rules and the right intentions if students are to be moral.	D. The teacher must provide practice in making moral choices based on situations and objective analysis of both intentions and rules.
E. Moral decision making is best done in a cost/benefit analysis format.	E. Moral decision making is a matter of identifying the proper motivating intention.	E. Moral decision making must be systematic, reflect the right intentions, and avoid offending our most deeply held intuitions about the worth of people.
F. Commonly used to solve questions of public policy today.	F. Commonly used by moralizers advocating the adoption of specific intentions.	F. Commonly used by moral psychologists as the epitome of moral development.

Figure 1.2 **A Comparison Between Consequentialist, Non-Consequentialist, and Rule-Utilitarian Perspectives of Morality.**

Alternative Policies	Good Produced	Categorically Prohibitive
Each alternative lays out a specific plan of action	(Practices or Acts) Total value in terms of pleasure produced (utils of pleasure)	Alternatives which treat one or more persons as a means to some other end thereby potentially victimizing them
Alternative A	22	X
Alternative B	13	
Alternative C	9	X
Alternative D	6	X
Alternative E	− 3	

Figure 1.3 Decision Making

Alternative A produces by far the greatest excess of pleasure. However, it does so only by treating one or more persons as a means, a tool, an instrument to some alleged higher objective (such as maximizing pleasure and minimizing suffering). This is not allowed from the rule-utilitarian perspective. Rather, morally upright people must choose alternative B since it produces the greatest excess of pleasure *while not risking the victimization of any other person!* Alternatives C and D both use one or more persons as a means to secure the well-being of others so they, too, must be abandoned. Alternative E uses no one as a means, but it produces a deficit of good consequences and so it, too, must be abandoned.

Imagine a white teacher who believes that by publicly humiliating a single student in class (perhaps the one wealthy, white, male student in class) she can motivate all the other students to extraordinary levels of achievement. (Perhaps in seeing the white teacher lean so heavily on the white male student, the students believe her to be free of certain expected prejudices and thus are more enthusiastic about working for her.) This situation would be similar to alternative A. Alternative B may be far less effective in motivating students, but it succeeds to the extent it does without victimizing students. This makes it a viable alternative under this approach to moral theorizing.

hostile and unreasonable confrontation among inquirers. The usual outcome of such potentially heated discussion is that adversaries become intolerant of other views, authoritarian, and irresponsible, and they fail to appreciate the fragility of even the most tenaciously held truths. This does not mean, however, that the search for moral universals should be abandoned. It only means that to claim there are absolutes for judging the good life is as ludicrous as saying that the good and moral life is a purely subjective affair. The search for moral universals may still be fruitfully pursued, albeit in a cautious and critical way.

Sociobiology

Many sociobiologists believe they have already identified two universals, one or both of which may be wholly constitutive of human regard for morality. The first is encompassed in what is called the selfish-gene theory. This theory claims that each individual human will do whatever is necessary to propagate his or her own genes. Under this theory, people are more protective of their own children than they are of the children of their brothers or sisters. Analogously, they are more protective of their brothers and sisters, their cousins, and their nephews and nieces than they are of the children of neighbors. Finally, they are more protective of their neighbors than they are of people from some other community. In short, individual genetic makeup determines people's concern for others.

The second sociobiological theory states simply that each organism tries to optimize the propagation of its species. Each person—regardless of cultural heritage— knows not only that members of the species must be encouraged to pass on their genetic inheritance to future generations, but also that each member of the species has a sort of genetic radar leading the strongest to match with equally strong mates. This strengthens the species over time as genetic frailties are purged, generation after generation. Such theorists claim, for example, that secret service employees protect the life of the president of the United States because they know down deep, down clear to their genes, that the species needs to retain this bundle of superior genetic material in hopes of passing it along to future generations.[8] To imagine human genes determining moral issues may be a bit overwhelming. The point to be retained here is that credible scientists from both biology and the social sciences have begun, in earnest, the search for moral universals, that is, prescriptions for behavior that transcend cultural influences and family upbringing.

A final note in keeping with the earlier discussion of the tripartite taxonomy of moral deliberation: most sociobiologists adopt a consequentialist approach to moral decision making. A few have augmented their generally consequentialist accounts with additional ad hoc hypotheses that allow for nonconsequentialist or rule-utilitarian decision making on a case-by-case basis within the individual organism.

Anthropology to Moral Psychology

Other social scientists, too, defend the idea that right-minded moral universals exist. For example, psychologist Lawrence Kohlberg and his many disciples have claimed their studies demonstrate what Jean Piaget's work in *The Moral Judgment of the Child* suggests, namely, that people in every culture esteem individuals who live a life dominated by respect for other persons. Psychologist Carol Gilligan sees two moral universals operative cross-culturally, one for men and the other for women. Kohlberg, she says, is right about how men think morally. Women, on the other hand, employ a more intuitive, though no less universal, ethic of caring. The ethic of caring is based on the sustaining of relationships. For Gilligan these gender-specific moral principles seem to be universal.[9] As noted earlier, Michael Scriven has shown how plausible it is to conclude that culturally diverse *conventions* may do nothing more than reflect different interpretations of a single moral universal (namely, respect for persons in Scriven's case). (See, for example, fig. 1.4.)

According to Bernard Gert, anthropological studies show that with few exceptions all cultures—even over time—have maintained eleven moral rules.[10] These moral rules prohibit such things as malicious brutality (brutality describes the effect of an action, while malicious reflects the intention) and incest. If nothing else, Gert's work illustrates clearly that the burden of proof is on those who want to claim morals are culturally relative and not the other way around. Finally, economists such as Robert Axelrod, John Elster, and Amartya Sen have each noted the need in economic theory

One Moral Universal Can Drive Very Different Sorts of Actions

Moral Universal	Social Context	Interpretation	Action
Respect for persons	A. Eskimos Long ago Eskimos were engaged in a desperate struggle for survival. Since they lived in a very hostile environment with few resources, they needed everyone's help for the community to survive. If an Eskimo became too old to contribute to the well-being of the community, he or she became a parasite on it. When old and feeble, the elderly Eskimo could still act heroically by leaving the community. Respect for persons could be shown by sacrificing oneself so that the able-bodied need only act to protect those who could similarly contribute to the survival of the community.	A. Eskimos With death imminent, the old Eskimo had a chance to show how much he or she valued all others in the end. The other Eskimos did not abandon the old person. But they also knew that if the old person chose to take when he or she could no longer give, he or she was depriving the community of its limited resources and was treating the able-bodied people as means and not as ends. By not leaving the community at this point, the Eskimo was failing to show respect for the other members of the community. The other Eskimos would not abandon the old person, but they would not attend to his or her feeding and care.	A. Eskimos The old Eskimo was expected by all to remove himself or herself from the community and travel over the glacier to a quiet place to await death.
	B. Yuppies Americans, and wealthy Western cultures generally, provide extensive medical treatment facilities to nearly anyone who needs it. This includes many of the elderly. They may be old but they still count as sick persons. Americans are committed to the idea that they should provide the best care available to every sick person. This is reflected most conspicuously in the physician's Hippocratic oath.	B. Yuppies Yuppies with lots of money should see to it that their parents are well cared for in their sunset years. To fail to address this need would be tantamount to dismissing them as persons, as something beneath or less important than the Yuppies themselves. Yuppies should seek their parents' comfort and care as much as they seek their own. Parents have reason to expect that this will occur since this is how young adults return respect for years of previous care.	B. Yuppies Yuppies arrange for their parents to have a cottage at a convalescent center with appropriate medical care.

Figure 1.4   Deep Structural Moral Universals

In these two scenarios, the motivating moral directive is the same, namely, to show respect for persons. However, the harsh environment of the northern slopes and the evolution of a hardy tribal society led to an interpretation quite different from that typically arrived at by most Americans. Where the Eskimos looked to the feeble to make way for able-bodied, the Yuppies expect the able-bodied worker to make way for the feeble. Since moral arguments must take note of the physical and social surroundings, it is not at all surprising that the same moral universal might lead to two such ostensibly different acts.

for some account of how universal moral principles affect economic systems. In particular, Axelrod argues that Anatol Rappaport's TIT FOR TAT computer program shows that in the long run, for any indefinite sequence, it is better to cooperate with neighbors than to betray them. This implicitly belies the human motivation for forgiving and other seemingly altruistic acts.[11] It also establishes the rationale for this strategy's persistence as a universal.

D. Getting at the Essence: Social Sympathy/Sense of Justice

Unlike expressions of personal taste or cultural preference, morality reflects a much deeper concern. It is a concern often debated by well-meaning people. Only the immature, the ignorant, and the immoral dismiss the value of discussion and thoughtful reflection in matters of morality. No value could be placed on such discussion and reflection if morality were simply a matter of personal taste. The fact that moral debate is common shows that people see morality as involving something more than the accident of social advantage or the contingent nature of each person's upbringing.

It is fairly easy to see that morality is about the proper regard one person ought to have for another, that is, for personhood itself. It is a matter of trying to determine what we owe ourselves and what we owe others. Finally, at its most superficial and yet immediately relevant level, morality is a matter of translating ideals into specific and explicit prescriptions for action. If moral universals exist, and it seems they do, then it is quite likely that common ground for agreement also exists at the foundation level of morality. On the other hand, as we move through the many translations to action possible in a pluralistic and culturally diverse society, we find much that provokes disagreement. In other words, while there may be only a handful of universal concerns, translating these into prescriptions and prohibitions at the level of practice forces morally sensitive individuals to take into account varying psychological dynamics, as well as social and cultural diversity. There may be, as philosopher David Hume once said, a sense of social sympathy in us all, or a sense that we are all destined to care about one another in some way.[12] What that means in practice remains to be seen.

The Humean idea regarding a sense of social sympathy continues to pique the imagination of scholars and researchers. Not only sociobiologists and psychologists but also philosophers hope to reveal something more about the motivating force of human morality. Perhaps the most influential attempt to identify this moral disposition is found in the work of the philosopher John Rawls. Rawls describes this sense of social sympathy, or sense of justice, as the product of an alert and powerful intellect common to the human species at large.[13] Our self-interest and our recognition that we humans constitute a common species lead us to seek minimal well-being for all while at the same time preserving an optimal amount of individual opportunity. Throughout the 1970s and the 1980s national meetings of political scientists, economists, and sociologists, as well as philosophers, attempted to draw out the implications of Rawls's work for all human activity. Kohlberg attributes to Rawls the insight that led him to conceive of a completable stage of human moral development.[14] And Gilligan readily admits that socially conscientious and morally upright men do, in fact, address the world just the way Rawls and Kohlberg claim.[15]

Whether Rawls, Hume, Scriven, and Kohlberg are right about a single moral directive for human beings, or whether Gilligan is right in insisting on two, one for each sex, the message seems clear: philosophers, psychologists, and all sociobiologists are convinced species-wide moral imperatives exist. The problem is identifying which ones are operative (and, presumably, *right*). Most important of all, teachers must decide which moral rules are central to their professional concerns. Teachers have considerable influence over students. This enables them to extinguish in children any tendency toward a given moral imperative the teachers themselves reject. They can also nourish instincts in children that ultimately lead to the adoption of sets of morals. Presumably, teachers should help students move toward those moral rules that are right-minded and potentially recognizable as such by nearly everyone.

E. Other Universal Features of Moral Life

Assume for the moment that there are moral universals. And assume further that these universals motivate human beings to seek both the individual's well-being and the common good. Then consider that moral rules themselves have additional features with universal appeal.

Prescriptiveness

At one time or another nearly every individual, and certainly every community, engages in some form of moral debate. As individuals, and as communities, we ask questions such as "Is it right for me to . . . , or should people refrain from such behavior?" The point of such debate and self-reflection is to arrive at conclusions. These conclusions take essentially the form of a public policy recommendation. When a husband concludes it is wrong to murder his wife's lover, he is not being whimsical. Rather, he is implicitly assenting to the wrongness of such actions for anyone in his shoes. The content of his decision may not be justifiable—and others may attempt to point that out to him—but in arriving at a decision he is not trying to alleviate his own psychological discomfort. Rather, he is genuinely trying to figure out the right thing to do!

This phenomenon is similar to what goes on at the community level. In Western society we have knitted our eyebrows and wrenched our hands trying to figure out if women should be permitted to abort an unwanted fetus. Good, well-meaning people present arguments on both sides. They do this not because it feels good to get their way—but because they genuinely want everyone to comply with what is right, what in the moral sense is most reasonable. To achieve these ends, the disputants try to identify some assumptions about right and wrong and about human nature that can be accepted as generally uncontroversial. If that can be done, then, through careful argument, they can arrive at a compelling conclusion about what ought to be done in a prescribed range of circumstances. All such conclusions take on a certain common grammatical form. They do not tell us about how the world is but rather how it ought to be. For example, a biologist might conclude that a natural human tendency is to be aggressive, but no mature moral agent would look at that alleged statement of fact and conclude that is how we ought to be. Rather, a moral agent could accept such a statement as true but then proceed to note that we ought to restrain ourselves in certain situations even though it is contrary to our nature!

Moral debate, which is successfully concluded, results in prescriptive statements that assert that people "ought" or "ought not" do something. In addition, moral deliberations are as vulnerable to contamination by vague, ambiguous, or other ill-conceived uses of language as are deliberations in other domains of human discourse. If people discussing the moral merit of educating illegal aliens cannot agree on the meaning of terms such as *fairness*, *duty*, and *right*, it is unlikely they will resolve any disputes to the satisfaction of everyone involved. It is difficult enough to secure agreement on a set of noncontroversial assumptions. But, even when disputants agree, their success will quickly erode if they are not employing a commonly understood vocabulary. Once the assumptions are identified and agreed on and the meanings of the terms are evident to all, successful completion of moral reasoning requires everyone to use logical operators effectively.

Effective logical operators connect "chunks" of thought together in such a way that a plan of action is seen to unfold. Specifically, these logical operators include words such as *because, so, if . . . then, consequently, hence,* and *therefore.* Each expression announces that sufficient reason has been given for some alleged conclusion. The words *possibly, probably,* and *maybe* are used to express doubt as well as confidence in the likelihood of the outcome of some event (such as a person's intention or the outcome of some action). These guarded assessments are often crucial in deciding how vigorously a judgment or course of action should be pursued. Words such as *subsequently* and *thereafter* denote a temporal order. These words help clarify the actual pattern (or sequence) of events leading to the present uncertainty. And, finally, words such as *but, yet,* and *nevertheless* are used to exclude some entity from a proposed generalization. In this way words protect the users from imprudent oversimplification. The effective use of all these terms is crucial to moral debate.

The expert use of logical operators is the stuff that constitutes courses in logic and critical thinking. If a person is to address the moral dimension of human experience responsibly, that person's deliberation must skillfully utilize each class of operator. These terms connect premises and conclusions together in a manner that illustrates the strength of an argument, moral or otherwise. (See the references at the end of the chapter for further information on logical operators.) The overwhelming strength of an argument ought to lead the responsible intellect to adopt it.

Purity of Moral Discourse

One final universal of moral deliberation needs attention. Moral deliberation and debate should not be confused with discourse whose sole interest is political or social efficacy. Despite the difficulties surrounding every attempt to distinguish what is good and right from what is evil or wrong, this is what moral reflection is all about. In contrast, the pursuit and exercise of power do not require that we feel constrained by any sense of duty or special regard for others. The political domain and many of our day-to-day social activities are preoccupied with just how well we can get others to do our bidding, in short, with the acquisition and exercise of power. These activities can be pursued quite effectively without any attention to morality. But, if morality matters, then it does place constraints on our exercise of power and our political maneuvers.

As long ago as the sixteenth century, a political theorist and aspiring statesman, Niccolo Machiavelli, noted that the study, acquisition, and exercise of power is a subject entirely separate from considerations of morality. A person may be quite saintly and yet wholly ineffective when engaging in power relations with others. On the other hand, a person may be a villain, such as Adolf Hitler, and yet quite adept at influencing others. The point of moral discourse is to figure out the right thing to do. It is not simply to get others to do our bidding or approve of our actions. Often the best results are achieved when people are motivated by the best possible moral concerns and are sufficiently skilled at social networking to "make things happen." Indeed, this very realization prompted Machiavelli to assert, "The ends justify the means."[16] Today Machiavelli's statement has become a slogan used to excuse almost any action that in the long run results in some unequivocal good. Hitler's policies brought Germany out of worldwide depression, but at great cost to a minority of people, namely, the Jews, gypsies, and the mentally retarded. Hitler was the kind of person who could get things rolling and "make things happen." Most Germans fared far better than their neighbors because of Hitler's policies and his charismatic leadership. But the cost, even at the beginning, was of great personal injury to German Jews (and ultimately to all people). Thus, there may be politically effective means for bringing about certain admirable states but presumably there ought to be constraints, moral constraints, on what ought to be allowed in the name of political efficiency. Even if Hitler's policies did result in a more pleasant lifestyle for many Germans, people the world over are in nearly unanimous agreement that morally conscientious Germans ought to have opposed any policies they knew to be so malicious and so prejudicial to minorities.

Two Types of Social Knowledge

Knowing how to make things happen and knowing moral duties and goals are two separate kinds of knowledge. Clearly, the most effective moral agents possess both types of knowledge and recognize that the first must be subordinate to the second.

Teachers like to think of themselves as people who make things happen. They also like to think of themselves as people who do good in the world. Since the most good can be brought about by a good person who changes the world the most dramatically, it is tempting and all too easy to confuse questions of social engineering with those of moral ends. But, the mature moral agent knows the two are separate issues. For example, a talented teacher can be effective in changing students' attitudes and in helping them learn new facts and skills. However, the professionally responsible teacher never acts in such a way that students become bigoted or less respectful toward others. An effective practice should never blind a teacher to its moral inappropriateness. In short, there must be moral constraints on how teachers go about teaching, counseling, or otherwise bringing about the advancement of both schooling and education.

Treating one child prejudicially so another can get ahead may do good for the second, but only by victimizing the first. This is an end our morals proscribe. Morality is about what we *ought* and *ought not* do. Politics is about getting people to act as we wish. For morally conscientious people questions of morality must be given precedence over questions of influence, effectiveness, power, and politics. This prioritization is part of what it means to be morally responsible.

F. Professional Ethics of Teaching

The following chapters will not attempt to specify which moral rules should govern practice. Rather, they will show only that the world of teaching is replete with subtle and yet important moral concerns. Furthermore, these chapters will show how to address the moral world of the practicing teacher in a responsible and professional manner. In doing so they will show that it is possible to preserve and respect cultural diversity while at the same time ensuring mutual respect on behalf of everyone.

Teachers must seek out those moral principles that bond us all together in potentially cooperative union. Educational philosopher John Dewey labored under this task for years and moral psychologists Lawrence Kohlberg and Jonathan Baron have since undertaken it.[17] The task is the challenge of designing a program of education, of moral education! A comprehensive education must be sufficiently humane to underscore how much humans should value one another and sufficiently fluid to allow adaptation to ever-changing circumstances. To achieve these goals teachers must ensure that children are free from all *unnecessary* dogmatism.

Our task at present is perhaps somewhat easier than that, say, of the moral philosopher. Whereas the moral philosopher seeks to solve grand questions about the ultimately moral, we begin with the fact that teachers or prospective teachers share a common professional perspective. Thus, several profession-wide universals can serve as our starting point. Mention of these few will set the stage for everything that follows.

Since the earliest times, long before recorded history, the role of teachers has been to move people away from their primitive natural state toward something more civilized. Humans came to see themselves as creatures able to learn from others and improve their lot in life through instruction. Formal instruction and the value of what was to be learned became a fact of moral life for teachers. This fact gave teachers license to exercise paternalistic control over students to help them manage their environment more effectively. Here rests the central justification for teachers' attempts to engineer the learning environment of students. Such engineering must aim at the betterment of the student. This is achieved by extending students' understanding of the world and, subsequently, their control over it.

Of course, there are limits to this authority. Teachers are not licensed to implement any and all possible means to achieve their ends. For example, teachers are bound not to undertake any action destined to frustrate the student's exercise of autonomy in the future. Making students memorize copious amounts of factual materials may increase the information they acquire, but they may become dependent on the fact giver and reticent about figuring things out for themselves. Consequently, teachers must be wary of indoctrinative practices whose ultimate effect is to hinder students' ability to make sense of the world independently. Teacher concern with helping others learn reflects a basic "other-regarding" attitude toward people germane to the teaching profession itself.

The value teachers place on personhood, that is, on respecting every person alike, is a value that they must maintain—not because teachers have thought this way in the past but rather because this is central to the ideal of student betterment itself. Surely no one, teacher or layperson alike, who genuinely cares about the well-being of others would deny this value to developing students. The nature of the teaching profession itself assigns us this starting point. Now we will see where this leads in the daily world of the practicing teacher.

QUESTIONS FOR DISCUSSION

1. What reasons are there for suspecting substantive moral universals exist?
2. If matters of morality are just a matter of personal preference or taste, why do earnest people bother discussing at length the appropriateness of a particular moral practice? (Keep in mind that people would never debate which is the best-tasting flavor of ice cream.)
3. If there are moral universals, why is it so important to maintain flexibility and openness in a moral system?
4. What are the features of moral reflection, moral debate, and moral experiences that distinguish them from other like events?
5. Why does moral thinking depend, in part, on the skillful use of logical operators?
6. Why must teaching, in essence, always remain a moralistic enterprise?

NOTES

1. For an extensive discussion of how media coverage can affect negatively the development of a subculture, see the essays collected in Kofi Lomotey, ed., *Going to School: The African-American Experience* (Albany, N.Y.: SUNY Press, 1991).
2. Michael Scriven, "The Science of Ethics" in *Science, Ethics and Medicine*, ed. H. Tristum Engelhardt, Jr., and Daniel Callahan (Hastings-on-Hudson, New York: The Hastings Center, 1976), 15–43. For an earlier psychological attempt to examine this same issue, see E. L. Thorndike, *Human Nature and Social Order* (Cambridge: MIT Press, 1940).
3. Kenneth Strike and Jonas Soltis, *The Ethics of Teaching* (New York: Teachers College Press, 1985).
4. See, for example, J. J. C. Smart and Bernard Williams, *Utilitarianism: For and Against* (Cambridge: Cambridge University Press, 1973), and Samuel Scheffler, *The Rejection of Consequentialism* (Oxford: Clarendon Press, 1982).
5. See, for example, R. B. Brandt, *Ethical Theory: The Problems of Normative and Critical Ethics* (Englewood Cliffs, N.J.: Prentice-Hall, 1959).
6. R. M. Hare, *Moral Thinking: Its Levels, Method and Points* (Oxford: Clarendon Press, 1981).
7. Strike and Soltis, *Ethics of Teaching*.
8. See, for example, Richard Dawkins, *The Selfish Gene* (New York: Oxford University Press, 1976). See also E. O. Wilson, *On Human Nature* (Cambridge: Harvard University Press, 1978) and Daniel Freedman, *Human Sociobiology* (New York: Free Press, 1979).
9. Lawrence Kohlberg, *The Psychology of Moral Development: The Nature and Validity of Moral Stages* (San Francisco: Harper & Row, 1984). See also Jean Piaget, *The Moral Judgment of the Child* (New York: Free Press of Glencoe, 1932), and Carol Gilligan, *In a Different Voice: Psychological*

Theory and Women's Development (Cambridge: Harvard University Press, 1982).

10. Bernard Gert, *The Moral Rules: A New Rational Foundation for Morality* (New York: Harper & Row, 1973).

11. Robert Axelrod, *The Evolution of Cooperation* (New York: Basic Books, 1984).

12. David Hume, *Enquiries Concerning the Human Understanding and Concerning the Principles of Morals* (Oxford: Clarendon Press, 1966).

13. John Rawls, *Theory of Justice* (Cambridge: Press of Harvard University Belknap Press, 1971). It should be noted here that Strike and Soltis's preference for reflective equilibrium reflects a strong appreciation for the work of Rawls.

14. Kohlberg, *Psychology of Moral Development*.

15. Gilligan, *In a Different Voice*.

16. Niccolo Machiavelli, *The Prince* (New York: P. F. Collier and Son, 1910).

17. See, for example, the culmination of Dewey's thinking in this matter in the pamphlet he wrote for the Progressive Education Society, *Experience and Education* (New York: P. F. Collier and Son, 1932). See also Kohlberg, *Psychology of Moral Development*, and Jonathan Baron, *Rationality and Intelligence* (New York: Cambridge University Press, 1985).

For Further Reading

Decision Theory

McClennen, E. F. *Rationality and Dynamic Choice*. New York: Cambridge University Press, 1990.

Resnick, M. *Choices*. Minneapolis: University of Minnesota Press, 1987.

Professional Ethics

Passmore, J. *The Philosophy of Teaching*. Cambridge: Harvard University Press, 1980.

Rich, J. M. *Professional Ethics in Education*. Springfield, Ill.: Charles C. Thomas, 1984.

Strike, K., and J. Soltis. *The Ethics of Teaching*. New York: Teachers College Press, 1985.

Logic and Critical Thinking

Barry, V. *Invitation to Critical Thinking*. New York: Holt, Rinehart, & Winston, 1984.

Salmon, M. *Logic and Critical Thinking*. 2d ed. New York: Harcourt Brace Jovanovich, 1989.

Moral Education

Baron, J. *Thinking and Deciding*. New York: Cambridge University Press, 1989.

Goodlad, J., et al. *The Moral Dimensions of Teaching*. San Francisco: Jossey-Bass, 1990.

Peters, R. S. *Ethics and Education*. New York: Scott, Foresman, 1956.

Scheffler, I. *Human Potential*. New York: Routledge & Kegan Paul, 1983.

Snook, I. A., ed. *Concepts of Indoctrination*. New York: Routledge & Kegan Paul, 1972.

Wilson, J. *Discipline and Moral Education*. Windsor, Borks, England: NFER-Nelson, 1979.

Moral Philosophy

Barrow, R. *Utilitarianism*. Brookfield, VT.: Edward Elgar, 1991.

Barrow, R. *Moral Philosophy for Education*. Hansden, Conn.: Allen and Ansuring, 1975.

Kohlberg, L. *The Psychology of Moral Development*. San Francisco: Harper & Row, 1984.

Rawls, J. *Theory of Justice*. Cambridge: Harvard University Press, 1971.

Rest, J. *Development in Judging Moral Issues*. Minneapolis: University of Minnesota Press, 1979.

Other Social Science Literature

Ardrey, R. *The Territorial Imperative*. New York: Atheneum, 1966.

Axelrod, R. *The Evolution of Cooperation*. New York: Basic Books, 1984.

Diegler, C. N. *In Search of Human Nature*. New York: Oxford University Press, 1991.

Elster, J. *Nuts and Bolts*. New York: Cambridge University Press, 1989.

Freedman, D. *Human Sociobiology*. New York: Free Press, 1979.

Wilson, E. O. *On Human Nature*. Cambridge: Harvard University Press, 1978.

Chapter Two

Social Contexts

OBJECTIVES

After studying this chapter you will be able to:

1. Understand ways the environment influences the actions of people.
2. Recognize that there are convincing arguments for concluding that cross-cultural moral principles exist.
3. Realize that cultures can learn from one another.
4. Understand that culture is influenced by wealth, sex, and geography as well as ethnic heritage.
5. Explain why it is important to protect cultural diversity.
6. Consider limits that ought to be placed on some cultural practices.
7. Cite at least eight considerations that merit attention in a thorough analysis of a moral dilemma.
8. Explain how participation in society helps people experience the sort of gestalt shift that makes them other-regarding.
9. Realize the importance of moral deliberation and recognize that as a teacher you can have much to do with how future generations care for the world.

I. From Igloo to Condo: The Role of the Environment in Forming Social Structures

A. Cultural Relativism: Society and Social Forces

In northern Alaska Eskimos were once said to rub noses to show affection. In New York people have long shown affection through kissing. In Houston numerous men wear cowboy hats all year long, while in Chicago they wear baseball caps in summer and heavy wool hunters' caps in winter. Why should such differences exist?

After all Alaskans and New Yorkers, Houstonians and Chicagoans are all residents of the same country!

In the past, there has been much speculation about the origin of Eskimo nose rubbing. (Was it just too cold to kiss?) Actually, while nose rubbing may seem a markedly different way to show affection to some Americans, it does not seem at all strange that people from a faraway place like Alaska might behave differently than other Americans do. Social behaviors seem to swim in and out of fashion for no particular reason. We have become so accustomed to such shifts of fancy that no one really gives them much thought—no one, that is, but social theorists who ponder the extent to which all our behavior may be conditioned by the social and environmental forces that surround us. If an Eskimo couple moved to Florida, would they adopt kissing behavior? If they did begin kissing, would this be a result of social influences, the warmer climate, or a decision for which they alone are responsible?

Men in Chicago may wear warm, wool caps in winter because such caps are serviceable. On the other hand, few men in Houston wear cowboy hats because of their utility. Instead they may claim the cowboy hat allows them to express their identity. But what are we to make of this latter claim? If so many men see wearing a cowboy hat as an expression of "their" identity, is this a collective decision of some sort, or is this an expression of individual free will? If we claim it to be an expression of free will, how do we explain the popularity of the cowboy hat in Houston and its absence in Chicago? If community spirit or cultural history makes the cowboy hat more popular in Houston than in Chicago, how can any man rightfully claim to be asserting his independence in wearing a cowboy hat?

Many "objective" social theorists would answer that Houstonians are simply caught up in a social milieu that eludes people from Chicago, and that is all there is to it. It would be pleasing if things could be explained away so simply. The problem, however, is that any adequate social theory must explain two things about the wearing of cowboy hats. First, why is it that even in Houston so many people never wear a cowboy hat? On the other hand, why do so many newcomers to Houston wear them? Second, what are we to make of ordinary people's commonsense claim that they wear cowboy hats to display a sense of independence and not to protect themselves from the environment?

Two things are clearly evident from these considerations. First, the social structures that characterize a person's environment often produce predictable behavior in individuals. Second, a variety of atmospheric and other physical events can also contribute to the behavior of individuals in predictable ways. What is not evident is the extent of such forces. Is individual behavior purely a function of personal history—a collection of social forces and physical conditions? Or is *chance* built into individual human behavior just as it is into the world of quantum physics and as it seems to be into the world of biological creation? Is there any reason to believe that humans *create* their world as much as they respond to it? Is the notion of free will really as unscientific and anachronistic as some behavioral scientists would lead us to believe? Can teachers assume all that needs to be done in the classroom is expose children to an effective set of reinforcement schedules?

These questions have not yet been resolved. Unfortunately, however, many teachers and prospective teachers have already concluded that such matters have long since been resolved decisively. They have not. To develop a responsible understanding of the role the environment actually plays in the genesis of individual behavior, it is instructive to reflect on some of the various attempts that have been made to account for this dynamic.

B. Origins of Cultural Considerations

Aristotle began his deliberations in the *Politics* by noting that a natural feature of human nature is to be social. Over two thousand years later, the French philosopher Jean Jacques Rousseau was also conscious of the potency of various social forces. In writing *Émile* (his prescription for an ideal education), he advised that Émile be removed from society so that none of the community's destructive influences could contaminate the developing character of the young boy. Rousseau believed that a child can develop the proper character only when his natural goodness has been allowed to come to fruition away from the corrupting influences of society. A child brought up in this way would have strong ideals capable of withstanding the prevailing and corrupting forces of society. Moreover, such a strong and independent individual on reentry to society could quickly identify its ailments and act to remedy them.

Nearly a century later, the German philosopher Georg Hegel declared that all that exists is little more than an expression of society's will. Collective thought and desire make the will all that it is and nothing more. This contrasts sharply to Rousseau's ambitions for the promise of individual free will. Throughout the nineteenth century, Karl Marx and other like-minded socialists came to believe that the future of humankind was at the mercy of various inevitable social forces. And, finally, twentieth-century philosophy came to be dominated by, or at least was most characteristically represented by, the Viennese philosopher Ludwig Wittgenstein. Wittgenstein claimed that language, concepts of personhood and self, and even science and mathematics are themselves a function of interacting social forces. The idea that science itself is an inherently social enterprise continues to be advocated by physicist Thomas Kuhn. Kuhn's *The Structure of Scientific Revolution* was the single-most cited book in the 1970s, according to the American Literary Association. Lesser-known philosopher Paul Feyerbend, educator John McPeck, sociologist Robert Merton, and many, many others concur.[1]

Present Determinism

Probably at no other time in history has humankind been so convinced that all human action is little more than a function of competing social forces. At the turn of the twentieth century, French sociologist Émile Durkheim spoke of a community geist (or collective spirit), explaining that the community itself is greater than the sum of its parts. Presumably, for Durkheim, society is more complicated, more viable than any number of human beings alone can make it. Only a little less modest is the Spanish philosopher José Ortega y Gasset's claim that societies change not because of the dissemination of good ideas or superb leadership, but rather because of the accumulating momentum of mass movements. In his book *The Revolt of the Masses*, Ortega y Gasset says that when the masses gain control the community's social fabric disintegrates beyond repair. For Ortega y Gasset, extensive social change is both inevitable and well beyond the control of individuals. Finally, American psychologists E. L. Thorndike, J. B. Watson, and B. F. Skinner each denounced free will as a grossly misleading myth. To know what makes an individual tick, scientists need only consider measurable elements in the individual's past and present experience.[2]

Even social scientists critical of the behavioral tradition typically remain strictly deterministic in their view of human nature. For example, psycholinguist and social critic Noam Chomsky, who unleashed a merciless attack on the behaviorist views of B. F. Skinner, remains resolute in his conviction that the human mind is a determined mechanism governed by natural laws. Specifically, Chomsky likens the mind to a computer-processing unit, forever destined to process all data input in accord with preexisting rules and genetically hard-wired into the brain.[3] In short, few scholars today attribute any self-determining powers to human beings.

More Than Culture

The idea that human beings are not, and cannot in any way be, self-determining strikes alarm into the hearts of many classroom teachers. Teachers know that the goals of education cannot be neatly encapsulated into a mechanistic model of humankind. Yet even in the educational literature the idea that humans are without autonomy is widely pervasive. For example, while teachers are told to teach children about various cultures, they are discouraged from having the children consider the superiority of one culture's habits, values, or beliefs to those of another. Of course, if the habits, values, and beliefs of one culture are meritoriously indistinguishable from one another, why should habits, values, and beliefs be studied in the first place? If all differences are simply a matter of geographical and historical accident, then no one needs to care what goes on in another culture. All that can be noticed is difference—not merit, intellectual sophistication, or moral goodness. This is, in fact, the position taken today by so-called deconstructionists.[4] Indeed, even the belief that people ought to know about other cultures must itself be demeaned by such advocates as just one more culturally contingent accident. For the deconstructionist, culture—and the individual's place in it—is a chance occurrence with nothing more to recommend it than the fact that teachers, media-types, and a few intelligentsia are currently in the habit of talking that way.

The Value of Studying Other Cultures

Curiously, the most persuasive voice protesting this relativistic thinking is political conservative Allan Bloom. Bloom denounces cultural relativism as an attack on the value of multicultural studies for reasons similar to those already stated. He states that the most persuasive argument for multicultural studies is that judgments of good and bad, right and wrong *can be made cross-culturally*. Students should study various cultures respectfully. They should look with an eye to the *goods* inherent in those cultures, goods that may be lacking in the students' own. When making judgments of cultural merit, students should be encouraged to incorporate the goods of other cultures into their own.[5] In practice, teachers may be encouraging this kind of thinking on the part of students. However, the longer teachers are subjected to college professors who demand adherence to the politically correct dogma that "truths" are all culturally determined and that individuals cannot get beyond the inhibitions imposed by their own culture, the more likely the earnest study of various cultures will be trivialized.

The point in studying various cultures should be to learn from them how to improve our own. Engaging in this process requires evaluation. While we must be careful not to be too jingoistic and make whatever evaluations suit our fancy (or seem most commensurate with our own community's way of seeing things), we should not shrink from the responsibility of drawing students' attention to the goods and evils of our culture as well as to the additional goods, or evils, of other cultures.

People do learn from other cultures how to change and improve their own. Schools should be the principal place for this learning to occur. For example, the ancient Greeks were often overrun by their adversaries. Nevertheless, Greek culture won out and the conquerors shortly fell under the ways of Greek culture itself. This shows that cultural goods have a life of their own—a life that merits serious study by students of all ages.

From Cultural Influence to Cultural Advance

The foregoing point must be reiterated. Not only do cultures have the power to change neighboring politically or militarily dominant communities, but also they have the power to do so to the moral well-being of both. For example, as noted in the previous chapter, slavery was generally accepted by most countries, in the East and West, just two millennia ago. Today no country anywhere in the world even attempts the public advocacy of slavery. Surely, that is a giant step for humankind, a correct step. Again, until just one hundred years ago women were accorded a negatively deferential status compared with their male counterparts in all Western cultures and in most Eastern cultures as well. This has now changed. In most societies today, women are accorded legal rights identical to those of men. Of course, numerous exceptions remain. The countries of the Middle East and parts of Africa are perhaps the most obvious. Still, women have achieved equality before the law in a majority of countries. In other countries resentment is growing between those advocating equality and those opposed to it. Thus, a seemingly inevitable social consciousness is emerging on these issues. Moreover, countries that refuse to grant lawful equality to women or to various racial or religious minorities are likely to incur the ire of the international community. Consider, for example, the Commonwealth of Soviet Nations and South Africa. In the case of the former, Jews are oppressed because of religious and ethnic background. In South Africa, blacks are oppressed because of skin color. In each instance citizens from other developed countries have decried the oppression in these countries. They may even encourage their own governments to enact sanctions against those morally deficient sovereignties.

In the United States, where equal treatment of women and minorities is assured under the law, there remain many areas in which these groups still suffer the disadvantage of a less overt, but often more insidious, kind of prejudice. Nevertheless, whenever this is pointed out, public outcry generally occurs and the relative moral and legal merits of such practices are discussed at length. More often than not, change is implemented to redress grievances or otherwise improve the lot of the oppressed.

Admittedly, changes in social practice do not always better society. We need only recall the Holocaust to be reminded of this fact. But even with such discouraging episodes in mind, we can note that the moral progress of humankind nevertheless seems to advance much the same way the stock market does. There are recessions and even an occasional depression in the day-to-day, and month-to-month, behavior of the market. Similar "peaks and valleys" occur in the moral behavior of large groups of human beings. Yet despite disappointing lapses of progress, over the long run, the market and moral achievements of humankind swing ever upward. As long as we do not blow ourselves off the face of the earth, saturate our environment with poisons, or give an antagonistic virus an evolutionary edge during one of the inevitable moral recessions, the future of humankind will reflect an increasing concern with doing right toward one another and toward all the other creatures of the planet. A given culture may prove to be in moral decline at any point in time. But, in the long run, it will usually acquiesce to cultural pressures from outside to reform itself in morally commendable ways.

Culture and physical environment do strongly influence the behavior of individuals. But individual behavior reflects more than mere responsiveness to such forces. Individual human behavior is often quite innovative and may, at times, lead to massive changes in society at large. Furthermore, there is reason to believe that moral thinking advances in much the way that scientific advance is achieved—not through steady progress toward "truth" but rather through fits and starts that eventually reveal a more self-conscious and deliberate human spirit. The principal agent of change in human behavior, moral thinking, and even science in all cultures has traditionally been and remains the schools.

II. Professional, Establishment, and Pluralistic Public Benefits and Dangers of Cultural Diversity

Every large nation is comprised of a set of cultures, or at least microcultures, each of which attempts to influence the direction of the nation. These competing interests can become aggressive and intolerant of one another. The 1990s have seen much of this sort of thing occurring in Eastern Europe and the Commonwealth of Soviet Nations. The conflict competing interests bring can be devastating to a nation and to its people. But the absence of any conflict can be destructive as well!

In the 1930s Hitler mandated the curriculum for German schools. Hitler wanted a single-minded nation to support him in his quest for world domination. He sought to destroy any interest group or person with interests not entirely commensurate with his own. Internally, Hitler very nearly succeeded. Externally, he failed. Not only did the victorious nations destroy Hitler's Germany on the field of battle but also they split Germany geographically for nearly fifty years and mandated a school curriculum directed at removing Nazi excesses from the behavior of future generations of Germans. Hitler attempted to impose a homogenous set of ideals on the German people. To the extent that he succeeded, the moral advance of the German people was preempted. The moral advance of any people requires a certain amount of diversity. Without diversity there are no seeds of creation from which a new and better society can evolve. Consequently, it is in every nation's best interest to encourage diversity. The question is, How much diversity is too much?

A. Schools and Culture

Hitler's Germany shows that for nations the most potent diversity is cultural. Consequently, if public schools are to serve the nation, they must preserve respect for cultural diversity. Only when cultural diversity is respected can individuals and groups coexist in a collegial manner, a manner that protects and serves the well-being of all. To accomplish this task the curriculum of the public schools must foster two aptitudes with respect to cultural diversity. First, students must learn how various cultures influence the United States. Second, students must examine specific cultural practices peculiar to each group and consider how incorporating these practices into the macroculture might help or hinder the nation.

The instructional techniques of teachers must also model and thereby encourage students to develop specific attitudes toward the study of cultural diversity. First, teaching techniques must encourage esteem in each student for different cultures. Specifically, the student must be shown the importance of reserving judgment about a cultural practice until the practice has been studied *in context* sufficiently to understand its intent as well as its outcomes. For example, if the intent of a practice is to honor people while victimizing no one, this would certainly count in the practice's favor. On the other hand, if the intent is merely to serve the interests of a select few while imposing considerable burden on many innocents, this would count against the practice. Requiring that everyone remain quietly attentive to a duly recognized speaker's remarks illustrates a practice of the first kind while discriminatory classroom seating arrangements illustrate the second.

High Culture and Establishment

The social forces impinging on the schools extend well beyond the cultural—or, at least, beyond ethnically derived forces. People may participate in the establishment regardless of race, creed, or ethnic background. This was equally true of access to high culture in Germany and Austria. For example, prior to World War I in both Germany and Austria, the ability to speak grammatically correct German was said to be indicative of "high culture." The term *high culture* then meant something very much like the current expression *establishment*. Obviously, it is no secret that white northern European and Judeo-Christians dominate the American establishment just as they did the high culture of turn-of-the-century Germany and Austria. But, if a person were fortunate enough to secure the proper schooling, acquire an understanding of the arts, accumulate a substantial amount of money, and demonstrate familiarity with rules of etiquette, then access to the establishment became relatively open. Of course, access to proper schooling was and remains a socioeconomic factor in virtually all countries and among all ethnic groups.

The terms *high culture* and *establishment* are important concepts for understanding the social phenomenon of class access. *High culture* ostensibly refers to sophistication, refinement, the good life—all those things that distinguish an individual from the masses, the common people. Yet the most distinguishing feature of the masses or the so-called common people is lack of control over the direction of government. Thus, while practitioners of high culture see themselves as persons of taste, refinement, and so on, there is no denying that political power does much to determine whose voice will decide what counts as "good taste."

The term *control* identifies the single-most important feature distinguishing the establishment from the rest of society. However, its connotative image is so alluring that we can easily forget that there is more to being a part of this social class than sharing in the exercise of disproportionate political power. The ancient Greeks, for instance, were enslaved by the victorious Romans. However, after a relatively short period, the rich and powerful Romans were smitten by Greek culture, including Greek art, theatre, philosophy, and science. Roman soldiers had defeated Greek soldiers in battle, but enslaved Greeks brought with them a culture that ultimately championed itself over the ruling class. A culture is not likely to survive the continued animosity of rich and powerful adversaries. But a rich and powerful intellectual tradition is often far more alluring than the high and mighty ever suspect. Still, the assets of a culture may erode before they are recognized as valuable by the ruling class. This is a terrible and not wholly uncommon event.

Valuable cultural innovations seem to have a forcefulness all their own. But, as noted, the collective power of an entrenched establishment is hard to overestimate. Things go best when the establishment is quick to endorse the merit of culturally distinct practices. Things are at best chancy when they do not. For example, in the early days of the American republic few people saw the value in reading, writing, and arithmetic. Even fewer adults saw much point in distracting students from their chores for something as frivolous as schooling. Nevertheless, pastors, merchants, plantation owners, and other establishment-types saw the value in these skills and implemented educational programs to instill them in their respective communities.

In contrast, there are times when the establishment endorses a conspicuously self-serving practice, and to no one's advantage but its own. Historian Joel Spring claims this was the case when the robber-baron philanthropists at the turn of the century made such a public display of supporting public education, in particular, public vocational education. According to Spring, the great industrialists saw that a productive work force must be orderly and able to follow directions. Whatever else schools may or may not do, they should at least produce graduates who are moderately well disciplined and willing to follow orders. Furthermore, since American business instructs its workers in English, it seemed imperative that at a time of great immigration, workers should learn the language of the establishment in order to serve the business interests of the establishment. In short, the schools were seen as vehicles for preparing a work force able to follow orders in the vernacular of the ruling class.

Vocational education offered industrialists the additional advantage of providing minimal training for future generations of skilled and semiskilled workers. In all this, Spring contends, the establishment was looking after its own to the detriment of the poor. The schools were becoming the tools of the rich and powerful. They were the unwitting instruments of oppressors who were securing a well-trained work force, while at the same time discouraging common people from seeking their own fortunes.[6] In Spring's portrayal of establishment interests and support for vocational education, the Marxist historian sounds very much like the conservative educational critic Mortimer Adler. Throughout the 1980s, Adler, the former editor of the *Encyclopaedia Britannica*, toured the country, encouraging state legislators to follow the educational reform program he outlined in two books titled, respectively, *The Paideia Proposal* and *The Paideia Program*.[7]

B. *Paideia Program:* An Educational Syllabus

In these two books, Adler advocated that everyone be taught the sorts of things establishment-types have always wanted their own children to learn, namely, reading, writing, arithmetic, the arts and sciences, and something approximating character education. In pursuing this program of general education for all, Adler reasoned, we can remove the barriers that prevent ethnic and cultural groups from sharing freely in the American dream. However, Adler assumed much about what counts as the American dream or, shall we say, his version of the American dream.

Defining the American Dream
If America chooses to accommodate greater variety in cultural pursuits and greater tolerance for inherent cultural diversity, then the American dream may no longer be definable simply in terms of access to the establishment. (See fig. 2.1.) However, it

The correlation between low culture and socioeconomic disadvantage is high. The path from low culture/socioeconomic disadvantage to establishment status is twofold. The path to the left, the solid black line, is the most common. Through acquiring the trappings of high culture, the individual's opportunities for entering the establishment expand greatly. Very few people are able to follow the path of the dotted line from the lowest classes directly to establishment status. Note, too, even if a person succeeds in this it is virtually impossible to acquire high culture. Hence, no dotted line goes from Establishment to High Culture.

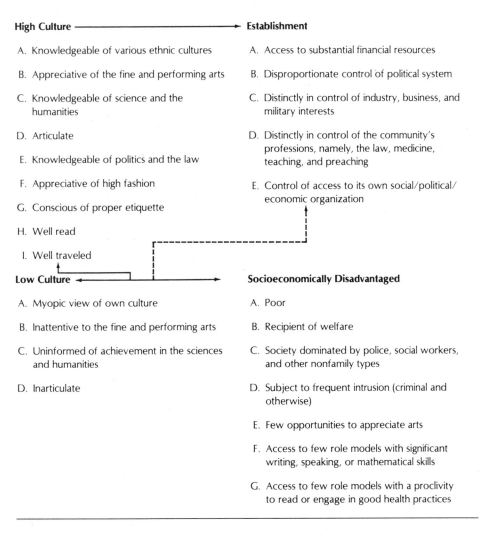

High Culture ⟶ **Establishment**

A. Knowledgeable of various ethnic cultures

B. Appreciative of the fine and performing arts

C. Knowledgeable of science and the humanities

D. Articulate

E. Knowledgeable of politics and the law

F. Appreciative of high fashion

G. Conscious of proper etiquette

H. Well read

I. Well traveled

Low Culture ⟵

A. Myopic view of own culture

B. Inattentive to the fine and performing arts

C. Uninformed of achievement in the sciences and humanities

D. Inarticulate

A. Access to substantial financial resources

B. Disproportionate control of political system

C. Distinctly in control of industry, business, and military interests

D. Distinctly in control of the community's professions, namely, the law, medicine, teaching, and preaching

E. Control of access to its own social/political/economic organization

Socioeconomically Disadvantaged

A. Poor

B. Recipient of welfare

C. Society dominated by police, social workers, and other nonfamily types

D. Subject to frequent intrusion (criminal and otherwise)

E. Few opportunities to appreciate arts

F. Access to few role models with significant writing, speaking, or mathematical skills

G. Access to few role models with a proclivity to read or engage in good health practices

Figure 2.1 Roads to the American Dream

must be admitted that as things now stand, access to the establishment is limited. It is limited because the individual shares little of the establishment's intellectual heritage or its moral sensibilities. Consequently, to ensure as much access as possible, it is advisable to incorporate the customs, mores, and intellectual pursuits of the establishment into the general curriculum of the public schools. Of course, in recommending this, we risk creating an atmosphere of intolerance toward ethnic and other cultural practices that are not easily accommodated by the elite—regardless of the ultimate value of such practices. This intolerance limits the cultural diversity required for advancing the moral growth of the nation as described earlier. (Also, while the foregoing point was specific to moral progress, similar arguments can be made on behalf of cultural diversity serving as a means for securing aesthetic and intellectual advance as well.) So what are we to do?

Unfortunately, no obvious and pat answers to this question exist. This matter of educational policy continues to perplex professional educators, politicians, and students of educational practice generally. On the one hand, the natural inclination of any establishment is to maintain the status quo. For the establishment to maintain the status quo it must ensure that a wide variance in curricular offerings and instructional techniques pervades the educational world and thus deepens the chasms between groups.

Children of the upper middle class will get a healthy dose of the liberal arts, mathematics, and the sciences. The instructional technique will be highly interactive, encouraging much discussion between student and student, and student and teacher. The results of such teaching have been shown to be highly successful. Psychologist Robert Sternberg of Yale has demonstrated that interaction between child and adult in the first seven years of life is much more predictive of how the child will do on standard IQ tests than is the child's socioeconomic status or the parents' IQ scores.[8]

Children who are encouraged to respond to open-ended questions and present their own view of the world tend to do better on IQ tests than do children who go through life answering adult queries with "yes," "no," and "I don't know." It is no accident that children in wealthy suburban schools tend to score high on IQ tests. They are encouraged to be loquacious. In contrast, children in inner-city schools not only tend to score low on IQ tests, but also, not unconnectedly, they suffer the endless drone of truth-giving pedagogues. The only relief they enjoy is occasioned by the rebellious and generally irreverent protests of the interred students themselves.

Access to the Establishment

All too often it is assumed that the establishment preserves its grip over the public by requiring disadvantaged minorities to study a curriculum tailor-made for the middle class. This just is not true. As Jonathan Kozol argued in his left-wing essay *Free Schools,* if inner-city children are to have a real opportunity, then teachers must be committed to helping the children score high on the SAT and the ACT and acquire whatever other academic skills maximize the range of opportunities society extends to the intellectually talented.[9] Range of choice is a relative concept in American society. It is relative to intellectual talent in some degree, but is mostly relative to *demonstrated intellectual precocity.* Economically advantaged children get to demonstrate whatever precocity they may have. Poor children rarely get the chance.

In this vein, the heroic story of Jaime Escalante, a high school teacher in East Los Angeles, illustrates the profundity of Kozol's charges. Escalante left a well-paying job as an engineer to return to the barrio and teach in a school populated by students both the establishment and the district had implicitly written off as uneducable. The school authorities and Escalante's colleagues tried to convince him that the students were intellectually disabled or emotionally beyond help. In either case, they explained, Escalante was wasting his time in trying to help his students learn calculus competitive with the best students in the country.

Escalante ignored the advice of the "experts" and other experienced teachers. Instead, he set out to achieve what others said could not be done. He turned an entire class of minority students into a group of mathematical superstars. Specifically, in his first year of teaching, Escalante succeeded in getting eighteen students through the calculus section of the National Advanced Placement Calculus Examination. This was the highest record of any school in the country at the time.

A short time before Escalante began his teaching, a black teacher, Marva Collins, was working miracles with minority children in Chicago. Collins was disgruntled with the subject matter and with the way the Chicago school district presented it to minority children. Seeing no way to work through the school district, Collins set up her own school. Her first students were minority children from the inner city. They were also children the school district regarded as among the least educable in the district. Collins set out to teach these children the basics, plus an understanding of some of the great intellectual achievements of Western culture. In contrast to school authorities who would have been happy if these children learned simply to read and write, master-teacher Collins set out to teach the children Plato, Shakespeare, and many other things essential to scoring high on the SAT. Like Kozol and Escalante, Collins believed that teachers maximize students' options by sharing with them the education routinely prescribed for the highest achieving group. The path to the upper middle class runs right through its education. And this is decidedly no accident. If a student graduates and decides to stay in the neighborhood, working at a menial job, then so be it. But, if young people never dream of leaving the neighborhood, never acquire the skills that would allow for their departure, then there is no free, informed choice.

Martin Luther King Jr., in his "I Have a Dream" speech, spoke of a world in which all races and all ethnic groups have an opportunity to seek their fortunes and find their rightful place in life. Teachers like Collins, Escalante, and Kozol make King's dream a reality. These radicals of the educational world mounted their frontal assault on the establishment by giving to minority children an education that for too long has been a birthright for a select few. These teachers did more to give their students access to the establishment than any large-scale governmental social program currently in existence. They shared the establishment's high culture with ostracized minorities. In doing this, they pioneered what is now called site-based management and promoted a universal, transcultural curriculum.

When Kozol wrote *Free Schools*, he was a young white man living and teaching in a black inner-city neighborhood. He was brash, filled with anger, and always ready to direct scorn toward the establishment. It is ironic that Kozol's recommendations for upsetting the hold of the establishment parallel the educational recommendations of former Secretary of Education William Bennett, Mortimer Adler, and others whom critics label as elitists and conservatives. Giving minority students access to the conceptual inheritance of the establishment is the surest way of opening doors to privilege and opportunity—doors that for too long have been closed to American minorities.

While curricular uniformity may seem to be in the establishment's own best interest, it is not. The theme of allowing for cultural diversity is easily exploited by a self-interested aristocracy to create social barriers that are all but impossible to overcome. Having vastly different curricula and educational goals dilutes the potential of minorities to succeed in the establishment's world. A strong uniform curriculum is by far the greatest threat to the establishment's intent to preserve the social privilege of its offspring. The preservation of the establishment over generations to come is assured only to the extent that the establishment controls access to its ranks. One principal and effective way to do this is to limit the educational opportunities of minority populations.

No wonder, then, that organizations like Jesse Jackson's Operation PUSH (People United to Serve Humanity) have been so aggressive in encouraging students to stay in school and, more importantly, to pursue a college-preparatory curriculum. Presumably, the motivation of interest groups such as PUSH is to increase individuals' freedom of choice. Succeeding in a college-preparatory does not preclude a person from doing manual labor, but few other curricular options preserve the range of choices the college-preparatory program allows. The college-preparatory curriculum is the student's entry into an increasingly global high culture wherein the achievements of Hispanic Nobel laureate Octavio Paz, black philosopher Frantz Fanon, and the Native American physicist Stephen Alvarez are all recognized alongside those of Pierre and Marie Curie, George Sand, Stephen Hawking, Aristotle, and Ernest Hemingway.

What is the appeal of the multifarious curricular options so evident in our large public school systems today? Supporters argue that some students simply cannot "cut it" in a college-preparatory environment. Maybe this is true. But, when the students identified as unable to cut it are routinely black, Hispanic, and other minorities, we cannot help but suspect some prejudicial arrogance on the part of those insisting that vocationally oriented options be made available for these "slower" students. The argument that more modest curricular offerings be preserved for these ethnically predominant, slower groups is highly suspect.

In contrast to such prejudicial sorting practices, Escalante and Collins create self-esteem in students by developing their true range of competence. This shows students they can succeed even when the establishment says they cannot. Apologists for diverse vocationally-oriented curricular options might retort that the number of minorities in slower and/or vocational curriculums is inevitable given the inflexible and culturally intolerant college-preparatory curriculum. These critics allow that minority students are just as likely as others to succeed in strictly academic ventures, but the literature and social studies components of such curricula are myopic in their vision. Rather than submit to any cultural retooling, minority students in the past, the critics claim, opt out of college-preparatory curricula and choose, instead, curricular options that are less jingoistic.

This argument has appeal on the surface, but it fails to explain the preference for economically less-promising curricular options. The college-preparatory curriculum is narrowly conceived and has focused on the European contribution to the American experience. However, this is no less true of the optional curricular paths in those same school districts! There is no more attention to minority concerns in noncollege-track programs than there is in college-track programs. There is simply less academic content and greater vocational emphasis in the noncollege tracks. Minorities rightly complain that too little is made of minority contributions. But opting out of the college track is no way to address this deficiency. Instead, they should insist on a college track with a greater scope of vision. By abandoning the college track, minorities preclude themselves from moving into positions wherein their collective voices can effectively cry out against deficient and prejudicial educational policies. A graduate from a college-preparatory program can secure a job as a welder one year after graduation as easily as the vocational education graduate. The vocational education graduate, however, is unlikely to pursue, much less succeed, in a college endeavor.

Opening Doors of Opportunity

An educational system that prepares students to move into positions modeled by their parents is likely to be applauded by all but those in the lowest classes. And, since people in the lowest socioeconomic classes represent a relatively weak position in society, there is little reason for anyone in the classes above to worry much about them. Thus, a social policy aimed at securing minimal economic benefits for minorities succeeds principally in maintaining the present social hierarchy. Practices that maintain the current hierarchical structure run counter to the egalitarian principles articulated by the nation's leaders, both past and present.

These two contrasting lines of debate lead to a rather peculiar dilemma. On the one hand, the debate stresses the fact that, if the American dream is to become a reality for everyone, then educational programs that distract students from sharing the intellectual riches of the dominating class are oppressive to minorities. Consequently, there should be one curriculum for all. On the other hand, if the one curriculum reflects the establishment's worldview, then we risk creating ignorance and intolerance toward any culture varying from that of the establishment. Neither prospect is likely to appeal to conscientious teachers wanting the best for all students. So once again we must pause and ask, What are we to do?

There is a way out. It begins by noting the truth in both arguments. First, a generally uniform curriculum for students throughout the country will do much to erode the citadels of privilege and the contaminants causing socioeconomic disadvantage. In future generations, if students share something of a common educational background, then nearly everyone will have a chance to pursue the career of his or her authentically made choice (as much as individual talent allows). Second, this uniform curriculum ought to incorporate the study of various cultures and of various racial, ethnic, and religious groups, as well as characteristics of socioeconomic classes and gender. In short, every graduating high school student should know something about the author of the Declaration of Independence, entropy, Odysseus, Caesar, Gandhi, pi, Cervantes, Picasso, Cleopatra, the Curies, King, DNA, HIV, the Magna Charta, pre-Columbian art, and the Boxer Rebellion to name but a few. The goal should be to achieve a transcultural understanding that goes beyond class structure and ethnic diversity.

This solution is intuitively obvious to every teacher dedicated to expanding the intellectual horizons of all students. In addition to preparing students for a world of work, every teacher seeks to prepare students for all the world has to offer—responsibilities, intellectual challenges, a sense of self and community, and so on. For most students the only opportunity they have to learn to express themselves effectively in speech and writing, to calculate, to develop some aesthetic sense, to learn of the social forces and structures likely to affect them throughout their lives, and to learn enough science so as to demystify its authoritative pronouncements comes while they are in public school. Students who learn a minimal amount of this material will likely seek appropriate vocational training or further education when their initial education is complete. Students assume a responsible role as citizens only if they learn the nature and rationale for our laws and the need to remain attentive to the practices of all the cultures influencing our pluralistic society.

Appreciating these arguments as only a dedicated professional can, the teacher is still confronted by an enormous task. Remember, neither the establishment nor the most oppressed minorities are likely to see a uniform curriculum as being in their own best interest. Only the vantage point of the classroom teacher, or the most talented social theorists, is likely to reveal that teachers alone must challenge the self-interest and inertia, respectively, of the establishment and the oppressed. In addressing this challenge, classroom teachers are forced to stand with only their colleagues to rely on. But stand and be counted they must for only then can this great country ever hope to fulfill its promise. Only then can this great country lead the way toward further moral advance for humankind, toward a time when each human will learn to address every other human as a focal point of mutual respect.

III. Sociopolitical Pressures and Ethical Behavior

A. Approaching Moral Issues

Teaching is a moralistic enterprise. Being moral in professional behavior is no small task. At least three commitments constitute professional conduct. First, the teacher must ascertain what is the right thing to do. Second, the teacher must act in response to conscience and never for mere convenience. Third, the teacher must remain mindful that other persons and even groups of people may set themselves against her or his efforts to do what is right. The responsible teacher must learn to recognize when this is occurring, why it is occurring, and how it might be avoided. The first of these challenges will no doubt strike the human mind as indefinitely perplexing. Much of this book seeks to provide a start in addressing these matters, at least so far as they demand the attention of the professional teacher. However, by way of preliminary summary to the rest of the book, we should now consider the fact that, essentially, there are eight elements that every ordinary moral agent ought to address. The eight can be summarized simply as follows:

Elements of Ethical Analysis

1. Due attention must be given to each relevant argument.
    a. This requires that the moral agent possess a certain amount of experience and a capacity for imagination. The imaginative recall of personal experiences allows the moral agent to develop a sense of the relative range of inquiry.
    b. This requires the moral agent to be wary of fallacious forms of reasoning. Arguments that are contradictory or in some other way unintelligible are not relevant to solving a dilemma at hand.

2. Due attention must be given to all relevant empirical information.
   a. The agent must know how to identify evidence descriptive of the circumstances at hand. This is acquired both through experience of similar cases in the past and knowledge of studies descriptive of characteristic patterns of behavior.
   b. The agent must understand the limitations of his or her own observations as well as limitations inherent in the accumulation of scientific data. (For example, optical illusions cause people to "see" things that do not exist. And, statistical studies describe features of *groups*, not necessarily attributes of any *one member* of a group under study.)
3. Moral nomenclature must be aptly employed. (This means that the moral agent will be fastidious about the use of words such as *duty, right, good, bad,* or *responsibility*. It just will not do to say different words mean different things to different people. If that were the case, then public moral deliberation would always amount to nothing more than an unintelligible set of grunts and groans.)
4. Due attention must be given to the role of logical operators in moral thinking. (Words such as *if . . . then, ought, thus, therefore, or, not, consequently,* and *hence* must be used with precision to denote the giving of sufficient reasons for a claim, to establish necessary conditions for conclusions, to denote the compellingness of a moral imperative, and to announce various disclaimers.)
5. Moral intuitions are not ignored. (This refers not to hunches about what should be done at the moment, but rather to deep-seated notions such as the importance of respect in human deliberations.)
6. Political effectiveness and ambitions must not control the agent's moral reasoning. (Political considerations are not wholly irrelevant to moral reasoning. However, if the agent's concern is to do the "right" thing rather than what will simply satisfy the agent's own immediate ambitions, then the grounds of moral reasoning cannot begin with transient reference to self-interest. One way to imagine what this means in practice is to insist that altruistic behavior be considered as a relevant consideration in every moral dilemma.)
7. Legal and social conventions must be reviewed to ascertain what the conventional wisdom may be in regard to the matter at hand. (As far back as Aristotle in *Politics*, it was recognized that laws and social protocols reflect an evolutionary resiliency that ought to be studied and respected. Revolutionary change of long-standing traditions ought to be considered only after intense and sustained deliberation.)
8. Professionals undertake special moral tasks that others may choose to avoid. The nature of these tasks is usually noted in a code of ethics. But, since a code of ethics can never be more than a sketch, the responsible professional must always look beyond the code to determine the range of moral obligations the agent has acquired in virtue of his or her standing as a professional.

The second of the challenges—acting with strength of conscience—lies beyond the purview of this book. Others may encourage you to be vigilant about matters of morality, but only you can decide to *be* a moral person. Even your college teacher, who can at least role-model a certain serious-mindedness with regard to moral matters, can do nothing to make you act morally. The profession you are about to join can only hope that you are coming to it already committed to doing good and avoiding evil.

Moral Courage

The third challenge—to do the right thing in the face of opposition—is the one to which we now direct our attention. Assuming teachers are sufficiently conscientious about ferreting out the morally right course of action and acting as their conscience dictates, we must still consider the matter of acting against the wishes of diverse social and political forces.

While history books describe many individuals who successfully championed various moral causes—both right and wrong—there are many more individuals who championed a cause unsuccessfully. Is it better to suffer a principled defeat than to escape to fight another day? Abolitionists lied, cheated, and deceived in order to carry on the mission of the Underground Railroad. Were they better persons than people who merely *proclaimed* the wrongfulness of slavery? Those talking against slavery were regarded as outcasts, were never above suspicion, and were never beyond the reproachful eye of the establishment. They were never in a position to contribute directly to the work of the railroad itself. Is avoiding confrontation always advisable? Are there occasions when standing by, while innocents are victimized, is cowardly and wrong? If a teacher colleague is being unfairly dismissed, what action are you prepared to take in his or her defense? If a quiet but insidious bigotry exists at your school, are you doing more good by making this public (and thereby risking your career), or do you do more good by staying in the system and trying gradually to change it from within?

Acting morally is never a matter to be decided in intellectual isolation. Humans are communal creatures. Ideally, we nourish our communities as they nourish us. But, if a community turns poisonous toward one or more individuals, what are you obligated to do to restore an environment that is nourishing in some way to all?

Presumably, we expect that the communities within which we live will in some fashion nourish our evolving quality of life. Citizens vote for candidates who share their vision of the future. This shared vision represents the best of available alternatives. People enter into a profession because, in part, they see in that communal endeavor an opportunity for fulfillment. Finally, teachers continue employment at a given school because it affords them some possibility for personal satisfaction. Admittedly, other factors do play a part in a person's decision to work at a given school—factors such as pay and geographic locale. Nevertheless, no responsible professional would continue working in a setting that destroyed the professional's sense of self-respect. In short, being a professional is a highly moral activity. A *community of professionals* is highly charged with moralistic concerns and allegiances. To foster development of teachers, an educational environment must be responsive to the motivations of the professional staff, motivations which first and foremost are, and ought to be, moralistic.

Moral Community

The local community of educators is part of a larger community of educators at the state and national levels. Beyond this is an international community of educators. It, in turn, is but a part of a noble tradition of educators spanning the millennia and including the likes of Socrates, Christ, Moses, Gandhi, Confucius, Collins, Escalante, and many others. Every educator is obligated to reflect on the traditions that have distinguished teaching from all the other professions and from what may reflect the current society's transient self-interest. From the moment the teaching profession first appeared on the human social horizon, it represented an attempt to shape the lives of the uninitiated in ways that would improve those lives. Individuals do not learn reading, writing, arithmetic, science, and the arts on their own or in isolation. These skills and sensitivities are often created and always nourished by responsible teachers. Clearly, value judgments are involved in the decision to teach students such "unnatural" ways of addressing the world, but it is hard for the professional teacher to imagine that any greater gifts, the gifts of learned civilization, could be passed on to future generations.

Responsible teaching from its very beginning has aimed at extending the student's understanding of bits and pieces of the world. As shown by the great teachers of the past, learning is instrumental in extending the individual's control over his or her own immediate world. But learning and its forum, education, are more than just instrumental endeavors. Great teachers of the past have correctly reminded their descendants that in giving people control over their environment, teachers must also pass along a sense of pride and responsibility for protecting that world for everyone's benefit today and in the future. Thus, from the smallest unit of teacher collegiality to the professional tradition itself, teachers have assumed the responsibility of helping each generation ready itself for its opportunity to improve self and world alike.

Apathy and Moral Challenge

The world is not always ready to be improved. Indeed, as alluded to earlier, people in general become entrenched in habits and beliefs, even after these habits and beliefs have outlived their usefulness. Establishment-types, as well as some who have accepted repression, often resist the efforts of teachers to improve the fortunes of all. Regardless, the teacher's general duty remains clearly in focus: prepare students to continue the quest for human progress—technical, social, and moral.

In the 1950s there was a great deal of prejudice in America. Some prejudicial practices were quite overt and even enjoyed the sanction of law. Other prejudice was less overt. Examples of the first kind of prejudice are the Jim Crow laws contrived to prevent blacks from voting, from using white-only public drinking fountains and restrooms, and from attending the same schools as whites. Covert prejudice during that same era is illustrated in the treatment of women. If asked, nearly every husband of the 1950s would have declared unequivocal commitment to his wife. While the notion of partnership sounds egalitarian, in point of fact the typical marital relationship was far from egalitarian. At best the partnership of marriage was limited. Men were generally the heads of their households (unless outmaneuvered by a spirited spouse), and women played a nurturing (but, at best, supportive) role for spouse and family. Educational and employment opportunities abounded for men, comparatively speaking, while their female counterparts were discouraged from seeking advantages males had come to recognize as part of their birthright. Generally, the laws did not actively seek to protect men from competition with women, as they did whites from blacks, but they seldom ensured women anything approaching equal opportunity. Things have changed.

In the well-known case *Plessy v. Ferguson* (1896), the U.S. Supreme Court said that conditions of equal treatment, as required by the Fourteenth Amendment, were satisfied if the facilities available to all citizens were equal. *Brown v. Board of Education of Topeka* (1954) overruled that decision. In *Brown*, the Court recognized that equality cannot be assured merely by maintaining access to equal physical resources. If a minority group is capriciously identified as deserving separate treatment because of skin color, that group becomes ostracized from the community at large. Such ostracism makes subsequent equality of opportunity a de facto impossibility.

In addition to *Brown*, the Civil Rights Act of 1964 did much to remove inequities affecting the access of blacks to equal opportunity in the political, social, and commercial arenas. While the law ostensibly opened up new vistas of opportunity for blacks and others, jurists and lawmakers actually created the demands for tolerance and integration in the first place. For decades, jurists and lawmakers had protected the status quo. From where, then, did the motivation on the part of jurists and lawmakers to change prejudicial practices come?

The need for change preceded the actual enactments and decisions that constituted the shift in law. The need was no doubt established in classrooms throughout the land. School teachers, perhaps Lyndon Johnson himself, extolled students to emulate the virtues of the mythical George Washington and Abraham Lincoln, men who were extraordinarily honest and committed to the well-being and equal treatment of all Americans. (See fig. 2.2.) The mythical Washington and the mythical Lincoln that teachers presented to students as role models in the thirties, forties, and fifties ultimately bore fruit. As mentioned in the first chapter, students emerging into young adulthood in the fifties and sixties observed the wrong suffered by minority groups and then joined forces with them to make America the land of equality and opportunity it claimed to be. For example, the student council of Ohio State University rented five buses to carry students, mostly white, to Alabama to march alongside Martin Luther King and his followers in the celebrated march to Selma. The Ohio State students were not the only students to actively support civil rights movement in 1965. The fact of the matter is that students from all over the country, many the sons and daughters of the privileged, acted to right the wrongs of the past. Their teachers had stirred them to capture the spirit of mythically portrayed giants of American history and they did just that.

This is not to suggest that schoolteachers urged their students to specific acts of protest. In fact, evidence suggests that most teachers advised against such tactics. Historically speaking, teachers in the 1950s protected the status quo unconditionally. Drawing attention to the attributes of mythical American heroes was probably more

Abraham Lincoln (Preserver of the Union and Signer of the Emancipation Proclamation, 1863)	George Washington (Father of Our Country)
1. Avid reader/self-educated	1. Never told a lie; the cherry-tree episode
2. "Honest Abe" walked miles to return a few pennies to a customer	2. Looked after minorities; freed his slaves
3. Champion of an enslaved minority	3. Man of the people; refused to be King George I
4. Steady and hardworking from woodsman to presidency	4. Member of no clique; looked after the poor and downtrodden (loaned his cloak to a soldier)

Figure 2.2 Mythical American Presidents

to create jingoistic support for alleged American ideals than to provoke monumental social change. Still, the actual effect of these efforts is unrefutable. A generation of Americans came to believe its duty was to secure so-called American ideals for all. In emulating the heroes schoolteachers narrated, students began looking for ways to right wrongs conspicuously apparent to anyone so morally inspired.

Consciousness of the inequities confronting women was similarly inspired by schoolteachers. Teachers were far from assuming the lead in the feminist movement. But their promotion of just and fair treatment for all sowed the seeds of a social conscience that could no longer abide previous inequities. This perhaps unintentional impact of teachers is, it seems, undeniable. The press remained generally conservative and supportive of establishment-endorsed social practices. Hollywood and other entertainment media continued to present the American consumer with female stereotypes. Only through education was there a mass effort to present a different ideal, an ideal that in the long run may have been contrary to the social mores of most practicing teachers, but an ideal that was, nevertheless, thoroughly consistent with all that teachers had to *say*.

Gore Vidal, in his excellent novel *Hollywood*, aptly portrayed the way in which Hollywood and political-types do far more than merely entertain or reflect the world as it is. Movie viewers, as Walker Percy also illustrated in his novel *The Moviegoer*, tend to model the behavior they see depicted on the screen. Once Hollywood moguls realized this they began to use the medium to create sympathies commensurate with the moviemakers' political and social worldviews. The power of moviemakers and other media-types is so prevalent today that teachers themselves often wonder aloud if they still have any influence at all on today's media-drenched students. Only time will reveal the answer to this question. However, if teachers become attentive to the moral conscience of their professional community, they can still achieve much. In any case, the influence of classroom teachers in the 1940s and 1950s has undoubtedly shown itself to be a powerful force in the 1960s and beyond.

B. Teacher Power

Teachers can wield considerable influence over the future of America. When teachers use their collective influence, the power they exercise is positively heady. But with power comes responsibility. Teachers are responsible for maintaining their sense of professionalism. This means they must recall that their profession exists first and foremost to provide students with greater knowledge and thus greater control over their environment. Furthermore, teachers must remember that they are duty bound to do something to contribute to the well-being of this world.

If Hollywood and Madison Avenue prove to be far stronger influences than the collective efforts of classroom teachers, this will not free teachers in the least from their primary responsibilities. If the media and profession come into conflict, teachers will just have to work that much harder to serve students, the community, and their disciplines. The difficulty of the challenge does not excuse the responsible professional from making the effort. In the best of all possible worlds, media-types, teachers, and politicos will be of one mind. But since this is not the best of all possible worlds, teachers must be vigilant in carrying out their professional duties in the face of opposing influences.

IV. The Social Psychology of Moral Development

A. Communal Morality

Morality is everyone's business. Achieving adulthood means achieving a certain level of moral maturity. Maturity is the idea that a person sets about to act responsibly. Responsible action requires intellectual effort and strength of will. A person must find the morally compelling and separate it from all that is morally reprehensible, as well as all that is morally inconsequential. Responsible action is typically regarded as the principal, if not the sole, designator of maturity. For example, in the Jewish tradition the ceremonies of bar mitzvah and bas mitzvah are public signs that a youth has demonstrated this maturity to the satisfaction of his or her elders, respectively. With or without ceremony, every group recognizes that developing maturity is a consequence of moral growth, along with social growth and worldliness.

In every society a person is duly honored when described by others as mature. In contrast, a person is denigrated whenever others regard him or her as immature. In short, it is good to appear mature and bad not to appear so. Hence, each individual is led by impending social forces to acquiesce in whatever actions are generally taken to be symbolic of mature, responsible behavior within the context of a given social fabric. One type of action universally regarded as responsible is any act exhibiting a concern for the appropriate development of the young.[10] In other words, seeking the moral development of others is a way of exhibiting our own moral development. In short, moral education is an objective of every maturing individual.

Self-interest and Moral Progress

Moral education serves individual self-interest in at least three ways. First, moral education may be pursued from time to time by individuals hoping to improve their own status within a community. Second, contributing to the moral education of others is a way of demonstrating how far individuals have come in their own quest to attain maturity in the public eye. Third, the more others are shaped through moral education the more tolerant they become of others' efforts in this regard and appreciative of other successes. Thus, moral education inevitably becomes a self-interested consideration in the mind of every maturing individual. But curiously enough there is a paradox in all this. The most characteristic hallmark of any moral hero is the person's ability to act in ways that extend beyond mere self-interest. This fact of moral experience has been alluded to throughout the present chapter. But, if we were to suppose even for a moment that the principal motivator for individual moral development is self-interest, how can we account for the fact that moral development aims at the abandonment of self-interest as a goal?

The Gestalt Shift of Moral Development

What looks paradoxical at first glance may not be so perplexing once we have had a chance to reflect on the psychology of moral development. In the *Politics* Aristotle admonished, "To become just one must do just acts, but to be just one must do just acts as a just person." Not being privy to the insights of Gestalt psychology, Aristotle was only clumsily recognizing an experience in the moral domain that today psychologists describe as a gestalt shift. In the perceptual domain, if we stare at a cube drawn on a flat surface for a sufficiently long period of time, we will notice that the face of the cube abruptly shifts to the back while the back spontaneously reappears as the face. (See fig. 2.3.) Sustained attention to the cube as we originally see it leads inevitably to a sudden shift in perspective. Aristotle's observation suggests that this is precisely what happens in the moral domain in the most successful cases. Teachers and various social forces focus students' attention on the performance of certain acts. Should this focus of attention be sustained something dramatic happens. The students no longer perform such acts to please others. Rather, they "discover" that *serving others is pleasing in itself!* The specific acts they perform are, at best, a contingent matter to be decided, in part, on the basis of the facts at hand and the desired results.

Aristotle was not the only one to observe this gestalt shift in the moral domain of human experience. The French mathematician, theologian, and father of decision theory Blaise Pascal argued that if people would wager the possibility (no matter how small) of an infinitely great and eternal reward, then no measure of sensuous pleasure in the temporally limited world could ever make the loss of eternal bliss worthwhile. Through such reasoning Pascal hoped to induce people to adopt a lifestyle commensurate with a religious worldview. Pascal was not so naive as to think that because individuals adopt a set of behavioral practices they are thereby committed to seeing the world in an unselfish and religiously orthodox way. He knew a gestalt shift from a self-interested focus to a "God-regarding" focus has to take place. He went to great lengths to explain that once a person adopts the wager, years of dutifully complying with religion's demands are only a beginning. Ultimately, the gambler will abandon mere self-interest (the very thing that made adoption of the wager so convincing in the first place) and accept instead a spiritually motivated source of inspiration.[11]

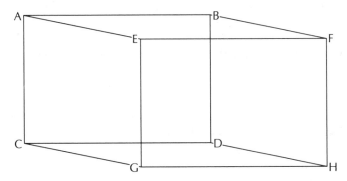

The Necker Cube was so named because of its use in the early work of psychologist L. C. Necker. Begin by identifying the corners of the front face of the cube. Is it GEFH or CABD? Now, stare at the cube and wait. Did you see the face of the cube shift to the back and the back flash to the front? The shift you experience in this case is sudden and abrupt. This is what is meant as a gestalt shift: an abrupt new way of seeing the world "happen." This shift usually occurs after much effort with no noticeable results beforehand, no "evolution" of perspective.

Figure 2.3 The Necker Cube and Perception

The Danish philosopher Søren Kierkegaard similarly wrote that after an individual adopts a repertoire of good practices, the truly enlightened person discovers that the point of it all stands beyond the pale of mere action. Ultimately, adopting the right attitude *while acting* is what matters.[12] In short, respectful actions breed respect-minded persons. In both Pascal and Kierkegaard, we find strong religious overtones, but that should not distract us from the point being addressed at present. In the moral domain just as in the perceptual domain, human beings are the sorts of creatures subject to dramatic shifts of perspective subsequent to sustained attention over time. Why this should be no one knows for sure. However, psychologists such as Jonathan Baron, economists such as Robert Frank, and philosophers such as Robert Nozick, Alasdair MacIntyre, and Charles Taylor have begun offering tentative hypotheses to explain this uniquely human phenomenon.[13]

While the cause of these dramatic shifts in human perspective remains a mystery to current researchers, developmental psychologists in the present century from Jean Piaget to Lawrence Kohlberg have documented time and again that people do undergo dramatic shifts in perspective in the world of moral experience and that in general these shifts exhibit predictable species-wide trends.[14] Even moral psychologists critical of Piaget, Kohlberg, and their disciples—most notably Carol Gilligan, Nel Noddings, and Robert Coles—all readily admit that throughout the world, people exhibit a pronounced tendency to become concerned with the well-being of others as they leave behind the egocentrism of their infancy.[15] The only exceptions are people suffering some obvious pathology or the aberrant examples provided by the lives of the so-called Wild Boys of Navarre and Borneo, respectively.[16]

Moral development cannot occur in a vacuum. No psychology of the individual can tell us all we want to know about the moral outlook of even that one individual. Moral development is a social enterprise. It is a matter of responding to others. More than that, it is a matter of how we *ought* to respond to others. Psychology has been increasingly successful in tracking the stages and range of responses humans are capable of in well-specified, moral-problem spaces. For example, a psychologically traumatized person is less likely to act in heroic fashion than is one whose self-esteem remains in tact. Similarly, sociology and anthropology have created extensive records recounting shifts of cultural expectations in matters clearly of moral relevance.[17] And, finally, even after the social sciences complete the record detailing the range of human responsiveness and the evolving habitual tendencies of various cultures, it still is left to the philosophically minded to determine what ought to be done from moment to moment and what morally relevant reasons form the basis for action. In short, mature individuals are philosophical when the situation demands responsible moral thinking. When their thinking leads to action, they are courageous.

B. Summary

The moral life of the educator is like that of other (traditional) professionals. In addition to the moral concerns confronting every adult, educators, by virtue of their profession, acquire an additional set of duties. While every adult must determine how best to increase his or her own ability to deal with the moral world, the educator is responsible for creating plans that will help large numbers of people become, as the commercials for the U.S. Army declare, the best that they can be. While all adults in a community ought to be concerned with matters of moral education in principle, and while parents have specific plans for advancing the cause of their own young, only teachers assume the public responsibility for shaping the environment of students so that in the end they become part of a generation that makes the world a better place. Through role modeling and compelling students to act respectfully toward self and others, teachers prepare the next generation for taking the world from the valley where they found it to ever-higher peaks of achievement.

Teachers find themselves inextricably bound up in their own culture. But that does not mean they cannot engender in their students a respect for other persons and other cultures and, most importantly, a desire to make their culture increasingly more civilized. As John Dewey proclaimed in "My Pedagogic Creed," among all society's citizens, teachers possess the unique and special duty to prepare the young for creating an as yet unspecified but somehow better world—a world more responsive to human needs and more inviting for the exercise of human talents.[18]

QUESTIONS FOR DISCUSSION

1. How do environmental conditions influence a person's ability to ascertain his or her moral duty in a given situation?
2. Why should people attempt to study other cultures?
3. Why should people be taught to respect other cultures and not just the people in those cultures?
4. What is a good reason for being intolerant of the cultural practices of others?
5. Besides the distinctions between the cultural practices of different ethnic groups, what other distinctions may be attributable to such things as gender and socioeconomic class?
6. If there were a single curriculum for all public schools to follow, who would benefit the most? the least?
7. Are politically effective decisions always the most moral? Explain. (Begin by explaining what you mean by "politically effective.")
8. What is being moral all about?
9. Why is it in anyone's self-interest to become moral?
10. Which of the elements of ethical analysis are most necessary? Why must all be addressed?
11. Does successful moral development result in the abandonment of an exclusive concern with self-interest? Explain.
12. How does a lack of self-esteem influence a person's ability to think about matters of morality?
13. What is the nature of a gestalt shift in the moral domain?
14. What are the special duties of a teacher?

1. Thomas S. Kuhn, *The Structure of Scientific Revolution* (Chicago: University of Chicago Press, 1962). See also Paul Feyerbend, *Against Method* (New York: Verso Pub., 1977); John McPeck, *Critical Thinking and Education* (New York: St. Martin's Press, 1982); and Robert K. Merton, *On the Shoulders of Giants* (New York: Harcourt Brace Jovanavich, 1985).

2. See E. L. Thorndike, *Human Nature and Social Order* (Cambridge: MIT Press, 1969). See also J. B. Watson, *Behaviorism* (New York: W. W. Norton, 1970), and B. F. Skinner, *Beyond Freedom and Dignity* (New York: Alfred A. Knopf, 1972).

3. See, for example, Noam Chomsky, *Language and Responsibility* (New York: Pantheon Books, 1977).

4. See, for example, Jacques Derrida, *Speech and Phenomena* (Evanston, Ill.: Northwestern University Press, 1973).

5. Allan Bloom, *The Closing of the American Mind* (New York: Simon & Schuster, 1987).

6. Joel Spring, *Education and the Rise of the Corporate State* (Boston: Beacon Press, 1972).

7. Mortimer Adler, *The Paideia Proposal: An Educational Manifesto* (New York: Macmillan, 1982).

8. See, for example, Robert J. Sternberg and William Sutter, "Concepts of Intelligence," in *Handbook of Human Intelligence* (New York: Cambridge University Press, 1982), 3–28.

9. Jonathan Kozol, *Free Schools* (Boston: Houghton Mifflin, 1972).

10. Owen Flanagan, *Varieties of Moral Personality* (Cambridge: Harvard University Press, 1991).

11. Blaise Pascal, *Pensees* (Paris: Editionis de Luremburg, 1962). See also Nicholas Rescher, *Pascal's Wager* (Notre Dame, Ind.: Notre Dame University Press, 1985).

12. Søren Kierkegaard, *Fear and Trembling and Sickness unto Death* (Princeton, N.J.: Princeton University Press, 1954).

13. Jonathan Baron, *Rationality and Intelligence* (New York: Cambridge University Press, 1985), and Jonathan Baron, *Thinking and Deciding* (New York: Cambridge University Press, 1988). See also Robert Frank, *Passion Within Reason* (New York: W. W. Norton, 1990); Robert Nozick, *The Examined Life* (New York: Simon & Schuster, 1989); and Alasdair MacIntyre, *After Virtue: A Study in Moral Theory* (Notre Dame, Ind.: Notre Dame University Press, 1981). See also P. T. Geach, *The Virtues* (New York: Cambridge University Press, 1977); Phillipas Foot, *Virtues and Vices* (Berkeley: University of California Press, 1978); and Charles Taylor, *Sources of Self: The Making of the Modern Identity* (Cambridge: Harvard University Press, 1989).

14. See, for example, Jean Piaget, *The Moral Judgment of the Child* (New York: Free Press of Glencoe, 1932); and Lawrence Kohlberg, *The Psychology of Moral Development: The Nature and Validity of Moral Stages* (San Francisco: Harper & Row, 1984).

15. See, for example, Carol Gilligan, *In a Different Voice: Psychological Theory and Women's Development* (Cambridge: Harvard University Press, 1982); Nel Noddings, *Caring: A Feminine Approach to Ethics and Moral Education* (Berkeley: University of California Press, 1984); and Robert Coles, *The Moral Life of Children* (Boston: Atlantic Monthly Press, 1986).

16. Some boys were reputed to have been abandoned by their parents and raised in the wilderness by animals (wolves are commonly believed to have served as the boys' surrogate parents). When found, each boy was on the verge of adolescence. At that age children of both sexes have begun recognizing that the interests of other people should matter very much in their private calculations. Furthermore, prepubescent youngsters have already begun cooperating in communal ways with their peers, if not yet with society at large. The wild boys exhibited no such inclination. How could they? Their lives were void of any communion with others.

17. See, for example, Crane Brinton, *A History of Western Morals* (New York: Harcourt, Brace & Co., 1959) and Robert N. Bellah et al., *Habits of the Heart* (Berkeley: University of California Press, 1989).

18. John Dewey, *Experience and Education* (New York: Collier Books, 1938).

For Further Reading

Educational Reform

Adler, M. The *Paideia Program: An Educational Syllabus*. New York: Macmillan, 1984.

Bredemeier, M., and H. Bredemeier. *Social Forces in Education*. Sherman Oaks, Calif.: Alfred Publishing Co., 1978.

Dewey, J. *The Child and the Curriculum: The School and Society*. Chicago: University of Chicago Press, 1956.

Graham, P. A. *Sustain Our Schools*. New York: Hill and Wang, 1992.

Kozol, J. *Free Schools*. Boston: Houghton Mifflin, 1972.

_____. *Illiterate America*. Garden City, N.Y.: Anchor Press, 1985.

Shimahara, N., and A. Scrupski. *Social Forces and Schooling*. New York: David McKay Co., 1975.

The Moral World

Dewey, J. *Moral Principles in Education*. Carbondale, Ill.: Southern Illinois University Press, 1975.

Flanagan, O. *Varieties of Moral Personality*. Cambridge: Harvard University Press, 1991.

Frank, R. *Passion Within Reason*. New York: W. W. Norton, 1990.

Nozick, R. *The Examined Life*. New York: Simon & Schuster, 1989.

Social Change

Bender, T. *Community and Social Change in America*. New Brunswick, N.J.: Rutgers University Press, 1978.

Bennett, W. *The De-Valuing of America*. New York: Summit, 1992.

Chafetz, J. *Gender Equality*. Newbury Park, Calif.: Sage Publishing, 1990.

Damon, W. *The Moral Child*. New York: Free Press, 1988.

Mead, M. *Continuities in Cultural Evolution*. New Haven: Yale University Press, 1964.

Toffler, A. *Powershift*. New York: Bantam Books, 1989.

Radest, H. *Can We Teach Ethics?* New York: Frederick A. Praeger, 1989.

Shaver, J., and W. Strong. *Facing Value Decisions*. New York: Teachers College Press, 1982.

Chapter Three

Ordering of Society: The Law and Its Effects on Education

OBJECTIVES

After studying this chapter you will be able to:

1. Give an account of why groups come into conflict with one another and contrast this with an account of why people organize into groups.
2. Explain the nature of freedom that social contract theorists such as Aristotle and Thomas Hobbes say people should protect.
3. Describe how greater civil control can actually help people enjoy more, rather than less, liberty.
4. Describe how interdependency among groups provides potentially competing groups with a collective sense of community.
5. Explain John Stuart Mill's concern about the "tyranny of the masses."
6. Discuss how education can be a device for securing a well-executed social contract form of community.
7. Explain why the law must be thought of as a subset of morality.
8. Tell why it is more natural to test the value of a law by comparing it with our deepest moral intuitions rather than the other way around.
9. Describe what expert moral thinking requires.
10. Distinguish between moral thinking and legal thinking.

11. Explain the value to the community of legal thinking and why judges try to settle the present case in light of previous decisions.

12. Explain why students and teachers are both expected to give up certain rights at the schoolhouse steps.

I. Thomas Hobbes: Two Different Freedoms

A. Foes and Friends

A favorite play of high school English teachers is Leonard Bernstein's *West Side Story*. Teachers tell students that *West Side Story* is essentially a contemporary version of Shakespeare's *Romeo and Juliet*. In both stories the plot revolves around lovers who are prevented from pursuing self-interest, friendship, and love because the groups to which they belong are antagonistic toward each other. Apart from the element of romance, the intolerance of families, tribes, gangs, and ethnic groups toward one another has long impeded successful social evolution.

History is replete with examples of how communities did irreparable damage to their own well-being because they allowed hostilities to continue between groups of antagonists. The biblical book of *Exodus* is the story of one ethnic group freeing itself from the oppression of another. The slave revolts led by Spartacus in ancient Rome and John Brown in the pre-Civil War United States were the consequences of sustained oppression. In each case, the majority as well as the oppressed minority suffered greatly because of bigotry and intolerance. Moving closer to our own era, we cannot forget the ravages inflicted on Germany by the pathologic prejudice of Adolf Hitler toward the Jews. When Hitler initiated his angry anti-Semitic policies, Jewish scholars from throughout Germany left for other Western countries. Those that remained were killed. The loss of so much trained genius sowed the seeds of disaster for Germany's subsequent military ambitions.

Today, the continued hatred and bigotry of Arab against Jew and Jew against Arab leaves the people of the Middle East anxious and forlorn. And here in the United States racist skinheads and Los Angeles-based groups such as the Bloods and Crips breed hatred and fear wherever their influence is felt. All this leads to the conclusion that wherever bigotry or a gang mentality exists, the community involved is forever in peril. This is the idea studied long ago in the seventeenth century by the English philosopher Thomas Hobbes. Without the benefits of civilizing social practices, Hobbes believed, humans are forever destined to be antagonistic toward one another.[1]

B. Hobbes's Theory of Social Competition

Thomas Hobbes began his study with the following thought experiment. Consider what it would be like to live in a world containing none of the restrictions imposed by government or other community social mores. Under these conditions individuals would be on their own, each one a bundle of self-interest. There would be nothing to deter aggressors, save for the apparent superior force of each competitor. Under such circumstances each human would remain ready for confrontation. Since humans seek many of the same necessities, conveniences, and pleasures, it is inevitable that they would compete with one another. Without prior agreement to the contrary, each contact with another person in Hobbes's hypothesis is a potential source of mortal conflict. With this potential in mind, Hobbes asked, What can prevent hostilities and the ever-constant threat of hostility? The answer, Hobbes declared, is a social contract.

C. Hobbesian Social Contract

In the social contract Hobbes described, each contracting party agrees to give up certain freedoms, pool powers, and establish a system for protecting the individual. This is an interesting ideal—one which continues to attract the attention of social theorists, scholars, and political interest groups.

In Hobbes's hypothetical, each person in the uncivilized condition possesses absolute freedom. That is part of what Hobbes meant by the "uncivilized condition." Without any socially contrived inhibitions, people are free to act as they please. This ranges from mundane acts, such as staying up late, to more dramatic acts, such as robbery, rape, or murder. As soon as restrictions are placed on any of these activities, people lose a portion of their absolute freedom. So what? After all, what good is there in absolute freedom? If a person lives in constant fear, dreading that he or she will be preyed on by others, what possible good can result from this condition of absolute freedom? The only protection a person has against dangerous or otherwise unwanted intrusions, Hobbes reasoned, is to ally with others.

For a mutually satisfying, self-protective network to function, certain conditions must be met. First, individual members must give up the idea that they are wholly free to act as they choose. The only way to be free of fear is to negotiate a set of limitations on individual action. So, for example, if each person agrees to steal no food from other members of the community, then all members of the community can feel somewhat relieved that the food each acquires will be available when needed. Of course, the matter cannot be left there. Humans, individually and collectively, may suffer a lapse of conscience. They forget their promises. Some further institutional device is needed to bind people to their word. Specifically, there must be a way to guarantee the property rights of community members.

A social contract must create procedures for arriving at decisions that protect the interests of the community (and thereby, presumably, the interests of each member— at least most of the time). To succeed, the contract must enforce adherence to all newly created rights. This is accomplished through the establishment of a central authority. Furthermore, the central authority must be suitably equipped with an effective mechanism for exercising power. The central authority could be a boss of some sort, a clique, or a mass vote followed by mass action. In any case, the idea is that through the social contract, people trade away some of the freedom they have by nature and, in return, gain greater liberty of action and freedom from anxiety. Note that, while in a state of nature people are free to do what they want, there is no assurance that any desires will, in fact, be satisfied. In a state of nature, if humans are paralyzed with fear and trepidation, they can enjoy little freedom of action. The social contract addresses this problem by decreasing absolute freedom and by increasing liberty—that is, actual freedom to act—proportionally. Another way of explaining Hobbes's reasoning at this point is to simply note that for any person to be at liberty

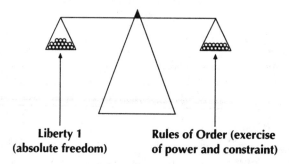

Liberty 2
(Protected freedom is optimal when there is a <u>balance</u> between absolute freedom and rules of order.)

Liberty 1
(absolute freedom)

Rules of Order (exercise of power and constraint)

In Hobbes's view every particle of absolute freedom that is removed and placed within a system of well-balanced rules produces an effect in which people enjoy license to exploit the freedoms that remain. The more liberty 1 in a person's life, the less liberty 2. Inversely, the more liberty 2, the less liberty 1. For example, a restrictive totalitarian regime amasses enormous amounts of control under the auspices of a central authority. As a result, it can provide nearly fail-safe protection for its citizenry, which it allows to pursue an especially narrow range of activities. In contrast, a society that goes to great lengths to maximize the range of activities its citizens may pursue must proportionately decrease the aggregation of power it exercises over them. As a result, a government of the latter sort will have difficulty protecting its citizens who are caught up in the enjoyment of many diverse freedoms.

Figure 3.1   Diminished Freedom vs. Protection and the Secure Exercise of License

to act there must be sufficient security to protect him or her when properly engaged in the act. The social contract is a device for creating this security. (See fig. 3.1.)

According to Hobbes, the nature of the social contract is that humans group together to protect themselves from one another. This is quite different from the thinking of another social contract theorist, Aristotle. Aristotle said humans group together simply because it is their nature to do so. Through community the individual experiences fulfillment and, conversely, it is the goal of the well-organized state to promote self-fulfillment for as many as possible. The family, the tribe, the nation, and even ethnic groups and gangs may easily be seen as institutions that draw support from the human inclination to seek protection for the exercise of self-interest. The control exerted by a group over its members protects constituent members from random violence. But, how does the group protect itself from the intrusions of competing groups? This is, after all, the reason some people group together and the query from which we began this chapter.

D. Group Competition

Each group has two choices. First, the group can selectively expand its numbers, recruiting a hardy membership that is larger and more intimidating than any of its nearby competitors. Through the sheer accumulation of power (economic, intellectual, muscle, anything that can be used to coerce outsiders to the will of the privileged), the group subdues or intimidates the competing interests of other groups. Second, the group can form alliances with other groups. If greater security can be secured for individuals by implicitly negotiating Hobbesian social contracts, then the same should be true for groups of individuals.

Problems are associated with both approaches to individual liberty through group affiliation. In the first case, there seems to be no end to the hostilities that arise as groups increase their ranks at the expense of competitors. Tyrants in the past have supposed that once all the world is brought under their command, humankind will be the ultimate benefactor. Maybe so, but the cost is far higher than most individuals are willing to pay. In addition, as the size of the group increases, the demand for surveillance and heavy-handed enforcement tactics increases as well. A point comes at which the central authority appears so aggressive that people become as fearful of it as they were in a state of nature. When the oppression of a central authority becomes uncompromisingly severe, the desire of the people to revolt festers. Hobbes himself advised that, if people are oppressed in this way, they need no longer honor any previously implied social contract. For Hobbes, people are free from obligations when previously agreed to accords no longer represent a mutually beneficial arrangement among a majority of the populace. Under such circumstances revolution is permissible and, presumably, inevitable.

If there are overwhelming problems with establishing a strong central authority over enormously large groups of people, then what about the alternative—establishing alliances among autonomous and mutually exclusive groups? In the nation's large cities, gangs often forge just such alliances with one another. However, as police records show, these alliances are usually short-lived. Conflict seems inevitable over the long run. Sooner or later each group discovers it has an interest in an enterprise or property that places it in stark competition with another group. At this point all cooperation seems lost as competing gangs go to war. To the victor belongs the spoils.

This phenomenon is not unique to gangs. We have ample evidence of conflict among nations as well. Karl Marx was so impressed with this seemingly universal experience that he concluded that as long as there are groups of "haves" and other groups of "have nots," confrontation is inevitable. Only when each person has what he or she needs will conflict end. If Marx is right, there will be no end to such conflict in the foreseeable future.

While the discussion here has focused principally on gangs and nations, competition between groups is everywhere—even in the teaching profession. Groups of faculty try to secure a larger portion of operating funds for their respective departments. In unionized school districts, groups of teachers compete to seize power over the union. Each school and its district leadership have at one time or another struck deals and compromises with groups both internal and external to the profession. Given what has been said thus far, we might conclude that prospects for a benevolent, well-organized school operation are as bleak as they seem to be for savvy youth gangs and nations alike. Recent research on schools has made this prospect vividly evident.[2]

E. Interdependency

In describing the problems associated with alliances among groups of people, we might find the phrase *mutually interdependent groups* helpful. Competing groups have no sense of dependence on their adversaries. Competitors and subservient allies are viewed as merely a means to the parent group's ends.

Dependence on others, however, can make us more appreciative of those others. When we suffer some trauma, our personal burdens are relieved by the friendly intervention of another. Benjamin Franklin once wrote that we can create bonds of friendship with others by allowing them to do us a kindness. This is true.

On the other hand, while occasional dependence on others can create feelings of friendship and accommodation, sustained dependence of one person or group on others tends to create fear and resentment. For example, slave holders and slaves both tend at times to fear their dependence on the other. This fear may erupt in painful ways. Similarly, welfare recipients often become antagonistic toward the employed. The employed resent the tax drain on their resources by welfare recipients. Once again, the resulting antagonism may lead to much distress. Finally, consider a simple school example. One child, call him Juan, may happily share an answer to a homework problem with his friend Erica. If Erica becomes dependent on Juan for answers to homework assignments, resentment will develop. For his part, Juan becomes resentful of being preyed on by Erica each day. Erica resents the haughtiness of Juan and the indignation of feeling forced to beg for more help. The key to avoiding these situations is to create networks that foster *mutual interdependence*.

Knowing that another may ask us for help, we do not feel guilty about requesting help from that person. In addition, helping a person who appreciates our effort makes the helping experience rewarding. Perhaps the person being helped will return the favor one day. Even if the favor is never returned, the other's appreciation indicates that, should the occasion arise, he or she will see it as an opportunity to reciprocate. A network that encourages giving, mutual concern, and respect fosters ultimately altruistic action. Recall Aristotle, Pascal, and Kierkegaard: when we get in the habit of doing considerate acts, then, after a time, for whatever reason, our initial efforts will ultimately dissolve and we will become considerate persons.

Where does all this take us? To ensure cooperation among groups and ultimately to produce social arrangements that are conducive to exemplary moral behavior, it is advisable to create as much mutual interdependence among groups and individuals as possible. One of the most widely recognized achievements of our own nation's founders is the system of checks and balances they contrived that forces the three branches of government to work cooperatively, one with another. When one branch of government bolts to secure a preponderance of power over the others, sooner or later the other two branches force temperance and cooperation. Failure to do so is recognized as devastating to all.

F. Mutual Interdependence in the Real World: The Historical Record

Creating systems of mutual interdependence seems the only way to protect us from ourselves. Consider as an example a chapter from the so-called war between the sexes: the right of women to vote. The failure to enfranchise women during the early republic was not a collective and conscious effort to take advantage of women. The injustices that existed were the result of the social inheritance of numerous generations. There had not as yet been sufficient insight, shared by significant numbers of those in power, to cry out to the injustice of it all. The deepest moral intuitions of those present had not awakened to the contradictions between what was espoused in documents such as the Declaration of Independence and the Constitution and what was suffered by an intolerably large and innocent segment of the community.[3] Fortunately, for all, matters were not left there interminably.

At the beginning of the twentieth century, the disenfranchisement of women still produced no inconvenience to men. As voters, men were the "haves" and women, the "have-nots." The group of haves saw no gain to sharing their property or the right to vote with outsiders. Feminists fighting for enfranchisement could have relied on strictly moral arguments to attract the attention of an alleged, morally upright electorate composed of all men. However, had they done so, their cries may well have fallen on deaf ears.

No doubt, some men were persuaded by the immorality of the current practice of disenfranchisement, but for most the women's suffrage movement was simply seen as the effort of a few disgruntled have-nots to steal away goods from the haves. The tactic feminists so successfully employed was to show the majority of as yet unconvinced men *and women* that a relationship of mutual interdependence already existed between men and women. Consequently, the well-being of women was seen as having a direct and immediate effect on the well-being of men. Through efforts at home and in public, feminists made the relationship of mutual interdependence palpably clear to men and to other women as well. The immediate result was a constitutional amendment. The long-term result was for women to begin talking about women's equality with men and for men to consistently acknowledge women's equality in word, if not, in deed. After years of *saying and doing* things that acknowledged the mutual interdependence of men and women, equality between the sexes became increasingly accepted throughout political and commercial domains.

At first, the story of how women came to acquire the vote seems to refute what has been said in earlier chapters about moral concerns universally appealing to and motivating of human beings. In particular, Hobbesian contract theory seems to underscore the idea that humans organize simply to accrue the benefits of "liberty 2," that is, that all is done out of self-interest. But this conclusion is not really as compelling as it may seem at the moment.

G. The Moral of the Story

There is an old story about a farmer who takes a mule to market. He stands the mule near the center of the market and tells all who will listen that the mule is the most cooperative and hardworking mule he has ever owned. He does all this to boost prospective buyers' interest in the mule. He ends each boast by noting that the mule is far too valuable to sell. By feigning no interest in selling the mule, the farmer piques the interest of an enterprising gentleman. The gentleman makes the farmer a handsome offer for the mule. A deal is struck. When attempting to take the mule home, the gentleman becomes chagrined to discover the mule will not move. Fearing he has been taken in, the gentleman implores the farmer to help him. In response to the petitioner's plea, the farmer picks up a board and smacks the mule in the forehead. The mule immediately lurches forward. Stunned by this act of apparent cruelty, the gentleman protests, "Why did you do that? You told me the mule was so very cooperative! Was that really necessary?" To this the farmer replies, "He is cooperative, but first you have to get his attention."

This story is not meant to make light of cruelty toward animals. Nor is it meant more generally to condone violence. The point is simply to note that for moral advance to occur, people do have to get the attention of others. Moral advance occurs when humans act to make it so. Lack of moral progress is, more often than not, a function of apathy or ignorance rather than immoral intent (that is, the intent to do evil to others).

American men and women who at the turn of the century remained unconcerned about the disenfranchisement of women were not out to do anyone harm. When feminists first attacked the injustice, the reaction on the part of many men was, predictably enough, to want to ignore the matter and maintain the status quo. As time went on and as feminists persisted, many men began to fear that a competitor, a have-not, was about to take something away (unjustly) from the haves. Once feminists succeeded in capturing the attention of voters and previously complacent women, due consideration was given to the problem. The more attention given to the problem, the more evident it became that the matter was not simply a contest between haves and have-nots. Rather, men and women came to recognize that an actual injustice was at hand. Opaque social forces had been confounding the attempt of groups (in this case gender-determinate groups) to work together in an unobstructive, mutually interdependent fashion. In short, once it was recognized by all groups that *each group* would benefit from extending the vote, the decision to enfranchise women became inevitable.

Tyranny of the Masses

Hobbesian contract theory explains why groups should act cooperatively with one another. This notion stirred later social contract theorists such as John Locke and, ultimately, Thomas Jefferson, John Adams, and others to advocate a republican form of democracy. But, as critics of Hobbes note, action taken for the mutual advantage of groups neither guarantees protection of the individual nor ensures his or her greatest advantage. Something more is needed. That something more, in the case of the United States, is the first five amendments to the Constitution. These amendments protect the individual from the "tyranny of the masses." In addition, laws denouncing individual tyranny, limiting length of term in office, separating realms of power, and limiting monopolies are all devices for preventing victimization of minorities as well as individuals.

While groups clearly benefit from mutual interdependence, individuals may selfishly take advantage of a group's well-meaning internal predisposition. Social theorists continue to address this problem, as do all practicing teachers. Specifically, in the case of the latter, teachers routinely struggle with individual students who recognize there is much to be gained personally from disrupting community and classroom efforts to act cooperatively. The malcontent often gets a disproportionate share of attention and other advantages by acting in a fashion contrary to group interests. Hobbes did little to explain why individuals should continue to cooperate rather than exploit the community agenda for personal gain. At this point our thoughts trail back to Aristotle.

Aristotle and the Good Guys

Recall that for Aristotle, humans are social animals. This means that it is natural and inevitable for humans to group together and live with others. For the spirit of community to succeed, schemes must be devised and practices implemented that preserve the security of each person and each group. At an emotional level this certainly seems true. Perhaps the philosophers Immanuel Kant and John Rawls are also right in their speculation that a sense of justice lurks in every mature individual.[4] As noted in the previous chapter, the very notion of maturity itself is a social concept, harboring within it regard for others. Both Lawrence Kohlberg and his oft-times adversary psychologist Carol Gilligan recognize that something other than self-interest motivates mature, fully developed individuals.[5] It makes great sense to give up the absolute freedom a person has in a state of Hobbesian nature to secure the liberties that only collective action can ensure. Still, when all is said and done, the best reason for humans to be *other-regarding* may be simply that it is right. And, as social philosophers Charles Taylor, Bernard Williams, and Hilary Putnam each independently conclude, it is commonly recognized as right and so there is little more that we could ask of a foundational principle in morality.[6] Similarly, even if the developmental psychologists and sociobiologists are right in their claims regarding the physical source of such intuitions, few doubt their universality.

II. John Stuart Mill: Respecting Pluralism and Protecting Against the Tyranny of the Masses

A. Humans Require More Than Freedom from Fear

Social contract theorists explain that in order to realize an optimal number of liberties, people organize themselves into groups. This affords them the protection to enjoy certain liberties free from intrusion by others. Laws, as well as many social customs, originate because they are seen as contributing to the purpose of the social contract. Would that things were so simple and straightforward. In truth, things are far more complicated.

No one, including Hobbes himself, ever thought people actually figured out the merits of a social contract and subsequently began to organize themselves accordingly. Hobbes was a theoretician, writing to lawmakers as well as to legal and social theorists. Hobbes wanted to show what "in principle" would justify a network of laws. For Hobbes, the law and the institutions it creates are justified to the extent that each serves the most basic needs of humankind. He wanted to construct criteria against which could be measured the extent to which a law contributes to the community's felicitous development. The most basic needs, from Hobbes's viewpoint, are (1) survival and (2) freedom from threat of aggression.

In a sense Aristotle foresaw that a list such as Hobbes's needed to include (3) the exercise of individual talents. According to Aristotle in the *Politics*, government and schools should help individuals learn to use their "excellencies excellently [as long as this does not endanger the state]." Finally, contemporary theoreticians extend the list further by claiming that (4) the community must provide for the individual's physical well-being and access to a minimal level of happiness.[7]

B. Pursuit of Happiness as an Educational Objective

Can happiness be a proper educational and social objective? The idea that the state is obligated to maximize the happiness of its citizens originated in the work of English jurist Jeremy Bentham. It received its most complete treatment, however, in the hands of John Stuart Mill and his disciples (which include nearly every leading liberal theorist of the twentieth century with the explicit exception of John Dewey).[8]

Mill, a nineteenth-century English philosopher and economist, thought that what motivated humans is, quite simply, happiness. He agreed there are qualitatively different levels of happiness. For example, the quality of happiness subsequent to completing some learning task varies with the merit of the thing learned. Thus, it makes a person happier, at the highest level, to understand Plato than to understand the rules for playing cricket or baseball. And, presumably, understanding Plato is both better and, in every way, more satisfying than stuffing ourselves full of pizza. To quote Mill on this matter, "It is better to be Socrates dissatisfied than a pig satisfied."

Mill, as with nearly every other social theorist before him, recognized that education is central to the successful development of the state. If the state is committed to the acquisition of happiness by all, then education has to achieve two goals. First, it has to identify what sorts of things make people happiest. Intellectual achievements are certainly high on the list, but even Mill, himself a child prodigy, in no way believed that the life of intellect is all that matters. In his autobiography Mill noted how much happiness he had missed by being so preoccupied with the pursuit of the intellect early in life.[9] Subsequent to his marriage, Mill noted that he learned much about the importance of love and other intangible elements of human relationships.[10] Furthermore, as evidenced by his very sensitive essay (for the time) *On the Subjugation of Women*, Mill believed superior levels of happiness can be achieved by crusading against evident social wrongs.[11] If education is to promote happiness, then education should illuminate for students the importance of nurturing relationships with others and the importance of crusading against injustices.

Second, education has to show people the way that they can secure the greatest aggregate happiness for the greatest number of people. If education is to promote happiness, it should take into account individual differences to extend each student's opportunities for achieving happiness. Only when students have an idea of all that might reasonably attract their interests can they move toward satisfying those interests. To expand students' horizons, Mill advocated a course of study that develops intellectual skills without deadening student emotional vitality. Tolerance is key to this task. Students learn at different rates and begin with different ideas of what is exciting and what is important. Teachers must be tolerant of all these differences if students are to move ever closer to optimal happiness.

C. Tolerance: A Condition for Happiness

Tolerance demands attention to many other related issues. For example, Mill denounced censorship as an affront to tolerance. Students must be free to let their minds explore various ideas without fear of reprisal and without the persistent demand that they learn only what their mentors take to be true. At first glance, Mill's rhetoric sounds akin to much liberal thought today. However, an important caveat should be heeded here. Though a champion of democratic action and a forerunner of the progressive education movement, Mill recognized a great potential for tyranny in democracy. In a pure democracy, the majority rule. A simple majority exists whenever 50 percent plus one agree upon a course of action. As noted in both this chapter and the previous one, simple majorities can be as oppressive to minorities as any tyrant.

Again, to quote a phrase enunciated originally by Mill, "The individual must be protected from the tyranny of the masses."

In short, Mill warned that there is a need to limit tolerance. A majority may identify a practice that will increase the immediate happiness of all but a small minority. The empirical efficacy of the practice is not in question. Still, Mill maintained, there must be limits that prevent the majority from victimizing a minority. Through education students learn both the virtues and the limits of tolerance and why citizens must be careful never to allow the victimization of any individual or any minority. Paradoxically, about right-minded attitudes toward tolerance there can be no tolerance. No amount of happiness, even on the part of a distinct majority, can ever license bigotry or prejudice.

The point to be gleaned from the first two sections of this chapter is that the law must create a network of government that is for the benefit of the governed. In a nation as admittedly pluralistic in ethnic richness as ours, the governed represent a broad diversity of peoples. Our nation is truly a nation of peoples. And, while each group of people is expected to abide by the laws and contribute as best it can to the well-being of all, all peoples are, in turn, expected to insist on the protection and respect due each minority.[12]

III.   The Law as Morality

A.   What Is law?

The study of the law remains a mystery to most people. The law is used to protect people, to obligate them, to ensure they keep their promises to one another, and, under certain circumstances, to provide remedies to injured parties. On the surface, the law is meant to keep things running in an orderly fashion—for better or worse. This surface appreciation of the law leads people to conclude that a distinct line of demarcation can be drawn between morals and laws. For example, people who fancy themselves moderates often respond to the abortion issue by saying the law ought to stay out of the moral domain. Those making this claim fall into two groups when addressing the legality of abortion. On the one hand, they say things like, "Issues such as this should be left to the states to decide," or, "Each individual should be free to decide these matters on his or her own. After all, what right has the state to interfere with the behavior of private individuals when such behavior affects no one else?"

Contrast the claims of these moderates with the challenges of extreme pro-choice groups and extreme pro-life groups. The former group asserts that the government should not interfere with the moral decision-making process of an individual (a traditionally conservative tact), and that the law has an affirmative obligation to protect women who have reached a decision regarding the unborn they bear. The latter group insists that the unborn have rights just as do all other persons (a traditionally liberal tact; for example, environmental groups considered liberal in their political leanings often champion the rights of future generations). Regardless of which side people take in this debate, they are addressing a moral issue. The claim that the state has a duty to protect the unborn is a blatant moral imperative, as is the claim that the law has a duty to protect, and perhaps even assist, an impoverished woman seeking an abortion.

And, finally, the claim that state laws ought to determine the legal status of the unborn is, once again, a straightforward moral claim—despite the fact that some have seen this as a strategy for ducking the immediate and personal implications of the decision! In truth, *whenever an individual engages in decision making that raises questions pertaining to personhood, that person is fully engaged in moral deliberation.* Specifically, questions such as who is to count as a person and the extent to which there might be degrees of personhood are questions of a strictly moral sort. So, too, are questions pertaining to what we owe persons and what considerations allow us to diminish the importance of a subject's personhood. For example, it is generally thought that persons should be allowed the broadest possible exercise of autonomy. On the other hand, the autonomy of a kindergarten student is greatly limited when compared with the autonomy extended to a senior in high school. In short, morality encompasses how degrees of personhood should be regarded as well as how persons should be treated. The law is but a subset of such decisions. *The law is that set of morals which those who hold the sovereignty of state are willing to endorse and (in some way attempt to) enforce.*[13]

Consider, for example, the law of contracts. This is essentially the law of promise keeping. It specifies what promises are to be kept and under what conditions. It further articulates what penalties are to be assessed on those who play loose and free with their promises. Finally, contract law provides (in principle) enforceable remedies for those who are evidently injured as a result of another's breach of contract. Those who shrink from the mere suggestion that the law and morals are one may protest that contract law is moral free and necessitated solely by our drive to associate with one another in matters of commerce and in other institutionalized relationships. In pressing their case, advocates for moral-free law quickly find themselves stumbling over their own words as they try to argue that various laws have sometimes arisen from strictly biological causes, from historical accident, or from the economic necessity of contractual arrangements necessary for human flourishing. Admittedly, each of these comes into play, but at no time can the body of law be regarded as a strict function of such elements. There are even times we can point to when laws are effected that offend the moral senses of nearly everyone. However, to keep from racing forward in error on this issue, we should consider what leads to a modification of the law.

B. Right-Minded Improvements in the Law

More often than not, legislative reform occurs when those who hold the sovereignty of state (in a democracy, this means the voting electorate) express dissatisfaction—moral indignation—with the present arrangement. Prior to a legislative enactment there is commonly much discussion about the *equity* or *fairness* of the situation at hand. *Legal reform is moral reform.*

This does not mean that legal reform always succeeds in the moral improvement of the world. More often than anyone would care to admit, it does not. Still, the point of reforming the law can never, in the final analysis, be freed from its home in the domain of moral rhetoric. (See fig. 3.2.)

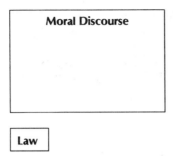

Figure 3.2 Law as Moral Discourse

Just as contract law is replete with moral implications and built from a variety of prior moral commitments, so, too, are family law, criminal law, welfare law, and even tax law. To repeat, the whole body of legislative law, and even matters of procedure, must be considered with an eye to the morality of it all. While all that has been said is true of law generally, nowhere is it more conspicuously true than in school law. Consider, for example, the laws surrounding the practice of punishment in the schools.

C. The Law and Morality of Punishment

Recall what punishment is not. Punishment is not brute force coercing one person to the will of a more powerful person. Bullies beat others into submission, but no one is so crass as to describe that as a proper example of punishment. Neither is punishment the deliberate infliction of harm. Some educational psychologists have carelessly described punishment as the deliberate infliction of a disadvantage on a student.14 Surely, this cannot be right. Imagine you are struck by a car and severely injured. The driver deliberately swerved in your direction to avoid hitting a school bus, thus avoiding a greater harm. In no sense have you been punished, even though you have been deliberately injured by another. And, in this case, by someone without malevolent intent. Punishment requires something more.

Finally, even if you suffer injury at the hands of someone who intends to injure you and reshape your behavior, does this establish an instance of punishment? Consider the following amusing, though once painful, account of an actual classroom event. A somewhat impetuous student, call him Tony, was reading his geography text per the teacher's instructions. Sitting next to Tony was another student, also named Tony. The latter student was reading a comic book he had secreted into his geography book. A fellow student told the teacher that Tony was reading a comic book. The teacher thought she knew which student the tattletale was talking about. Consequently, she immediately walked to where the boys were sitting and struck the arms of the first Tony with a yardstick. Tony yelped and looked up to see the grimacing teacher raise the yardstick again demanding, "Give it to me!" Whereupon she again brought the ruler down across Tony's hands. Tony wailed, "What? What do you want?" As the teacher raised her arm to inflict yet a third strike, the tattletale spoke up and said, "It's the other Tony!" Before the teacher could fully turn about "the other Tony" pushed the offending comic into her hands. Properly speaking, was the ill-fated Tony "punished" or merely victimized?

To say that Tony was unfairly punished is to admit obliquely that he was not punished at all but rather made to suffer a brutality. He deserved no infliction of disadvantage. Thus, he could not have been punished anymore than the victim of a crime is punished by the perpetrator of the crime. Wrongdoers are punished, not those who suffer wrong. So then, what is punishment?

The Real Thing

Punishment is the deliberate infliction of a disadvantage for a wrong (a moral offense) committed against some person. (The next time you receive a traffic ticket look on the back for the schedule of fines. These are described as penalties, not as punishments. Yet it is quite clear that when talking about the consequences of committing a felonious act, the topic at hand is one of punishment.) In punishment, properly speaking, the disadvantage is suffered at the hands of a person who is legitimately empowered to enforce certain rules. Furthermore, punishment is meant to ensure that due attention is given those rules in the future.

Teachers, and parents, are appropriate arbitrators of punishment under certain conditions. Each routinely and legitimately exercises a right to punish children. In fact, we are often prompted to criticize a teacher or parent for not punishing a child! Again, so the point is not lost here, the reason for the authority's action and accompanying explanation is to make a moral point in the mind of the punished, and not merely to execute a bit of behavioral technology.[15]

Not only do teachers and parents have a *right*, but also they sometimes have a *duty* to punish children. And, correspondingly, children have a *right* to expect punishment at times. Similarly, children themselves are *under a duty* to comply with properly punitive action. There are, and certainly ought to be, limits to punishment. In fact, the law is rather explicit about those limits. The basis of these limitations solidly reflects the community's moral sensibilities. Punishment properly executed is always a matter of maintaining moral order. Whenever this is not the case, an event cannot be regarded as punishment. With all this in mind, let us now turn to a direct and positive characterization of punishment.

Elements of Punishment

First, any infliction of a disadvantage on a student must be in response to the violation of a duly recognized prohibition; otherwise, the act is no more than the brute exercise of superior power to secure personal control over another. Second, the disadvantage inflicted must not exceed the harm created by the student's wrongdoing. In other words, the punishment must not be excessive. Teachers might address minor infractions by putting marks on the board, thus publically recording the student's transgressions. An extensive record of misbehavior may result in some further odious consequence: writing a violated rule five hundred times, sitting in the corner, or standing in the hall. In short, teachers can successfully employ a number of annoyances for a wide range of student infractions. As the seriousness of the student's misdeeds increases, the character of the punishment should change and intensify as well. Detention hall assignments, banishment to the principal's office, and even paddling or some other form of corporal punishment may be in order according to local school policy.

Third, any genuine punishment must be vividly educative. This means that any act of punishment must be portrayed in a way that reminds the student that the "crime" offends the moral sensibilities of the community. Failure to fulfill this last condition suggests to the student that he or she is merely the victim of a system of control. If the moral elements of punishment are not made conspicuously clear to the student through reasoned explanation, the student may regard the act as simple control—in short, a threat to his or her personhood. Control tends to demean personhood; punishment aims at enhancing it.

The Practice of Punishment

Most of your professors will discourage the use of corporal punishment in the schools. Still you may find that your school district allows it. What you may find even more surprising is that in some states children may be subjected to corporal punishment without any prior solicitation of parental consent. In *Ingraham v. Wright* (1977), the Supreme Court upheld the legality of corporal punishment. Specifically, in condoning the practice of corporal punishment, the Court declared, "Teachers may impose reasonable but not excessive force to discipline [punish] a child. . . . The prevalent rule in this country today privileges such force as a teacher or administrator reasonably believes to be necessary for the [child's] proper control, training, or education." Note the word *excessive* in the Court's ruling. While the law condones corporal punishment in principle, the caveat that the punishment must not be excessive leaves schools and school personnel vulnerable to civil suit. The result is that corporal punishment is diminishing in frequency, not so much because of professional advice to the contrary or legislative prohibitions against it, but rather because the economic and psychological costs of litigation are oppressive.

If corporal punishment is falling into disfavor, to what extent can the school punish a child by expulsion or suspension? In *Quinlan v. University Place, South Dakota* (1983), an exemplary high school student, with no previous disciplinary record, was suspended for sixty-four days because she was caught violating the school prohibition against the use of alcohol. (She had consumed a glass of champagne with her date shortly before a school dance.) According to case documentation, South Dakota state law permitted long-term suspension but subject to specific limitations, namely "The nature and circumstances of the violation must reasonably warrant a long-term suspension. . . . No student shall be suspended unless the other forms of corrective action or punishment reasonably calculated to modify his or her conduct have failed or unless there is good reason to believe that other forms of corrective action or punishment would fail if employed."

State and federal courts ruled against the suspension because it was based on a principle of "automatic suspension" for specific transgressions. Automatic suspension was said to be unduly harsh since it allowed no consideration for mitigating circumstances or for the student's general disposition toward behaving in a disruptive fashion. In short, the courts underscored their evolving commitment to *education*.

Schools are expected to have enforceable rules that contribute to a decorum necessary for learning. Systems of punishment that are so severe that they diminish the educational function of the school, even in individual cases, are not to be permitted. Sanctions should ensure compliance with the rules, but that is not all that matters. Educators are, or at least ought to be, committed to extending education to as many people as possible (so the South Dakota case reminds us). To forsake that commitment merely to strengthen the internal control structure of the school is to lose sight of the priorities that drive forward educators' moral sensibilities.

In the schools, punishment serves a purpose when it contributes to and protects the educational development of students. When punishment fails to serve that purpose, then it ought to be abandoned. This message has grown ever-clearer during the past three hundred years of legislation and court rulings.

While students may not think so, removing them from school is a serious matter. The American tradition maintains an unequivocal commitment to the principle of equality of opportunity.[16] Equality of educational opportunity is one way to ensure equal opportunity in general. Thus, jingoistic historians and educationists proudly recall the famous General Court of Massachusetts law of 1642 that declared, "[We] do hereupon order and decree that in every town the chosen men appointed for managing the prudential affairs of [children] shall henceforth . . . have power to take account from time to time of their parents and their masters and of their children, especially of their ability to read and understand the principles of religion and the capital laws of the country."

This law was followed by additional legislation in 1647 requiring towns to maintain schools. Gradually, access to equal *schooling* has become a right of everyone in the United States—a right secured by constitutional amendment and formally recognized as such in *Brown v. Board of Education of Topeka* (1954) and in *Plyler v. Doe* (1982). Furthermore, as education came to be seen as necessary to both the well-being of the community and the individual, attendance at school also became compulsory. Throughout the 1880s and the 1890s, states passed laws making school attendance compulsory. With the case of *Stuart v. School District No. 1* (1874), the state supreme court of Michigan upheld a compulsory attendance law. In short, this sort of law demonstrates that it matters very much in this country whether or not children go to school. It also matters whether or not all children have access to equal educational opportunity. It even matters to the citizens of the country that illegal aliens have access to education, as shown in the following chapter.

The nation's commitment to educational equality has even resulted in collisions between what appears to be conflicting constitutional rights. For example, the Bill of Rights guarantees both freedom of speech and religious freedom. Indeed, in *Pierce v. Society of Sisters* (1925), the Supreme Court declared a state law unconstitutional that would have ensured a state monopoly over the education of the young had it been allowed to stand. However, the Court, while noting the interest of the state in securing high quality education for its youth, emphasized that this interest cannot be used to deprive students of a competent education that includes religious instruction. In other words, the Court spoke as if two conflicting rights were at stake. This event is astonishing for no constitutional provision directly cites education as a right! Americans simply embrace it as one. Indeed, they hold equal educational opportunity in as high a regard as any right explicitly detailed in the Constitution. Access to an equal education is uncontroversially an *American good*.[17]

Just as punishment is always an effort to restore moral order in the schools, so, too, an equal education is esteemed as a good. Given that equal educational opportunity is an accepted good, commensurate with the American sense of moral order, expulsion or suspension as a means of punishment raises awkward moral (and legal) issues. On the one hand, to ensure that teachers can teach effectively and to remind a seemingly incorrigible student of the seriousness of his or her misbehavior, it seems reasonable to suspend or even expel a severely disquieting student. On the other hand, suspension and expulsion interfere with the individual's quest to secure equal opportunity.

These two interests run contrary to one another. Rather than try to figure out all the legal loopholes that may allow a school or teacher to get away with certain methods of control, the most simple and direct approach to issues of punishment is simply to recall that a teacher's first duty is to teach every student to the best of the teacher's ability.

Punishment that is educative makes sense. Punishment that makes it impossible for the student to continue in the educative process runs contrary to the most basic moral tenet of teacher professionalism, namely, teaching students all the good things we can. Thus, common sense dictates that every effort should be made to keep the child in school, to keep the child in some sort of environment wherein access to equal educational opportunity remains a possibility. When schools and teachers follow this simple moral dictate, neither are likely to run afoul of the law on the issue of punishment. This may seem too simplistic at first, but a review of our legal tradition reveals that as rules of thumb go, we will not find anything better. And, as more than one Supreme Court justice has reminded us, this is as it should be. The law is supposed to enrich and clarify our common-sense intuitions, not confound or befuddle them.

The discussion of punishment in the schools should illuminate much about the relationship between school law and our communal moral sensibilities. The law not only formalizes the morals the state wishes to enforce, but also it attempts to articulate resolutions to conflicting moral claims.

D. Systematic Thinking and the Law

Before continuing it must be noted that while the law is, at its roots, a subset of moral rhetoric, *legal thinking* is quite different from *moral thinking*. In the last chapter, the elements of ethical analysis were listed. An examination of the role of each element should have made one thing palpably clear: we can no more be certain that a current moral policy is free of error than we can conclude that current physics is free of error. Commendatory ethical reasoning produces conclusions with far more utility and promise than does ethical reasoning performed in a sloppy and haphazard way. Again, the same is true in physics. We cannot secure *grand truth* in either physics or ethics, but careful attention to our theories does help improve our science as well as our ethics. This is why we should be deliberative and systematic in reasoning about both. This is also why we should submit our moral conclusions to the scrutiny of other serious-minded moralists. And, finally, assuming all has been done to get our moral thinking into order, we should act in the most deliberate way possible to ensure our actions are commensurate with our conclusions. We are far more likely to do good in the world if we approach matters with care than if we approach them in a callous and careless way.

Moral Thinking

Moral reasoning leads to conclusions about what ought to be done. Once formalized, much of moral thinking becomes law. Once moral thinking becomes law it attains an emergent property (a property that exists in none of the component parts alone). It demands attention in a way that previous moral reflection did not. For example, we may all agree that prejudicial thinking in matters of race is a bad thing. Presumably, having arrived at that conclusion, we will try to discourage others from prejudicial beliefs. But, since there are no "thought police," no way to enforce legislation condemning prejudiced thinking, there is no law preventing such beliefs. There is, however, considerable law directed at decreasing prejudicial actions. One conspicuous feature of well-made law, as opposed to moral thinking generally, is that actions the law prescribes or prohibits are enforceable. Another emergent property of the law distinguishes it from the rest of the moral domain. Those charged with the administration of the law are duty bound to treat it as right-minded. Justice Clarence Thomas, a recent appointee to the U.S. Supreme Court, may disagree with the moral rightness of the law regarding abortion, but as a justice he is duty bound to decide all like cases in a manner commensurate with previous Supreme Court decrees. As a justice, he can no longer adjudicate matters through the lens of his own personal morality.

Legal Thinking

The task of jurists is to administer—not create—the law. The Latin phrase stare decisis prescribes how jurists ought to interpret the law. It means that the present case is to be decided in accord with the decision reached in the last such case. Officers of the court are not at liberty to use the court to inflict their own moral view of the world on others. They must treat the law as a "given" and adjudicate matters brought to them accordingly. A judge must set aside personal moral inclinations and decide matters in a manner consistent with previous judicial reasoning (and, where relevant, legislative intent). When wayward jurists begin imposing their own moral sensibilities on the behavior of litigants, the system of checks and balances fails. If a piece of law, as it currently exists, confounds our deepest moral intuitions, then we must act to change the law through appropriate legislation.

Precedential Thinking

In short, while enacted law may be rightfully described as a subset of moral discourse, legal reasoning is significantly different from that involved in more general ethical analysis. *Legal reasoning* is precedential. That is, whenever possible, decisions reached in current cases are to be consistent with previous decisions in the most similar cases. In contrast, *moral reasoning* is principally preoccupied with getting matters right on some grand scale. Nothing is taken as absolute. Human fallibility is freely recognized. Introspection into a person's deepest intuitions is considered legitimate. Morally sensitive people remain ever-ready to shift commitment from one moral dictate to another should they discover some universal reason for doing so. That is, when all reasonable people, considering the roles of all agents involved, are likely to consent to a revision of a given rule, then not only should they adopt the revision but also, presumably, they are duty bound to do so. The initial fluidity of moral reasoning is a luxury legal reasoning can ill afford. *The point of moral reasoning is to create laws and conventions that advance the nobility of the community and, perhaps, even the species.* The point of legal reasoning is to ensure stability.

IV. The Law as Politics

A. Changing State's Attitudes

In the last section, a major objective was to show that the law is inseparable from morality. This is contrary to a myth preserved by some lawyers and laypeople advocating a particular (usually libertarian) cause. Equally misleading is the myth that politics and law are inseparable. Again, as noted earlier in the story of the woman's suffrage movement, to force a change in the law moral agents must sometimes become immersed in powerful political movements to "get the attention of those in power." Politically aggressive movements often bring about significant changes in the law. There is no secret in this. Neither is it a secret that some changes represent a clear moral advance for society (such as the Civil Rights Act of 1964), while court decisions reaffirm the status quo and may even lead to transitory regression. This latter phenomenon is exemplified by the administrative laws and subsequent court decisions that led to the internment of Japanese-Americans during World War II. The Supreme Court appeared to be ruling in a manner consistent with earlier judgments. However, while the net effect of earlier judgments was to expand freedom, the internment cases threatened to greatly diminish it.

While the courts and legislatures are vulnerable to pressure from special interest groups, the courts at least are restricted from ever collaborating in a nonjusticiable issue (that is, an issue wherein no constitutional protection is at risk and the legislature has presumably represented the will of the people through the enactment of appropriate legislation). This principle was most recently reassessed in *Elrod v. Burns* (1976). The importance of this mind-your-own-business principle was cited again and again by Texas State Representative John Culbertson in an amicus curiae (friend of the court) brief in the recently settled *Kirby v. Edgewood Independent School District* (1989). Edgewood, an economically impoverished school district, sued the Texas State Board of Education claiming that the district was unable to offer equal educational opportunities to its students because of legislated fiscal policies. In the *Kirby* case, the appellate court declared that a state could not distribute its resources in a way that systematically led to the disadvantage of already impoverished school districts.

Culbertson insisted that the courts have always maintained that unless a constitutional protection could be shown to be at risk, they must refuse the temptation to make current administrative or legislative law "better."[18] And yet, Culbertson declared, this seemed to be precisely what the court was prepared to do in *Kirby*. Cases such as these make students of the courts frustrated and constitutional law scholars irritable.[19] Even if the *Kirby* decision is on the moral high ground, by ignoring a fairly powerful precedential history to the contrary, the court seemed willing to abort the normal checks and balances and force a practice it believed central to the good of the people. Further elaboration on the dangers of this sort of vigilantism on the part of the courts should be left to journalists and legal scholars for debate.

From the point of view of this text, two things merit continued attention. First, the teaching profession is dedicated to extending the educational benefits of every student. Thus, teachers cannot help but be cheered by the *intent* of the *Kirby* decision. Second, teachers should be aware that the law, even court-made law, may undertake a matter that had previously been held beyond its bounds. Consequently, inattention to the political drift of the courts is an error that could prove costly to individual teachers or, as in the *Kirby* case, to an entire state.

Funding for Head Start programs, bilingual education, English as a second language, various programs for special students, and even meal subsidies often depends more on the political climate than on the morality involved (or any other set of reasons that may make a given practice a good idea on a day-to-day basis). This does not contradict earlier statements in the text. Moral advance is neither linear nor evenly paced. As mentioned previously, moral advance can be compared to the stock market. It is a process governed by uneven fits and starts, recessions and advances of unpredictable duration. The morality of the species, like its control over the market, proceeds in curious fashion. Money invested in the market over long enough time has always shown itself to be money well spent. Similarly, moral recession occurs. It occurs because of apathy or, more often, because of the self-serving efforts of political demagogues and unscrupulous special interest organizations. Nevertheless, as in the market, the heroic efforts of moralists have, over the long run, proven to be quite effective in making the world a better place to live.

B. Individual Professionalism and Political Liability

The person entering the teaching profession is under a special obligation to be wary of the twists and turns of society's moral fortunes. Not only do teachers have the same duty as everyone else to live a decent life and to be an accommodating neighbor, but also teachers have special duties to assist in the upbringing of future generations. Consequently, teachers are obligated to *feel responsible* for the continued advance of civilization. That is, they must be determined to create a society in which people learn to be more civil to one another. And they need to know that it takes different techniques to get that message through to students from different backgrounds.[20]

Community Gadfly

The teacher's role in questioning society's morals is illustrated by the very famous constitutional law case of *Pickering v. Board of Education of Township High School District 205* (1968). In the early 1960s, Marvin L. Pickering was a schoolteacher in Illinois District 205. Pickering perceived himself to be an advocate of intellectual rigor and high academic standards. For him, there was no doubt that the first mission of the school should be the education of the students. He had become convinced that neither the district administration nor the board shared his enthusiasm for academic excellence. From his position as a teacher in the district, Pickering had noticed that a great deal of money was spent on athletics—too much money to his way of thinking.

Disturbed over the disproportionate amount of money the district committed to athletics, Pickering decided to speak out. In a letter to the local newspaper, he accused the administration and the board of being irresponsible in their expenditures on athletics and of misleading the public regarding how much of the district's budget actually went to underwrite athletic programs. He accused the superintendent of trying to prevent teachers from opposing or criticizing a school bond issue in 1961. Pickering's crusade went largely unnoticed by the public. It did not go unnoticed by the district officials or the board.

The board, pursuant to Illinois state law, held a hearing charging Pickering with dereliction of duty and libelous behavior regarding his superiors. During the hearing the board demonstrated that, technically, some of the figures cited by Pickering in his public letter were in error. The board noted further that in other matters Pickering's opinion honestly differed from that of his superiors. Nevertheless, they claimed, he was under obligation to the district not to make those differences a matter for public debate. Specifically, on this latter issue the board wrote that "the teacher has a duty of loyalty to support his superiors in attaining the generally accepted goals of education and that, if he must speak out publicly, he should do so factually and accurately, commensurate with his education and experience." At the conclusion of the hearing, Pickering was fired. Setting issues of legality aside for a moment, answer this question: Was the board's action in this matter morally right?

The Issues in *Pickering*

What sorts of things strike you as relevant in this case? Is the teacher obligated to be a team player? Did Pickering fail to be a good team player? What should happen if a teacher's individual sense of duty conflicts with explicit school policy? Is he duty bound to exercise restraint, making recommendations to his superiors and thereafter keeping silent to all others? The expenditure of public funds on public education is a public matter. Public funding of education is intended to be for the public good. As a public matter, shouldn't everyone feel free to express his or her ideas on the rightness or wrongness of public decisions? To what extent should teachers be held accountable for the accuracy of information they make public about their school district?

Teachers have the education of students as their principal responsibility. Administrators and board members are committed to the maintenance of the system. Do we want those whose principal professional concerns are with the education of students to be silenced by those whose principal concerns are with the health of an administrative system? Is it in the public's best interest to have access to the impressions of teachers as well as to the formal declarations of administrative officers?

Pickering sued the board for restraint of free speech as guaranteed by the First Amendment of the U.S. Constitution. The Circuit Court of Will County, Illinois, was unpersuaded by Pickering's arguments. Instead, it agreed with the board that Pickering had violated Illinois law (Ill. Rev. Stat., c. 122, sect. 10-22.4[1963]) stating that a school employee may not engage in any action "detrimental to the efficient operation and administration of the schools of the district." Pickering's letter to the newspaper was taken by the court to be just such a detriment. Everyone agreed Pickering was telling things as he saw them. He was addressing a public issue in a public forum, and he was relying on the best information he had. Some of his information regarding dollar figures was inaccurate. There was no evidence, however, that his letter had affected his working performance or that of his colleagues. Is there any reason to believe that Pickering was a bad person? Is there any reason to believe that Pickering did a bad thing? If Pickering did no harm and was acting with good intent and without malice toward any person, should the law protect him?

The Illinois Supreme Court upheld the lower court's ruling. The court appeared to say that even if Pickering did no more than what we allow other citizens to do, the fact that he was a teacher placed him under special constraints to abide by all policies, implicit and explicit, clearly endorsed by the district. Thus, the supreme court agreed with the lower court ruling emphasizing that employment with the school district diminishes the range of rights a citizen might otherwise enjoy.

Trading Away Rights

Is it right to force a person to trade away constitutional rights as a condition of employment? We require people in the military, the CIA, weapons laboratories, and various other government agencies to trade away rights as a condition of employment all the time. But what about this case? Should trading away rights be expected of teachers? Should it be expected of teachers who are commenting on priorities in education? More particularly, should it be expected of experienced teachers commenting on the very district with which they have personal and immediate experience? If teachers do not speak out on conditions within their district, where else can the public hope to get expert insight at the level of classroom practice?

At this point, all levels of the establishment in the state had decided against Pickering. From the superintendent's office and school board to the courts and even to the state supreme court, Pickering's behavior was judged wrong. Each agreed Pickering should be fired from his job as a schoolteacher. Alone with only the First and Fourteenth Amendment of the U.S. Constitution to protect him, Pickering presented his case to the Supreme Court of the United States. The Court granted a writ of certiorari (meaning it selected Pickering's case as one of the few cases it would hear that session) and ultimately reversed the lower court decisions. In doing this, the Supreme Court showed that genuine constitutional issues were at stake, issues that if subverted would result in great injustice to individuals. In making its ruling, the Supreme Court was well aware that it was confronting a powerful set of special interest groups including the state of Illinois and the fraternity of educational bureaucrats from throughout the country. Still, constitutional protections guarantee right-minded treatment for everyone, not just the majority and not just the powerful.

The Supreme Court's Answer

The Supreme Court pointed out that there was no compelling reason to diminish the equal protection clause of the Fourteenth Amendment in Pickering's case. The Court unhesitatingly declared that the Illinois Supreme Court erred in suggesting that conditions of state employment could be used as grounds for diminishing a person's constitutional rights. The Court cited numerous previous decisions wherein this precedent had been established and upheld. (For example, *Weiman v. Updegraff* [1952], *Shelton v. Tucker* [1960], and *Keyishian v. Board of Regents* [1967] from which the Court quoted, "The theory that public employment which may be denied altogether may be subjected to conditions, regardless of how unreasonable, has been uniformly rejected.")

The Court further rejected the trial court's reasoning that since some of Pickering's facts had been in error his action was libelous and therefore appropriate grounds for dismissal. The Court pointed out that teachers should be held to no greater standard of accuracy than a journalist researching a story. (The Court cited specifically the benchmark case of *New York Times Co. v. Sullivan* [1964] in this regard.) According to the Court in *Pickering*, the standard in such cases is as follows: To be legally actionable, statements must be made "with knowledge that [they were] . . . false or with reckless disregard of whether [they were] . . . false or not." The evidence presented by both sides showed no ill or reckless intent on Pickering's part.

Finally, Pickering had accepted a job with a school district in a state in which *statutory law* declares that teachers must behave, as it were, as team players. Did he give away his right to free speech by accepting the teaching position? Did he then later double-cross his employers by speaking out and thereby divorcing himself from the team effort? On both these matters the Court concluded that

> What we do have before us is a case in which a teacher has made erroneous public statements upon issues then currently the subject of public attention, which are critical of his ultimate employer but which are neither shown nor can be presumed to have in any way either impeded the teacher's proper performance of his daily duties in the classroom or to have interfered with the regular operation of the schools generally. In these circumstances we conclude that the

interest of the school administration in limiting teachers' opportunity to contribute to public debate is not significantly greater than its interest in limiting a similar contribution by any member of the general public.

More specifically, the Court in conclusion quoted from *Garrison v. State of Louisiana* (1964) that " 'statements by public officials [such as those made by Pickering] on matters of public concern must be accorded First Amendment protection despite the fact that the statements are directed at their nominal superiors.' "

Teacher Rights to Free Speech

The *Pickering* case is well worth the extended treatment given to it here. This case is cited as the benchmark example of the Supreme Court's willingness to protect teacher rights to free speech (even when that speech is directed against the teacher's own school district). But for this present chapter, *Pickering* also illustrates something important about the relationship between law and politics.

It has been noted that the courts are prohibited from infringing on the political domain. That is, when the will of the people is expressed through appropriate legislation, the courts will not act regardless of any apparent injustices that may result *unless* some constitutional issue is at stake. In *Pickering*, the state of Illinois had legislation in effect that presumably condoned actions such as those undertaken by the school board. Because a constitutional issue was at stake, each higher level court felt compelled to enter into the debate. That Pickering's rights were in jeopardy on numerous grounds is evident by the unequivocal language of the U.S. Supreme Court and by the numerous precedents it was able to cite grounding its decision. In so many ways, the *Pickering* case should not have been a difficult case for the state courts to decide. Not only did the state courts fail to protect Pickering, but also they failed to give way on a single issue, even though precedents to the contrary were easily at hand and relied on in numerous jurisdictions throughout the country.

Reviewing the *Pickering* court records brings a David-and-Goliath analogy to mind. Prominent local community members supported the power of other equally prominent people. Surely, that was not all that mattered to those involved, but neither can it be ruled out as altogether irrelevant. Furthermore, what person in power has not found himself or herself irritated to distraction by the self-appointed gadfly? Leadership is more enjoyable and institutions more steady when criticism is kept to a minimum. All the leading actors in the *Pickering* case were male, and as such all were no doubt well versed in the dogma of team play. Not that being a team player is bad. But it is not always good either. Mobs are given over to "team" action. It is the independent thinker who keeps the mob impulse in check.

Pickering was not a team player. It is easy to imagine how that alone could have lost him sympathy among the other actors. When Pickering's case went to the Illinois Supreme Court, all the external influences that may have affected the decisions of previous arbiters were still present. The state law, which the court is sworn to uphold, was vulnerable. How could the Illinois Supreme Court decide against the board without itself feeling it had not been a team player? After all, against all these considerations stood only the rights of one uncooperative and noisy schoolteacher. Despite so many legal precedents to the contrary, each one of the Illinois courts ultimately endorsed the most politically attractive decision. There may have been no ill intent toward Pickering on the part of any of the jurists, but the fact that not one saw reason to give way on a single issue suggests that political, and not strictly legal, issues were contaminating judicial thinking.

Much to its credit the U.S. Supreme Court, though admittedly greatly removed from many of the political influences affecting Illinois residents, decided a case consistent with precedent, faithful to the ideal of protecting individuals from all unjust exercise of power—even state power itself. Not surprisingly, the final adjudication of *Pickering* reflected good legal reasoning and produced a morally satisfying decision. Skeptics take note. The American system has many flaws, but somehow we keep muddling along and, over the long run, we do progress.

V. Court Cases Describing Teacher and Student Rights

A. Understanding Further the Idea of the Law

The purpose of this last section is not to give an exhaustive account of all student and teacher rights. That task would require an extensive book-length treatment in its own right. Rather, the purpose is to show that in teaching, the intimacy between morality and the law is a determinant affecting the most ordinary and routine practices of teachers. Television shows are filled with exotic portrayals of courtroom dilemmas. The viewing public becomes familiar with terms such as *objection, sustained, illegal search and seizure, due process, constitutional rights,* and *dismissal for cause.* And, if teachers have occasion to employ an attorney on a private matter, they may be further awestruck by the challenge of litigation and the use of terms such as *res ipsa loquitur, lack of venue, no jurisdiction, tort,* and *ex testamento.* While not to minimize the merit and intellectual challenge of the study of law, it need not be as mysterious as it at first seems. To reiterate a point made earlier, the law is a statement of the morals those who hold the sovereignty of state wish to endorse and enforce.

The Holders of Sovereignty
In a democracy the holders of the state's sovereignty are the electorate. This means the law is truly intended to be "by the people and for the people." Admittedly, this process gets subverted at times. Even when the law accurately portrays the will of the people, that will may be arrived at in haste and carelessness. Enacted law may reflect short-term popular preferences, and these may harbor difficulties that the holders of sovereignty will later need to change. The law is supposed to serve the people. After all, people make the law for their own purpose. Unfortunately, its apparent complexity limits the number of people who actually set out to study and understand it. The word *apparent* is important. While there is much to study in the law, it is not as inaccessible or as rigid as many people suppose.[21]

The law is an expression of community common sense and is more easily understood when viewed as a record of our deepest, collective moral sensibilities. Pay attention to the word *deepest.* The law is not directed at the unreflective hunches that pop into people's minds when a problem first arises. Rather, it embodies the conclusions that are reached subsequent to much commonsense deliberation.

B. Common Sense and Order in the Schools

Keeping these preliminary remarks in mind, consider a recent schoolhouse issue involving the media—popularized topic of illegal search and seizure. Followers of "Perry Mason," "L.A. Law," and cops-and-robbers television shows are well aware that the police cannot just pull suspicious-looking people over and search them for drugs, weapons, or other contraband. These shows contain much talk about search warrants and about the need for an arresting officer to observe a crime in action before searching a suspect for evidence. Much of this is accurately presented. But how does this translate into the schools? Are teachers akin to police officers? Are school policies and procedures to be likened to those of the criminal system? Are teachers and school administrators supposed to be knowledgeable of the most subtle intricacies of constitutional law? Is there a schoolhouse version of the *Miranda* statement (reading the accused their rights at the time of arrest)? Are schoolchildren full-fledged citizens possessing the same rights as every other citizen in society?

Policing the Schools

In answering these questions, consider the reasonableness of requiring teachers to be more than teachers in the classroom. Consider, too, the fact that not all adults have equal rights in all contexts. In the discussion of the *Pickering* case, it was noted that certain government employees sacrifice rights because of superior state interests. For example, CIA employees cannot publish classified information. Felons can never vote. The severely retarded and emotionally disturbed cannot vote, and they may be locked up against their wills and subjected to unwanted medical treatment. While no one would suggest that students are anything like select government employees, criminals, or the severely mentally impaired, they are not full citizens either.

No one under eighteen can vote. Until the early 1970s most colleges still labored under the doctrine of *in loco parentis* (meaning that the institution was expected to care for the student as would a parent). The law allows for students to be paddled. Yet nowhere are authorities allowed to paddle even the most vicious of criminals! There are clear and distinct differences between children and adult citizens, but on what grounds are these distinctions based?

School-aged children possess limited experience and are both physically and emotionally immature. In short, there is good reason to conclude that they cannot engage in the reflective deliberations and care we demand of adults. Children are not victims of diminished mental capacity, but neither are they adequately equipped with the adult's intellectual and emotional repertoire. The doctrine of in loco parentis no longer applies at the college level though it is still very much in effect in the public schools. Thus, nutritionists in the role of parents determine the content of cafeteria menus. School newspapers are not allowed the same range of freedoms as the adult media, dress codes continue, and exercise regimens and detention halls abound. All of this contrasts sharply to the conditions under which most adults live.

What's Left on the Schoolhouse Steps?

So how does in loco parentis relate to the issue of illegal search and seizure? Can teachers shake down students as they can their own offspring? That would be a serious mistake! Ever since the benchmark cases of *In Re Gault* (1966) and *Tinker v. Des Moines Community I.C.S.D.* (1969) the Supreme Court has insisted that children do retain some constitutional rights while at school. The colorful phrase *children's rights are not left at the schoolhouse gates* originated with the *Tinker* case. But powerful remnants of the in loco parentis doctrine continue to limit the range of rights students enjoy while in school (see also *Ingraham v. Wright* [1977]).

In *Irby v. State of Texas* (1988), the courts upheld the right of school officials to search students' property when *reasonable cause* exists. This is a much weaker constitutional protection than exists in criminal searches in the society at large (*probable cause* that a crime has been committed is required in the latter case). Specifically, in the *Irby* case, Sean Irby was searched by school officials after another student, found carrying marijuana, claimed Irby had given him the contraband. Irby claimed that to search his person on the grounds of another student's complaint violated his Fourth Amendment rights. The court noted that "the underlying command of the Fourth Amendment is always that searches and seizures must be reasonable. What is reasonable depends on the context within which a search takes place." The court then went on to declare, "It is evident that the school environment requires some easing of the restrictions to which searches by public authorities are ordinarily subject." Specifically, the court noted,

> We join the majority of courts that have examined this issue in concluding that the accommodation of the privacy interests of schoolchildren with the substantial need of teachers and administrators for freedom to maintain order in the schools does not require adherence to the relevant requirement that searches be based on probable cause. . . . Under ordinary circumstances, a search of a student by a teacher or other school official will be justified at its inception when there are reasonable grounds for suspecting that the search will turn up evidence that the student has violated or is violating either the law or the rules of the school.

In short, the accusation of an alleged accomplice establishes reasonable grounds for searching the accused. The *Irby* case is wholly consistent with the most recent Supreme Court ruling in this matter, *New Jersey v. T.L.O.* (1985). In *New Jersey* the Court stated that

> the legality of a search of a student should depend on the reasonableness, under all the circumstances, of the search. Determining the reasonableness of any search involves a twofold inquiry: first, one must consider whether the "action was justified at its inception," . . . second, one must determine whether the search as actually conducted "was reasonably related in scope to the circumstances which justified the interference in the first place" . . . Such a search will be permissible in its scope and not excessively intrusive in light of the age and sex of the student and the nature of the infraction.

Reasonable Expectation

Thus, if a school official has reason to believe that a student is guilty of a crime, then the official may initiate a search of the student's property. In the case of *Irby*, the reasonableness of the search at its inception was established by the accusation of an alleged conspirator. Moreover, had it turned out in *Irby*, as it had in *New Jersey*, that in the course of searching for drugs officials came on another, but initially unsuspected, contraband such as a knife, the newly discovered evidence would be admissible either in any school adjudication of the crime or in any subsequent court proceeding.

Students do not leave their rights at the schoolhouse door, but neither do they maintain a full complement of them. While *Tinker* represented the upholding of students' rights, recent decisions show the Court to be increasingly vigilant and protective of the needs of today's school officials in carrying out their educational mission.

What Do Teachers Leave on the Schoolhouse Steps?

The *Pickering* case shows that the right of teachers to speak out against perceived injustices within the public schools is protected by the Constitution. Does this mean that teachers also do not abandon their rights on the schoolhouse steps? Yes and no. Yes, the courts want to afford every teacher an optimal range of the protection the Constitution identifies. No, the reality is that the context determines the reasonableness of limiting or denying the full array of constitutional rights to both student and educator alike.

Criminal behavior and outlandish sexual behavior have both been upheld by the courts as legitimate grounds for teacher dismissal.[22] However, matters do not end there. Even self-expression through dress may be limited for teachers just as it is for students. Court cases have upheld school disciplinary actions against teachers for such seemingly minor violations of school policy as failing to wear a tie. In *East Hartford Education Association v. Board of Education of Town of East Hartford* (1977), the courts upheld precisely such a dismissal. In explaining its reasoning the court said

> The very notion of public education implies substantial public control. . . . In view of the uniquely influential role of the public school teacher in the classroom, the board is justified in imposing this regulation. As public servants in a special position of trust, teachers may be properly subjected to many restrictions in their professional lives which would be invalid if generally applied . . . a school board may, if it wishes, impose reasonable regulations governing the appearance of teachers it employs.

Thus, as *Pickering* demonstrates, teachers do not lose all constitutional rights by entering the profession. But, as *East Hartford* demonstrates, the rights they retain are limited.

Teachers hold an office of state. As a result, the state makes demands on their time and limits their range of rights in a manner dissimilar to anything we would expect to see in the private sector. As professionals, teachers labor under additional restrictive burdens that nonprofessionals can ignore. The best teachers are an unselfish lot. Only unselfish teachers are emotionally prepared to bear this burden of service—service to the public, to the school, to the disciplines they represent, and to the children. Teachers especially cannot forget the children from a variety of cultural backgrounds and family unions whose only sense of community arises from that which the school and classroom teacher create.[23] Society wants a better tomorrow. How ironic that its expectations should be left to the unselfish nature, good will, and skill of such an underpaid and inadequately valued group of professionals. Students have no choice but to live with the limited set of rights society preserves for them within the schools. Teachers, on the other hand, freely accept the diminished range of rights they incur in order to serve students, discipline, and community. People who enter the profession in full knowledge of all that it will cost and all that will be expected of them truly represent a class of American heroes. They need to remember their heroic stature and remain vigilant in their efforts to advance the well-being of their students.

In *Board of Education v. Rowley* (1982), the Supreme Court emphasized that it indeed expects the schools to seek the well-being of all students. In this case, the Court said that as long as handicapped students were "mainstreamed" and advancing like any other student, the school would be required to offer no other special services. In other words, the Court limited the district's financial commitment. But there are no limitations on time, duty, and compassion for the professional teacher. Such people know no limits when it comes to serving students, subject matter, and community. Only old age, illness, and other limitations of the body relieve the professional teacher of further effort to serve.

How can we understand what it means to be a good American in a pluralistic society? Maybe, we should begin by studying the role of the teacher. No greater exemplar of commitment to community and respect for individuality exists than in the person of the highly professional teacher.

QUESTIONS FOR DISCUSSION

1. Why does it matter how we choose to group together?
2. What danger is there to individuals and minorities in a strictly democratic form of government?
3. What is the relationship between the law and morality?
4. In what ways do the courts try to free themselves from the activities of political interest groups?
5. In what ways have the moral sensitivities of the community improved the direction of American education?
6. In what respects have political influences produced laws destructive to the educational mission of the schools?
7. In what ways have court decisions been instructive in informing teachers of the public's expectations?
8. On what grounds do the courts limit the rights of teachers and students alike?

NOTES

1. Thomas Hobbes, *Leviathan* (Oxford: Clarendon Press, 1909).
2. J. Johnson, H. Colliers et al., *Introduction to Foundations of American Education,* 2nd ed. (Boston: Allyn & Bacon, 1991), 505–7.
3. See, for example, Crane Brinton, *A History of Western Morals* (New York: Harcourt, Brace & Co., 1959).
4. Immanuel Kant, *Groundwork to a Metaphysics of Morals* (New York: Harper & Row, 1964); John Rawls, "A Sense of Justice," in *The Philosophical Review* see especially R. S. Peters, *Moral Development and Moral Education* (London: Allen and Unwin, 1981).
5. Lawrence Kohlberg, *Moral Stages: A Current Formulation and a Response to Critics* (New York: Karger, 1983). See also Carol Gilligan, *In a Different*

Voice: Psychological Theory and Women's Development (Cambridge: Harvard University Press, 1982).

6. Charles Taylor, *Sources of Self: The Making of the Modern Identity* (Cambridge: Harvard University Press, 1989), and Bernard Williams, *Morality: An Introduction to Ethics* (New York: Harper & Row, 1972). See also *Ethics and the Limits of Philosophy* (Cambridge: Cambridge University press, 1985); Hilary Putnam, *Reason, Truth and History* (Cambridge, England: Cambridge University Press, 1983); Hilary and Putnam, *The Many Faces of Realism* (La Salle, Ill.: Open Court, 1987).

7. Derek Parfit, *Reasons and Persons* (Oxford: Clarendon Press, 1984).

8. Robert Nozick, *Anarchy, State and Utopia* (New York: Basic Books, 1974).

9. John Stuart Mill, *Autobiography* (London: Longmans, Green & Co., 1873).

10. Peter Glassman, *J. S. Mill: The Evolution of Genius* (Gainesville: University of Florida Press, 1985).

11. John Stuart Mill, *On the Subjugation of Women* (New York: Henry Holt & Co., 1898).

12. See, for example, Laurence H. Fuchs, *The American Kaleidoscope: Race, Ethnicity and the Civic Culture* (Middletown, Conn.: Wesleyan University Press, 1991).

13. This seems well in accord with the minimal sense of the matter held by nearly every major judicial theorist of the twentieth century. See, for example, R. A. Wasserstrom, *The Judicial Decision* (Stanford: Stanford University Press, 1961); Patrick Devlin, *The Enforcement of Morals* (Oxford: Oxford University Press, 1965); Lon L. Fuller, *The Morality of Law* (New Haven: Yale University Press, 1969); H. L. A. Hart, *Law, Liberty and Morality* (Stanford, Calif.: Stanford University Press, 1962); Ronald M. Dworkin, *A Matter of Principle* (Cambridge: Harvard University Press, 1985).

14. Nathaniel N. Gage and David Berliner, *Educational Psychology*, 4th ed. (Boston: Houghton Mifflin, 1988).

15. P. S. Wilson, *Interest and Discipline in Education* (London: Routledge & Kegan Paul, 1971), chap. 4.

16. See, for example, Catherine Emihovich, "Toward Cultural Pluralism: Redefining Integration in American Society," *The Urban Review* 20: 3–7. See also Geneva Gay (January 1988), "Multiethnic Education: Historical Development and Future Prospects," *Phi Delta Kappan* 64 (8): 560–63.

17. James Banks, *Multiethnic Education: Theory and Practice* (Boston: Allyn & Bacon, 1988).

18. For example, Culbertson noted that in the area of draft registration the Supreme Court had rejected an equal protection challenge to a selective service regulation that excluded women as a nonjusticiable controversy because of the textually demonstrable constitutional power of Congress to raise and support armies (*Rostker v. Goldberg* [1981]). In short, the Court said this is Congress's business; the courts must stay out. Culbertson went on to cite *Chiaramine v. Immigration and Naturalization Service* (1980) wherein the courts refused to second-guess congressional decisions pertaining to immigration; *Lead Industries Ass'n. Inc. v. Environmental Protection Agency* (1980) wherein the courts refused to second-guess

standards established by the EPA; and *Desedare v. Schweiker* (1982) wherein the courts refused to tamper with the definition of disability as it pertained to individual access to social security disability benefits.

19. Albert Bork, *The Tempting of America: The Political Seduction of the Law* (New York: Touchstone Books, 1989).

20. James Anderson, "Cognitive Style and Multicultural Populations," *Journal of Teacher Education* 39(1): 2–9.

21. In commenting on the ease with which a person can come to understand tort law, one rather famous law professor routinely commented to his first-year students, "As you explain this stuff to your clients they may discover it's not nearly as elusive as they initially suspected. Consequently, they may balk at paying their bill. Whenever you sense the client is getting to that point, it's time to throw in a Latin phrase. A Latin phrase is always worth another hour of billing!"

22. See, for example, *Gaylord v. Tacoma School District No. 10* (1977) wherein the Supreme Court upheld the dismissal of a teacher for his "flagrant" pursuit of a homosexual lifestyle and *Gillett v. Unified School District No. 276* (1980) wherein the court affirmed a school board action supporting the dismissal of a teacher on grounds of having committed a criminal offense outside of school activities.

23. Gerald Pine and Asa Hilliard, "Rx for Racism: Imperatives for America's Schools," *Phi Delta Kappan* 71 (April 1990): 593–600.

For Further Reading

Educational Foundations

Bloom, B. *All Our Children Learning.* New York: McGraw-Hill, 1982.
Bruner, J. *Acts of Meaning.* Cambridge: Harvard University Press, 1990.
Kagan, J. *The Nature of the Child.* New York: Basic Books, 1985.
Kant, I. *Education.* Ann Arbor: University of Michigan Press, 1960.
Oakshott, M. *The Voice of Liberal Learning.* Cambridge: Harvard University Press, 1989.
Rut, J. *Development in Judging Moral Issues.* Minneapolis: University of Minnesota Press, 1979.

Law and Legal Theory

Bork, A. *The Tempting of America: The Political Seduction of the Law.* New York: Touchstone Books, 1989.
Devlin, P. *The Enforcement of Morals.* Oxford: Oxford University Press, 1965.
Dworkin, R. M. *A Matter of Principle.* Cambridge: Harvard University Press, 1985.
Fuller, L. L. *The Morality of Law.* New Haven: Yale University Press, 1969.
Hart, H. L. A. *Law, Liberty and Morality.* Stanford, Calif.: Stanford University Press, 1962.

Moral Theory

Crane, B. A *History of Western Morals*. New York: Harcourt, Brace & Co., 1959.

Gilligan, C. *In a Different Voice: Psychological Theory and Women's Development*. Cambridge: Harvard University Press, 1982.

Hare, R. M. *Moral Thinking*. Oxford: Oxford University Press, 1981.

Kant, I. *Groundwork to a Metaphysics of Morals*. New York: Harper & Row, 1964.

Kohlberg, L. *Moral Stages: A Current Formulation and a Response to Critics*. New York: Karger, 1983.

Parfit, D. *Reasons and Persons*. Oxford: Clarendon Press, 1984.

Williams, B. *Morality: An Introduction to Ethics*. New York: Harper & Row, 1972.

Pedagogical Theory

Dewey, J. *Democracy and Education*. New York: Macmillan, 1916.

Feinberg, W. *Understanding Education*. Cambridge: Cambridge University Press, 1983.

Howard, V., ed. *Varieties of Thinking*. New York: Routledge & Kegan Paul, 1990.

Nieto, S. *Affirming Diversity: The Sociopolitical Context of Multicultural Education*. White Plains, NY: Longman, 1992.

Passmore, J. *The Philosophy of Teaching*. Cambridge: Harvard University Press, 1980.

Scheffler, I. *Of Human Potential*. New York: Routledge & Kegan Paul, 1985.

Schrag, F. *Thinking in School and Society*. New York: Routledge & Kegan Paul, 1988.

Philosophy and Social Theory

Fuchs, L. *The American Kaleidoscope: Race, Ethnicity and the Civic Culture*. Conn.: Wesleyan University Press, 1991.

Hobbes, T. *Leviathan*. Oxford: Clarendon Press, 1909.

Mill, J. *Autobiography*. London: Longmans, Green & Co., 1873.

——————. *On the Subjugation of Women*. New York: Henry Holt & Co., 1898.

Nozick, R. *Anarchy, State and Utopia*. New York: Basic Books, 1974.

Putnam, H. *Realism and Reason*. Cambridge, England: Cambridge University Press, 1983.

——————. *The Many Faces of Realism*. La Salle, Ill.: Open Court, 1987.

——————. *Realism with a Human Face*. Cambridge: Harvard University Press, 1990.

Taylor, C. *Sources of the Self: The Making of the Modern Identity*. Cambridge: Harvard University Press, 1989.

Chapter Four

Cultural Pluralism, Ethnism, and Multiculturalism Related to Education in America

I. The Historical Precedent for Enculturation: The American Experience

America has a rich tradition of religious, racial, and cultural diversity, and indeed this country was founded by those seeking refuge from bias, discrimination, and bigotry. Our earliest history lessons in school are narratives of how America was settled by a myriad of cultural and ethnic groups, all of which were united to form an unusual and diverse society. Equal justice, opportunity, and fair play are all important elements in American life. But equal opportunity and justice for all may be just rhetoric—a story we have heard in school. The history of America is full of inconsistencies. Rights are not always distributed equally, representation is internally disproportionate, and equal opportunity and social justice are often an illusion. With the exception of Native Americans, America is primarily a nation of immigrants, but not all immigrants or natives have had the same benefits. This chapter is about issues of cultural pluralism, ethnism, and multiculturalism in America. It is also about how Americans have come to a critical breaking point in discussing these issues.

Despite the initial hardship and alienation many immigrants experience, America remains their most popular choice. Whether the immigrants come from Russia, Asia, Africa, Central America, the Caribbean, or any other part of the world, America is still the "promised land." Immigrants from many different backgrounds remember their first glimpse of America. Some are old enough to remember what Ellis Island and the Statue of Liberty looked like in New York harbor in the early twentieth century. Others remember more mundane sites like San Francisco airport and the Fort Smith, Arkansas, relocation center in the 1970s. Still others more recently remember crossing the Rio Grande to flee oppression in Central America. Immigrants remember their first experience in part because of the new opportunities, justice, and freedom this country promises. As Americans we are all too quick to forget how free and just America is compared with other parts of the world. The United States is by no means consistent and equal in its treatment of immigrants, but it does provide more promise and more equitable opportunity for improvement than the homelands of most immigrants. Although Americans can look with pride at America's record of tolerance, social justice, and personal freedom and opportunity, there is still much to do in these matters.

Has America evolved to become both culturally plural *and* distinctly American? Why have some ethnic and cultural groups been so easily assimilated and accommodated while others have had great difficulty? Why are there still inequity and discrimination in this the most free and just country in the world? Answers to these questions are found in the country's early history and in the historical accidents that determined who came first to settle the land. America did not begin as the land of the free and just, but rather it evolved into a model of democracy and human rights.

This section describes the histories of a representative sample of ethnic and cultural groups and their assimilation into American culture. Some of the more common terms and concepts used in ethnic and multicultural studies will also be explained in detail. These histories and terms are not intended to be all-inclusive and exhaustive, but rather they are an example of why and how cultures vary in their assimilation into the American culture.

A. The Meaning of Culture, Ethnic Groups, and Other Terms

In almost any country schools have been at the forefront of the struggle to "socialize," "enculturate," or "civilize" their populations. In America this has meant that individuals, other cultures, and ethnic groups accept and assimilate the Anglo-Saxon culture, language, values, beliefs, heritage, and social conventions. The term *culture* can be defined as a particular stage of development in a civilization or group with a shared sense of values, language, heritage, and experiences.[1] To be an American, therefore, is to experience acculturation of several ethnic and cultural groups into a mainstream culture, having common properties, values, and language. *Acculturation* is described as intercultural exchange between groups resulting in a new blend of cultural patterns, values, and traits.[2] It is a dynamic process and continues as long as there is interaction among the cultures. The American culture, although predominantly Anglo-Saxon, is still multicultural. Each new culture brings with it both similarities to the American culture and differences that change the larger group. America is both an acculturation or blend of many cultures as well as a multicultural conglomeration of different backgrounds sharing some traits, but not sharing others.

Norris B. Johnson describes *multiculturalism* as "a process through which a person develops competence in several cultures."[3] This process is absolutely necessary in a country like America because no matter what an individual's culture of origin, there is always a larger cultural context. Additionally, multiculturalism is the study of a broad range of cultures for the purpose of appreciation and understanding. More recently, multiculturalism in education has included knowledge of women, handicapped students, and even religious groups.[4]

Transculturation is the interactive process of cultural exchange promoted by two-way communication. The major difference between multiculturalism and transculturation (transculturalism) is the two-way exchange and acculturation that transculturation requires. Multiculturalism requires a person to know and appreciate other cultures, but not necessarily to interact with and accommodate them. Transculturation requires interaction, assessment, and selective inclusion of cultural traits into a larger whole. Transculturalism does not assume that all cultures are equal. As chapters 1, 2, and 3 have already noted, the reason to study cultures is to incorporate strengths and exclude weaknesses through moral discourse. Figure 4.1 illustrates the differences among monoculturalism, multiculturalism, and transculturalism.

Enculturation, unlike acculturation, is defined as a process by which an individual learns traditional content of a culture and assimilates it in practice and valuing.[5] Both individuals and groups are assimilated and accommodated into the larger American culture. How much acculturation and enculturation are absorbed by each varies from individual to individual and from group to group.

Figure 4.2 illustrates how American culture comprises many cultural and ethnic groups. These smaller cultural groups are called microcultures by social scientists and anthropologists. The larger American culture is called a macroculture. Polish-American, Irish-American, Mexican-American, and Nigerian-American cultures would be examples of microcultures. Not all of the circles in the figure are the same size because some microcultures have more impact on the macroculture and have more members. Microcultures *assimilate* into the macroculture (aspects of the microculture are absorbed and incorporated as part of a larger whole). Microcultures *accommodate*

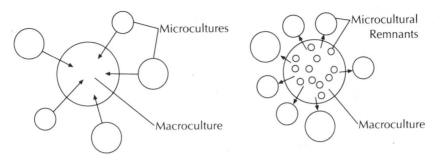

Monocultural Evolution (assimilation and accommodation of microcultures and the macroculture)

Phase 1 (assimilation)

Phase 2 (macroculture accommodates some microcultural elements and rejects others)

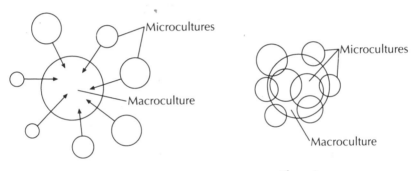

Multicultural Evolution (enculturation and partial one–way acculturation of microcultures and the macroculture)

Phase 1

Phase 2

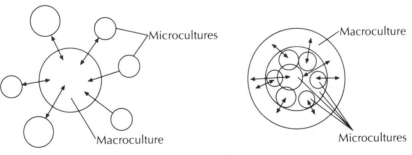

Transcultural Evolution (two–way continuous acculturation among microcultures and the macroculture)

Phase 1

Phase 2

Figure 4.1 **Monocultural, Multicultural, and Transcultural Evolutions of Societies**

Microculture

Language and Dialects
Values
Priorities
Methods of Communication
Knowledge Bases
Sense of Identity
Ethnic Origins
Economic and Social History
Other Variants

Phase 1

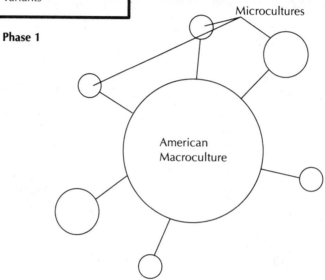

Microcultures

American
Macroculture

Phase 2

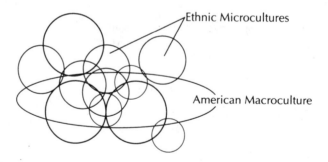

Ethnic Microcultures

American Macroculture

Figure 4.2   Assimilation and Accommodation of Microcultures with an American Macroculture

the macroculture (they accept the macroculture's traits and give up microculture traits that conflict with those of the macroculture). For example, Italian-Americans accommodated American culture when they accepted its form of government, laws, and democratic ideals. They were also assimilated when other Americans accepted their foods, music, art, and Roman Catholic religion. Phase 1 of figure 4.2 shows how initial interaction occurs between microcultures and the macroculture. In this stage the microcultures interact and confront the demands of the larger culture, as required. Phase 2 shows how the microcultures are assimilated and accommodated, but in varying degrees. As the figure depicts, some of the microcultures are almost entirely accommodated and assimilated, while others have been impacted minimally. The variation in accommodation and assimilation is due to the similarity or difference between the immigrant's culture and the establishment's culture (commonly titled the White Anglo-Saxon Protestant, or WASP, culture). Each *is* part of the macroculture, but each does not assimilate or accommodate entirely. They all retain unique aspects of the original culture.

This description of assimilation is similar to Jean Piaget's notion of assimilation and accommodation in individual cognitive learning.[6] Piaget argued that learners assimilate new knowledge when that new knowledge does not force them to rethink their schema or patterns of thinking. Accommodation occurs when learners are forced to change their thinking to meet new ways of thinking and valuing. So it is with the assimilation and accommodation of new cultures in American society. Some groups have to accommodate a great deal, while others have to change only a small part of their values and beliefs.

The term *ethnic*, as in ethnic groups, is defined as an involuntary grouping of people classed according to common traits, customs, common identity, and shared interdependence.[7] Part of a person's ethnic origin may be black, white, red, or brown, but race or color is not the sole determinant of ethnic standing. Biological differences like skin pigmentation are only a part of the total ethnic makeup of a person or group. The ethnic identity of people could be Chinese, Japanese, Chicano, Latino, Hispanic, Siouxian, or Micronesian, just to name a few. *Ethnism*, simply stated, is common ancestry that separates one group from other groups. A person's ethnicity does not change. Race is an ethnic trait. In contrast, culture is dynamic and is always in flux. An example of our changing American culture may be useful here.

As discussed in chapter 1, moral reasoning and ethical conduct require not only understanding moral imperatives but also taking a moral stance. Values in societies and cultures change just because there *is* a need to weigh consequences. In America reverence for motherhood may still be an important value, but the meaning of motherhood may have changed in the last fifty years. American mothers and fathers no longer must have large families to be of worth, nor must they put the preponderance of their energies into child-rearing as a manifestation of womanhood or manhood. American culture has changed to reflect this redefinition of the family, women's and men's roles, and the value of children. Our macroculture reveres the family, but it does not necessarily believe families have to be large as a form of social convention and acceptance. Better medical facilities, lower infant mortality rates, social security, and better working conditions have also contributed to smaller families in America. Older Americans no longer need to rely on children when they stop work and reach senior years. Children no longer take the same jobs their parents did as a way for the family to survive. All of these factors contribute to change in the value of family life as we know it today.

To summarize by means of a further example, a person's *ethnicity* may be Chinese, something which is an accident of birth. Whether Chinese-Americans revere their elders the same way mainland Chinese do is a matter of *cultural* interpretation. While the rest of America seems to worship youth, Chinese-Americans often retain profound respect for their elders. They have been acculturated, but not entirely assimilated. Another way to demonstrate the meaning and difference between cultures and ethnic groups is to compare some of the groups of America. Mexican and Vietnamese cultures have the ethnic traits shown in table 4.1. Yet it is difficult to generalize about all of the people within each ethnic group.

Table 4.1

A Partial Ethnic Comparison Between Mexican and Vietnamese Societies

	Mexicans	**Vietnamese**
Racial Origin	Amerindian/Spanish	Asian-French
Language(s)	Spanish, other Indian	Vietnamese/French
Customs	Combination of Amerindian, Spanish, French, other American	Combination of Chinese, Indo-Chinese, French, others
Ethnic Diet (due to original locality)	Beans, wheat, corn flour, tomato, beef, goat, fish, tropical fruit, chicken, pork, eggs, peppers	Rice, fish, pork, greens, eggs, leeks, spices, tropical fruit, peppers, shellfish

For example, not all Mexican-Americans are Amerindian, but there are few who are not at least partially so. Table 4.2 describes some of the cultural traits of Mexican-Americans and Vietnamese-Americans, once they have been assimilated into the American macroculture. Some of their original cultural traits remain, but many also change.

Table 4.2

A Partial Comparison Between Mexican-American and Vietnamese-American Microcultures

	Mexican-American	Vietnamese-American
Religion	Roman Catholic, animist, Protestant	Confucian, Buddhist, Roman Catholic
Music	Traditional Indian, Spanish, ballad, Caribbean, Latino	Traditional Chinese, ballad
Values (representative sample)	Knowledge, family, socialization, respect for elders, cooperation, communal life	Ancestors, knowledge, harmony with nature, respect for elders, family
Diet	Mexican, Italian, French-Asian, American, other	Vietnamese, Mexican, Asian, Italian, American, other
Language	English/Spanish	English/Vietnamese/French

Historically, microcultures have been assimilated and accommodated into the American macroculture with varying degrees of success. The following subsections are thumbnail sketches of some of the major microcultures in America and the struggles they have endured to be American.

B. Early European Acculturation and Enculturation

As a way of surviving the first few years of transition, many European immigrants found refuge by forming ethnic neighborhoods. There was a black ghetto, a Jewish ghetto, a Chinatown, and possibly a Little Italy in almost every major American city. Some of our greatest cities still have remnants of these neighborhoods today. Poles, Czechs, Greeks, Italians, Irish, Germans, and many more groups were able to ease the transition to a new culture and language through generations of their children. Parents found it difficult to adapt to a new way of life, but America's schools were adept in managing the transition of their children to an already established culture.[8]

Neighborhoods like those in Brooklyn, Chicago, Boston, and Cleveland went through several ethnic changes, as earlier immigrants found success in assimilation and new ones arrived. Hell's Kitchen in New York City, for example, evolved from German to Polish, then Irish, then Italian, then black, and finally to Puerto Rican neighborhoods. Each ethnic group settled there until it was at least partially assimilated into the culture.

Part of this transition from one culture to the next can be attributed to improved political and economic conditions. When able to afford it, each microculture moved out of squalid, depressing environments. Each gained political power by electing its own people or at least people who were responsive to the group's needs. The fact that blacks and Puerto Ricans still live in ghettos like Hell's Kitchen is not by choice. Although white cultures have found the transition out of poverty difficult, they have not had the same difficulties as nonwhite ethnic groups.

Many white cultures were easily assimilated into the mainstream of what many call the "American way." We must recognize, however, that the mainstream is still predominantly Anglo-Saxon in origin. With all its success in enculturating groups, America still faces racial discrimination and bias. Multiethnic neighborhoods exist, but the ghettos remain as well. Despite judicial, moral, and legislative resolve, inequities persist among cultures, ethnic groups, and individuals.

C. The African-American Experience

America indeed has some proud moments in its multiethnic history, but it also has bleak moments of ethnic and racial intolerance. Most Americans are aware of the hardship and suffering blacks experienced on the way to this country. They saw no Statue of Liberty from the hold of a slave ship in the seventeenth and eighteenth centuries. Their future was predestined and closed to alternatives. They were "assimilated" into America's culture as chattel or property. Their cultures were essentially lost through centuries of bondage and deprivation. Their religions and heritages were nullified and replaced by their owner's cultural background.

Unlike white ethnic groups, African-Americans had no political, economic, or social power. Andrew Billingsley states four main reasons why black immigrants were different from any other groups: (1) blacks came with norms and values that were different from those of their American masters; (2) they were made up of many different tribes, with different languages, cultures, and traditions; (3) in the beginning they came without women; and (4) they came as slaves.[9] One other factor, the fact that they were racially and ethnically different, should be added to this list.

Although other groups came with some of the same traits, none came with *all* of these traits. These factors were to place blacks in a much more difficult position when it came to enculturation and assimilation into the American way of life. The stigma of once being slaves was to haunt African-Americans to the present. Stereotypes of slave behavior (laziness, ignorance, living a carefree life, etc.) are still difficult for African-Americans to outlive. Part of the dominant culture still views this behavior as a "fact," rather than as a way for people living in slavery to survive the experience and *appear* as no threat.

Even after slavery was abolished, the cultural discontinuity blacks experienced provided no mechanism for them to overcome centuries of dependency and suppression. In 1865 the southern states enacted Black Codes, which limited voting rights, working rights, and educational opportunities. Blacks often could not own land, work at anything but farming, or even get an education beyond sixth grade. The first Civil Rights Act of 1866 abolished these Black Codes, but African-Americans did not experience true freedom from slavery until the twentieth century.[10]

The Freedmen's Bureau was instituted after the Civil War to provide "Negro education" in 2,600 different regions throughout America. Although the idea was to educate blacks for a better life and opportunity, it also separated them from whites, particularly in the southern states. This new form of discrimination guaranteed a subservient role for blacks for the next one hundred years.[11] Even though the Thirteenth and Fourteenth Amendments to the Constitution freed the slaves and guaranteed them rights regardless of race, color, or creed, hate literature continued to be printed, like this document in 1900:

> The Negro was never a slave . . . The Negro is an ape; hence his status in the universe, his relation to Man, like any other animal, was fixed irrevocably by God in the Creation, and no act upon man's part . . . can change it.[12]

Many people in America justified the harsh and inhumane treatment of African-Americans because they were somehow "subhuman." As noted in chapter 2, *Plessy v. Ferguson* (1896) allowed separate-but-equal educational facilities and services for blacks, thereby ensuring discrimination, racial isolation, and inequality of opportunity. It was not until *Brown v. Board of Education of Topeka* (1954) that the Jim Crow laws and separate-but-equal provision were overturned. The U.S. Supreme Court concluded that

> to separate them from others of similar age and qualifications solely because of their race generated a feeling of inferiority as to their status in the community that may affect their hearts and minds in a way unlikely ever to be undone.[13]

Education of blacks in the northern states was less discriminatory, but still was not on a par with education of whites. Many states did not even have mandatory school attendance laws until the late nineteenth or early twentieth century. By 1900 thirty-one states and territories had such laws, but they were not enforced until later in the century.[14] *Green v. County School Board* (1968) required school boards to provide plans for implementing desegregation, thereby ensuring the elimination of "black" or "white" schools. Although this case provided for the de facto end of segregation in classrooms, many schools still have segregated populations.[15]

Violence, poll taxes, and difficult literacy requirements were used to politically disenfranchise African-Americans for many years.[16] The battle for civil rights was first fought in the schools. Blacks believed a better education would give better opportunities, but they faced what Joel Spring calls "institutional discrimination" in all parts of the country. Examples of this kind of discrimination include inferior quality of teaching, a lack of books and materials, poor classroom facilities, and the tracking of black children into vocational and nonacademic programs.[17] Although blacks have made great strides in improving their opportunities and political power, they have not yet overcome the inequities and repression experienced in almost four hundred years of American history. As Diane Ravitch summarizes the African-American educational experience, "Black educational history is not a story of schooling imposed on unwilling black masses, but rather of schooling denied black masses."[18]

D. The Native American Experience

Native Americans have fared no better than the blacks. The history of America is replete with inhumane and immoral treatment of tribe after tribe of Native Americans. For example, when gold was discovered on Cherokee lands in 1838, whites obtained a fraudulent treaty to move the tribe west. The Cherokees did not consent to their removal or to the treaty drafted by the government. They were forced to move anyway, partly by rail, but mostly on foot. The thousand-mile trek killed four thousand men, women, and children on the way. A Georgia volunteer soldier on the trek depicted it this way:

> I fought through the Civil War and have seen men shot to pieces and slaughtered by the thousands, but the Cherokee removal was the cruelest work I ever knew.[19]

Although these Native Americans had their own alphabet and newspaper, owned slaves, and had their own governing body, they were treated as savages and forced off their lands at the point of a gun.[20] This forced migration called the "trail of tears" removed the Cherokees from Georgia, Tennessee, and Kentucky to Oklahoma. It is just one example of nineteenth-century administration of the "Indian problem" by the U.S. government. Similar examples of greed and immorality on the part of the whites exist as a sad testament against tolerance and respect for personhood.

"Custer's Last Stand" is one of few stories in American folklore conceding victory, no matter how brief, to the Indians. The battle against the Sioux at Little Bighorn in 1876 is not, however, a good description of how the West was settled. The Indians may have won this battle, but victory was short-lived. The sheer numbers of immigrants and those seeking new opportunities were to be the Indians' undoing as a nation. "Americanization" of Native Americans included not only relocation but also genocide. Phrases like "the only good Indian is a dead one" were used to express white-expansionist solutions to land ownership disputes.

Much of the literature written about westward expansion was sensationalized to depict Native Americans as bloodthirsty, primitive monsters. More recent research shows that this sensationalization was a ploy for greedy settlers, traders, and speculators to take land. The personal annals of military leaders active in the Indian wars often depicted the Indians as victims of unscrupulous, scurrilous, and greedy government agents and settlers. A large number of the officers agonized over the moral injustice the Indians had to bear. Sherry L. Smith in a recent book about military leadership in the West surmises that the officers did not agree wholeheartedly with Indian policy, and often found their work distasteful and inconsistent with present definitions of humane treatment.[21]

There are hundreds of examples of how and when Native Americans were taken from their lands and relocated. Treaties were often broken the day they were implemented. This part of American history, although colorful and the topic of many Hollywood films, is truly a tragic chapter in our nation's development. Modern depictions of Native American mistreatment in movies, although graphic and enlightening, are still directed by, produced by, and told by whites. Native Americans have a very different depiction of how the West was won.

Many white Americans believed the solution to the "Indian problem" was to separate Indians from the land they occupied, put them on reservations, or exterminate them. Native American cultures probably survived just because they were not willing to give up everything to be "Americans." Attempts to "Americanize" and enculturate Native Americans have only been partially successful as many groups continue to maintain tribal and cultural heritage. Despite efforts by the federal government to systematically enculturate these Americans, many tribes exist intact. What many other Americans have called stubbornness and a lack of initiative are really one of the few ways Native Americans have had to fight back and resist complete loss of their heritage.

Many misunderstandings about Amerindians abound today. Some whites believe that the whole race is dying out, while others believe Indians rely almost entirely on the U.S. government for survival. Still another popular stereotype is that the majority of Native Americans live on reservations and make trinkets for tourists in order to survive. These and other myths are part of the reason why Native Americans face continued apathy, isolation, and lack of understanding. Adding to the ignorance about Indians is the lack of research actually going on, whether pertaining to the colonial era or to the present. American historians have treated the Indians as a separate topic rather than as an integral part of history. James Merrill, a noted colonial historian, states, " 'Because Indians don't intrude on our consciousness today, historians assume they can write about colonial times without them.' "[22] This type of mindset causes a continued lack of understanding of Native American problems and their influence on American culture. Between 1950 and 1980 the number of Native American children attending school has increased by one million, yet research about these Americans has actually declined in the last quarter century.[23]

E. The Hispanic Experience

Like the Native American, Hispanics have been part of the United States from the beginning. Yet they are sometimes labeled the "forgotten minority" or the "hidden" Americans. When land in Texas, California, Florida, and the rest of the Southwest was settled, Hispanics were already there to meet the new settlers. Their history is as old as the history of the New World. These early settlers have a rich tradition and culture, yet they have experienced discrimination similar to other minorities who settled much later. America's oldest immigrant people, the descendants of Spaniards and Indians, not only faced political, racial, and educational discrimination from Americans, but also from their own native populations south of the Rio Grande.

Although it would take volumes to discuss all Hispanics, Mexican-Americans, the largest group, are a good representation of the enculturation process experienced by all. Not only were Mexican-Americans given less opportunity and political power but also from the beginning they were at an educational disadvantage. Although Mexico gave its settlers in the Southwest the right to start their own schools in 1824, most of the settlements did not have any financial support for formal education. Western settlers described the "natives" as illiterate and poor "remnants" of an earlier civilization.

Following the Mexican-American War of 1848 between Mexico and the United States, discrimination and negligence continued. In most of the American Southwest there were property restrictions, voting restrictions, and laws limiting rights of Mexican-Americans. For example, one historian has depicted the Texas Rangers as "the region's Ku Klux Klan against Mexicans—ever since they were established in 1835."[24] Although the rangers had other police duties besides controlling and disenfranchising Mexican-Americans, their greatest efforts were spent settling land disputes between whites and Hispanics in what one ranger described as "keeping Mexican-Americans on the other side of the track."[25]

Their plight continues. These hidden Americans have been forced into barrios in most major metropolitan and rural areas throughout the country. They continue to be, in effect, second-class citizens when it comes to education, social services, voting rights, and employment opportunities. Only about half of Hispanic students graduate from high school. Less than 38 percent of those graduating in 1990 were able to read at the twelfth-grade level.[26]

Yet with all the years of suffering and deprivation, there has been some improvement in recognizing the needs of this hidden or forgotten minority. Title IV of the Civil Rights Act of 1964 ensured that school districts provide bilingual education for children unable to understand English. Recognizing the need for proficiency in two languages (native and English), lawmakers intended Title IV to help children in the transition from one culture to another. The 1974 *Lau v. Nichols* case set new guidelines for bilingual education, requiring specific programs dealing with language problems in schools. The *Lau* decision obligated schools to: (1) identify students using language other than English as a primary language, (2) provide special services when necessary for these students, and (3) employ instructors who speak languages spoken by the children having language difficulties.

Since the Reagan administration, however, the education and improvement of conditions for Mexican-Americans and other Hispanics continue to be at issue. Support for expensive bilingual programs has waned, and alternatives like the total-immersion method (teaching everything in English) have again been suggested and used in some states.

Legislation by states like California, Illinois, Virginia, Kentucky, and Georgia to make English the official language is another example of a conservative response to the influx of minorities into these states. Many other states like Texas and Florida have suggested such legislation. In 1990 California already had a "minority majority" in its public schools, with Arizona, New Mexico, Florida, and possibly New York projected to follow shortly. Demographic projections for Texas indicated in 1986 that minority students would become a minority majority by the year 2000.[27] These projections were off by nine years—Texas reached minority-majority status in 1991. The implication for states with present and projected minority-majorities must be improve performance of "at-risk" students (students who face hardships and poverty, lack English-speaking skills, or suffer emotional instability) or all of America will bear the consequences of an uneducated, unprepared, and unemployable population majority. Children labeled "at-risk" include Native Americans, African-Americans, and Hispanics.

The League of United Latin American Citizens (LULAC) has been active since 1928, defending the rights of Mexican-Americans and other minorities in Texas and throughout the country. Other political groups are springing up. For the past twenty years the silent or hidden minority has been more vocal, but the struggle for equality of opportunity is a long way from being won. At-risk students will continue to be in jeopardy unless institutions like the public schools break the cycle of poverty and inequality of opportunity.

F. The Asian Experience

Of all of our microcultures, the Asian group may be least known by the American macroculture, and thereby least understood. Despite decades of discrimination, Asian cultures have been assimilated and accommodated without the same kind of uprooting and racial strife experienced by other minorities. Fear of Asians was a common reality in nineteenth-century America. While groups from Europe were allowed to emigrate in large numbers, harsh limits were placed on Asian countries. Treatment of Chinese in the American West was best described as inhuman.

The Chinese

The most menial and difficult labor was the fate of most Asians, whether it was working on the railroad (for particularly low wages), doing laundry, cooking, or similar employment. Stereotypes of Asians doing this kind of work remain in American mind-sets even today, but the fact remains they were *forced* to work at jobs that were not competitive against anyone else. Many Chinese were *invited* to America in the 1860s by railroad and mining industries with promises of high pay and good benefits. Chinese labor built the first transcontinental railroad and excavated a good amount of the gold and silver in California and Nevada mines. When the railroad was completed and the mines were played out, the Chinese became "unwelcome." They were labeled as "a yellow plague," "Chinks," or "opium fiends" by the white population competing for the same jobs.[28]

Asian ghettos and Chinatowns sprang up in almost every major city—many remaining even today. While some Asians may want to remain in cultural enclaves in America as a way of preserving cultures and ethnic lifestyles, the continued existence of these enclaves is partly due to historical precedent and discrimination initiated by the establishment culture.

The Japanese

Japanese migration to America grew significantly in the 1890s. Most came with the intention of staying only a few years. After making money, they would return for a new life in Japan. Many immigrants, however, remained on the Pacific Coast or in Hawaii, returning to Japan only to find a spouse or to bring the rest of the family to America. Many males sent for "picture brides" through a marriage broker in Japan until new American laws banned the practice in the early twentieth century. These *issei*, or first-generation Japanese, soon faced laws like the California Land Laws of 1913 and 1920, preventing them from owning land or even farming it. They were also denied U.S. citizenship. Most had to give the land they had bought before 1913 to their children, who were *nisei*, or second-generation Japanese born in America.[29]

The internment of Japanese-Americans during World War II is yet another example of fear, discrimination, and bias against Asians in America. Executive Order 9066 by President Franklin Roosevelt in February, 1942, placed 110,000 Japanese into internment camps until the end of the war. Although their nisei sons and daughters distinguished themselves in the war effort, the issei and other noncombatant Japanese-Americans were under the control of the War Relocation Authority until 1945. Only recently has the federal government tried to apologize to these Americans and reimburse them for the loss of land and property, as well as loss of freedom.

G. New Immigration

Asian immigration after the Vietnam War was titled the "new immigration" by many social scientists in the period. The Immigration Act of 1965 not only allowed more immigrants from South and Central America, Mexico, and Cuba, but it also allowed many from Asia and the Pacific. Two parts of this act have changed immigration patterns in the last twenty-five years; one part gives preference to those having relatives already in America, and the second part gives preference to skilled professionals. Many students from foreign countries have studied here, gained professional status, and then been allowed to remain. On the basis of the first part of the act, they have eventually been able to bring other members of their families into America. Recently, more Asian and South American students have taken advantage of this opportunity; hence, the "new" immigration patterns are coming from those regions rather than from Europe.

The new immigration has been a different racial mix than before. This has caused a variety of reactionary responses in some states, such as efforts to ensure English as the official language. Other "safeguards" against the perceived "yellow peril" are quotas for Asians getting into universities and restrictions on professional memberships. Particular ramifications to education will be discussed in chapter 5.

America, therefore, is becoming more culturally plural and ethnically diverse than ever before, but it is also a multicultural society with a common language and a common set of beliefs and lifestyles. Americans have been enculturated into a larger whole, but also acculturated to many other cultural groups. The larger question now is whether America will be transcultural (a two-way street of shared cultures) or merely multicultural (mostly a one-way street of assimilated and accommodated cultures).

II. The Need For Diversity and Cultural Pluralism

Because America remains ethnically diverse and yet espouses equal opportunity, the issues of cultural pluralism and diversity in goals, values, and learning remain as important topics in the future. The central purpose of multicultural education is to gradually enculturate a person from a microculture (culture originating outside the larger group) into a macroculture (a group having common goals, values, and lifestyle). Bilingual programs in our schools are a good example of this enculturation process. Title VII of the Elementary and Secondary Education Act of 1965 and the Bilingual Education Act of 1968 appropriated monies for the special educational needs of non-English-speaking children. Children are taught subjects in their own native tongues, but at the same time English is being taught. They are able to bridge the transition from one dominant language to another with the least amount of cultural shock. Students often have up to three years of bilingual instruction to bridge the transition to a new culture. The children are placed in a "regular" classroom once they have learned to communicate in English.

Other examples of programs intended to create equality of opportunity are Head Start, school breakfast and lunch programs, VISTA, the Teacher Corps, "bootstrap" programs of all types, and job training programs. Many Americans saw the War on Poverty started by the Johnson administration in the 1960s as a war on a subculture of poverty, inequality, and three centuries of deprivation. Title I of Public Law 89–10 gave school districts extra money to help educate children of low-income families. Although great strides were made against poverty, some racial, cultural, and educational discrimination and inequality remain. Education is still seen as one of the major ways out of the problems experienced by minorities, whether they be newly arrived minorities like the Vietnamese-Americans, or historically older minorities like the African-Americans.

These examples of enculturation and acculturation of individuals and groups are designed to produce people with a commensurate set of cultural beliefs and values. For decades this has been and remains the major policy of most states in America. Why, then, would someone argue for plurality and diversity in a culture? Why would a nation change to a policy of multicultural or transcultural teaching when it would be much easier and safer to teach, instruct, and direct people to one culture? Why has there been more recent concern for cultural or ethnic pluralism and multiethnic education in America? *Cultural* or *ethnic pluralism* can be defined as the promotion of an individual's own ethnic or cultural identity in order to gain power among competing ethnic or cultural groups. Part of the answer to these questions is in the history of the discrimination and neglect already mentioned. New immigrants also realized that they would never be truly equal in opportunity if they were not white, or from northern Europe. The Immigration Acts of 1917 and 1924 made it abundantly clear that even immigration from eastern Europe was to be drastically curtailed, and that any subsequent group was to face much harsher entrance requirements. Knowing how to read and write English, converse in English, and pass extensive literacy and intelligence tests are just a few of the new requirements aimed at all new immigrants.

The need for ethnic studies, multicultural education, and bilingual education came from a realization by the *newer* immigrants that their own cultural identity must be preserved, if they were to get equal opportunity and recognition. In the 1960s and 1970s the oldest minorities in America—namely, African-Americans, Native Americans, and Mexican-Americans—became active participants in the struggle for equal treatment and opportunity (instigated somewhat by the successes of new immigrants). Many conservatives viewed this resurgence as a struggle for individual lost identity, rather than as a struggle to maintain cultural identity. The earlier American minorities countered that it was as much a cry for freedom and equal opportunity for the future as it was a search for a past. Afro-American studies, women's studies, and Native American studies sprang up on several university campuses in the 1960s as one of the ways minorities sought new opportunities. Because minorities in America did not get to share their culture in their own enculturation, and because tolerance, respect for human dignity, and interdependence are needed, cultural pluralism and diversity of thinking have become more acceptable concepts for study on America's campuses.

A. The Myth of the Melting Pot

Few American sociologists or historians in the early twentieth century believed cultural pluralism was an acceptable principle, mainly because of the perceived need for a predominant culture (namely, the Anglo-Saxon culture) as an "Americanizing" force. There was an abject fear that too many of these immigrants would be disruptive and would need to be controlled. Immigrants were expected to drop their old ethnic and cultural traits and embrace the established culture. Schools, the media, government agencies, and even religious organizations assumed the role of "Americanizer."

A myth known as the "melting-pot theory" flourished in early-twentieth-century America. The term *myth* is used because the melting-pot theory was really a fictional characterization of America's cultural goals. The concept of this myth was to bring all aliens and immigrants together to assimilate the "American" (namely, the establishment or White Anglo-Saxon Protestant) culture and beliefs. James Banks believes this myth started with Israel Zangwill's play entitled *The Melting Pot*, which described how America would be a boiling pot of culture melding into one.[30] As long as most of the immigrants were white and from northern Europe, the myth of a melting pot survived.

The 1908 opening of this play in New York might have been the beginning of a new era in American culture; but, in fact, the doctrine of the "tossed salad" (a hodge-podge of cultures thrown together, but still separate) was rapidly becoming the real America. When most of the immigrants started coming from eastern Europe, Asia, and Latin America in the early part of the twentieth century, the melting-pot ideology began to disintegrate. The identifying characteristics of these cultural groups could not be so easily blended with those of the dominant culture. Xenophobia (a fear of other ideas, cultures, and beliefs) became a powerful weapon against any tolerance for cultural diversity. World War I, the "red scare" of communism in the 1920s through the 1950s, union violence, and the Depression all contributed to a xenophobic backlash against cultural diversity and "un-American" activities. Many of these historical events were blamed on "outside agitators" and "foreigners" preaching rebellion.[31] America, in effect, had become a tossed salad but continued to feign the transformation of all cultures into a melting pot.

Ellwood P. Cubberley and William James—and even John Dewey to an extent—were influential in the idea of assimilation and socialization of children into a social whole. All children would share the same beliefs, aspirations, and values. Cubberley, for example, noted that of the eleven million people who came to America just before World War I, 26.5 percent could not read or write in any language.[32] This fact led to his suggestion that it was better to teach all children the same way and the same curriculum and forego multiethnic diversity, than to have the ignorance and suffering caused by unequal schooling and the educational practices of previous cultures. Schools were to be the great equalizers.

The progressive education movement in the 1930s proposed the socialization and cooperation of children in all learning situations. Minority groups might see this as placing the individual at the mercy of the majority rather than as a liberating experience. In defense of the progressives, however, they truly wanted *all* to participate in the democratic process rather than the few. William Drake stated the role of progressive education this way:

> It is the function of education in our society to give expression to the elements
> of the democratic process in the everyday life and activities of individuals. . . .
> We must break the monopoly of learning.[33]

Drake wanted to give minorities and others unable to get an education the opportunity to be educated. Progressive education encouraged all to participate in the democratic process. Progressives realized that education must be available to all, rather than continue as a monopoly of the privileged.

Fragments of the melting-pot myth were to remain through World War II. During World War II, propaganda was used to show how *all* Americans were behind the war effort. Every week in movie theaters throughout the country, "Movietone News" showed workers, parents, and military groups as "all American."Although we *were* all Americans, we were still segregated into black, Asian, and women's military units, work forces, and volunteer organizations. Racial and ethnic groups were Americans, but they stayed with their own and, in fact, were expected and legally bound to stay with their own. There was little interracial or interdenominational marriage, and many ethnic groups remained isolated in ghettos. America's minorities and majority were to continue this voluntary and involuntary separation and myth until the Vietnam era brought the whole issue of racial inequity to the fore again. This was a time when the myths of both American equality and racial integration were to die in the riot-torn black ghettos of Los Angeles, Detroit, and Cleveland. The myth of the melting pot was officially dead.

B. Multicultural Versus Monocultural Education: Problems and Possibilities

The concept of multicultural education for America is on the surface a good idea. Its faults may be in the implementation of rules and regulations that actually discriminate against or even divide people rather than acculturate them. If there is one positive note to this concept, it is that true multiculturalism attempts to preserve some of the original culture and language of the immigrants. It also serves a tangential role, eliminating prejudice and discrimination in all.[34]

One of the weaknesses of multicultural education in America, however, is that it continues to be an assimilation and accommodation into a monocultural rather than a transcultural ideology. If diversity of thinking and preservation of culturally prized traits for the macroculture are desired, then present multicultural education in America tends to place limits on those ends. Students are allowed to express some cultural identity, but they are expected to cede most traits to the larger macroculture. The transformation is still a one-way street when it comes to "Americanization." Students are expected to think and act in establishment-type ways, even though the Constitution guarantees freedom of religion, speech, and press. Many supposed multicultural education practices are more monocultural or monoethnic in their results today than they were when the country was first settled by whites. For example, teaching multicultural awareness to all prospective teachers is part of almost every state's requirement. The results of this kind of instruction are questionable if there is no requirement for teachers also to act on multicultural differences in learning, teaching, and perception. Mere *knowledge* of different cultures could accentuate differences and possibly throttle educational efforts.

Educator James Banks recommends an intermediate step toward a true multicultural society: a policy of multiethnic education. He argues that if nations want to truly "promote the integration of structurally excluded ethnic groups into the mainstream of society . . . a curriculum that reflects cultures, ethos and experience of the diverse groups within the nation will reduce ethnic polarization and weaken ethnic revival movements."[35] Banks is not alone in his advocacy for the multiethnic view of education rather than the present monocultural view. Although his position is a step above present multicultural practices, he falls into the trap of separatism rather than unity of cultures.

Cultural Pluralism

Another disturbing trend is cultural pluralism, which breeds hate rather than unity. Some have divided multicultural education into divisions of ethnic and cultural studies—distinct curriculums—thereby separating groups even further than before. Unfortunately, ethnic studies have been used on our college and high school campuses to distinguish groups from other groups, often in ways that stereotype and blame anyone outside the cultural group. African-American studies, Native American studies,

Asian-American studies, and women's studies have all contributed, intentionally and unintentionally, to this kind of separatism. Dinesh D'Souza in *Illiberal Education* suggests that the debate on American campuses is not about ethnic inclusion but, rather, "politically correct views of cultures." Campuses are not really being used for cultural studies, but rather for politicalization of the issues. He concludes that the behavior of administrators toward minorities and women is "condescending," and that antiharassment codes on campuses are there to enforce "a social etiquette" rather than to show respect for women and minorities.[36]

This trend is by no means restricted to colleges and universities, for what happens on college campuses trickles down to American secondary and elementary schools as well. Many states have incorporated minority studies in the high schools. A pluralist position assumes that if we provide each culture with its own studies, the minority students will gain pride, identity, power, self-actualization, and a sense of ethnic cohesion. At the same time, however, pluralism also creates factionalism, hatred, bias, and stereotyping of those outside the cultural study. People can and do end up placing loyalties and trust in only those like themselves. Furthermore, they often expend great effort creating a political position of being victims, thereby gaining public sympathy and attention. This is a "win-lose" mind-set that can only create an ethical wasteland for America's future. It is a failure to appreciate what social contract theorists from Aristotle and Hobbes (chapter 3) to the present have been trying to help us realize. Nobody wins that kind of game. The attempt to pervert the evolving process of interdependence among groups leads to failure. We already have Lebanon, South Africa, Iran, India, Northern Ireland, Sri Lanka, Nigeria, Iraq, and many more countries as models of this kind of separatism, suspicion, and aversion.

Part of the difference between the pluralists (those who want a myriad of curricula emphasizing each particular culture) and the assimilationalists (those who support a monocultural view of education) is that they view the role of education differently and have *very* different views of how consensus about goals and purposes should be reached by a society. They also have *very* different views of how multicultural education should be taught. Solutions to this separatist dilemma will be addressed in chapter 5.

C. Consensus and the Role of the School

Whether we as Americans follow a monocultural (assimilationist) stance, a multicultural (pluralist) position, or a more transcultural (acculturation, with tolerance, interdependence, and mutual respect as key elements) perspective in the future depends a great deal on our view of consensus. Our schools have always been active in the process of "Americanization," which requires consensus of goals, values, and priorities. A major purpose of education is to prepare children for civic and social duties. The depth and breadth of any consensus require a person to take a philosophical position about what *should* be, rather than what is or has been. The social contract we use for governing our lives should be one *each* of us would choose if we thought about what would be in the best interest of *everyone*.

For example, we as a society might argue that all children must be given equal educational opportunity, but how that is interpreted and accomplished may vary. We have a broad consensus about providing equal educational opportunity, but the details necessary for full consensus are extensive and generally left unelaborated. Table 4.3

demonstrates that problem in America. As the table shows, there may be almost total agreement about providing equal educational opportunity (the main issue), and there may be a fairly high consensus that one of the first things to do is integrate the schools (option 1). However, as we go into the resolution of the problem in further depth and detail (options 2 through 7), there is less consensus on moral, legal, and other grounds. For example, there would be little agreement (about 35 percent consensus) that minority parents should be required to participate in school activities. Not surprisingly, it is against the law. The Family Educational Rights and Privacy Act of 1974 gives not only children over seventeen the right of privacy in grades, but also ensures parents access to their children's grades and activities throughout high school. It does not require parental participation, but rather gives them the *option* to do so. First Amendment rights prevent the government from forcing parents to participate in educational activities.

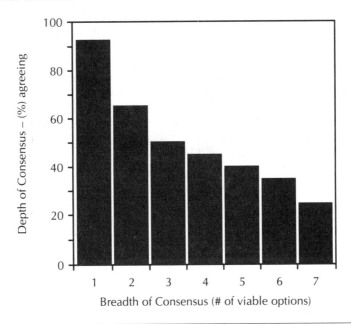

Breadth of Consensus (# of viable options)

Options for Equal Educational Opportunity

1. Integrate schools

2. Require same curriculum for all students

3. Spend more time on minority students

4. Teach multicultural education in the school

5. Monitor students' progress

6. Require minority parental participation in schools

7. Require remedial classes

Many schooling issues have breadth, but often have little depth of consensus. Some educators believe that the majority of educational purposes in America end up as sloganeering (for example, the just-say-no campaign), thereby having little depth as to how the goals are to be accomplished. With each new leader comes another tremendous pendulum swing in yet another direction, creating instability and upheaval in our schools. It is difficult for educators and administrators to try to meet the latest method or newest fad in instructional design when years of research have shown that most methods and designs have not really made much difference.[37] One reason may be that no plan is being given enough time to make a difference. When the how-to aspects of general educational goals are treated as political footballs, consensus in depth is lost, thereby creating unneeded turmoil in one of our most important social institutions.[38]

Slogans per se are not all that bad—they are useful starting points for educational consensus—but more in-depth analysis and evaluation of the issues are needed. America's schools (including the teachers) must be active in the analysis and resolution of social problems. As stated in chapter 1, practice in this kind of consensus and moral decision making is necessary. Many past and present educational models in America have reflected very different ideas about consensus or decision making. Additionally, these models of education have incorporated very different ideas about multicultural education. Which model of education should be used? What type of multicultural education should emerge from this model? What has been learned from previous models of education that might be useful in the search for a more desirable result?

Many images of America's schools have not survived as models for public education. Figure 4.3 depicts three of the major images that *have* survived as models for American education. One is as old as America's earliest schooling practice, while the others are more recent. Each has had its popularity, and vestiges of all three still exist in our public schools. The important point to make is that each image is a partial description of our public schools today, but each reflects a different idea of consensus educational goals and the role of multicultural education.

School as Protector

Earliest Puritan models of schools depicted them as places where morality and the work ethic are instilled into youth. This first image or model can be called the "school as protector." Children are protected from their own natural evildoing and sinfulness. In this instance, the teacher maintains authority and is a model whom the students are expected to emulate. Students learn virtue by being around virtuous teachers who practice what they preach. Many private and parochial schools follow this model today, but the model had its origins in the works of Plato.

Mortimer Adler's *The Paideia Proposal* and Allan Bloom's *The Closing of the American Mind* are two recent books supportive of the school-as-protector model. While Adler espouses equal educational opportunity for all, he also demands higher standards, required subjects, and common objectives for all students.[39] Students are given moral instruction, "right" thinking, and time-tested truths through didactics, coaching, and inquiry. Bloom proposes using the university as a "temple of the regime," again requiring a liberal arts education for all attending the university and thereby ensuring a time-tested curriculum based on the "Great Books" of the Western world.[40]

Name	School as Protector	School as Job Finder	School as Social Forum
Origin	Puritan ethic; parochial ideology	Industrial era; scientific revolution	Information age; post-industrial era
Philosophies	Idealism; Christian realism; perennialism; neo-Thomism	Realism; rationalism; essentialism	Pragmatism; progressivism; reconstructionism
Rationale	Rely on time-tested solutions and universal truths and values	All problems can be solved scientifically; learning should have utility; we have made great strides using scientific principles	Search for things that work; negotiate to solve problems
Teacher/Student	Protector and model citizen/ sinner	Knowledge expert/receptor or client	Facilitator and activist/ participant
Consensus	Narrow breadth but very deep; based on time-tested values and goals. Liberal studies provide greatest basis for answers to very old questions.	Based on scientific principles; great depth because of the use of technical language and analysis. Not much breadth because of a limited recognition of interrelationships, highs, and cross-impacts of events/ solutions.	Wide breadth and depth because of the use of schools as agencies for change. Consensus reached in tested enactment of proposed solutions. Must be more global in scope.
Multicultural Outlook	Be acultural or assimilate into monoculture reflecting the ''Great Books''	Tends to reject multiculturalism in favor of science	Must be multicultural to understand other opinions/solutions; eventual development of transcultural society

Figure 4.3 **Three Major Images of American Public Education's Role in Society**

Name	School as Protector	School as Job Finder	School as Social Forum
Educational Objective	Produce the intellectual	Produce the scientist	Produce social activists
Basis of Problems in Society	Amoral or immoral decisions; lack of intellectual knowledge based on the past	Not cost-efficient; lack of knowledge base to make decisions; need for more technical expertise	Inappropriate use of technology; inability to recognize consequences; faulty logic; lack of social activism
Curriculum	Liberal arts; Great Books of Western world; general courses, using lecture and dialogue for instruction.	Sciences, math form core curriculum. Objective tests; lecture, demonstration, teaching machines. A transmissive approach.	Group learning; test ability to solve problems and cooperate; core curriculum of science, math, English, and social studies but also apprenticeships in community. Real-life problems studied.

Figure 4.3—*Continued*

Consensus in this model would have less breadth. It would have great depth, however, since time-tested, universal, and liberal studies would show the consistency and validity of perennially honored ways of thinking. Bloom even suggests in his book that America should be *acultural* (having no specific cultural position) and rise above any cultural bias by pursuing universal "goods" of human nature. He contends that when America has used multicultural education as a means of "Americanization," the results have actually been culturally biased toward each specific culture—none of which was objective enough to advance understanding of humankind generally. Bloom feels ethnocentrism, (viewing the world only from one's own cultural perspective), a lack of standards for judgment based on more universal criteria, and creeping relativism have resulted from the other two models of education.

School as Job Finder
The school-as-job-finder model assumes the school's role is to fit the student into the industrial/technological complex. Schools should be efficiency models, providing the most knowledge possible in the shortest time. This image of education emerged in the late nineteenth century and blossomed in the twentieth century with the advent of technology, the machine age, and scientific methods of investigation. The answer for America's problems is to produce an adaptable, scientific thinker capable of using the scientific method to solve all problems.

This model proposes an education enhancing the senses and espousing empirical research as the way to salvation. Consensus would again be somewhat narrow in breadth because of the faith in science as the answer to all problems, but it would be very deep because of the use of specialized language and investigation techniques. The school-as-job-finder approach tends to discount multicultural perspectives and studies in favor of nonpartisan sciences. In this model's view, science has no "culture" and is "pure."

School as Social Forum

The school-as-social-forum model emerged in the early twentieth century as a result of the information age. The solution to America's problems is to give the student real problems to solve, while at the same time providing a forum for *all* of society to deal with social problems. Consensus in this model is very broad, but only moderately deep because of the interrelatedness of problems and their global consequences. Consensus is theoretically enhanced because one of the major roles of education in this model is to encourage continual participation in problem solving throughout life. Reaching consensus about social problems requires a forum for testing and discussing results. In this case, the school *is* the forum, preparing students to fulfill that role.

This model supports both multicultural and transcultural education by providing students a forum for the intellectual commerce of ideas and beliefs. Since global education is part of the objective, tolerance for other cultural perspectives and respect for the rights of individuals are practiced with an eye to the resolution of real-life problems.

Multicultural Education and the School Models

As figure 4.3 depicts, each image of American schools requires different solutions to a single set of broadly stated goals. Varying degrees of consensus are required; but, more importantly, multicultural education is taught and emphasized differently. While the school-as-protector model has lasted a long time in America and is still the mainstay for private schools, the answer to the multicultural education issue is to appeal to a universe of truths, realities (philosophy), and values that are acultural (that is to say, beyond any ethnocentric position). Hence the education of children is not oriented to transient cultural differences, but rather to human nature itself. Time-tested liberal studies promoting universal knowledge are believed to be the answer to all problems of cultural conflict.

The school-as-job-finder model of education continues today as the dominant approach in public education. It is decidedly subject-centered in its ideology, placing great faith in science and technology as the answer to most problems. Any differences in culture are placed aside in favor of scientific explanation, based on hard, empirical data. Producing productive, scientific thinkers is the goal of this model. A bottom-line businesslike definition of profitability is the definition of educational success. The rationale for having multicultural studies is to show merely the value and consistency of science to all cultures.

The school-as-social-forum model has been around since the 1930s but is not in vogue in most states today. This model's concern for participatory problem solving, cultural cohesion, and multicultural analysis of global problems is appealing to professional educators. However, it is not politically astute to advocate this model in a world demanding behaviorally demonstrable competencies as the measure of educational success. Most people do not want to recognize that there is a "crisis in the culture" that would warrant dramatic shifts in educational emphasis and goals.[41] To apprentice children into the community to solve real-life social problems requires educators to evaluate student success with measures other than so-called standardized and objective testing. In this model, students are evaluated for cooperation, tolerance, interdependence, extensive analysis of problems, and creativity in addition to the mastery of information. Multicultural education is required because the model's goal is to produce tolerant, concerned, adaptive participants in problems of global social concern. The school-as-social-forum approach assumes there will be analysis of cultures and two-way exchange to produce a more transcultural society.

The school-as-job-finder model of education remains predominant in America because Americans want not only economic utility in education but also facility in measuring learning. This model teaches from a content base, evaluating teachers, students, and schools on the basis of standard test scores. This model is politically exploited by elected officials whenever the society criticizes the schools for Johnny's not being able to read, write, or cipher. It is not, however, the best model for producing diverse thinkers. Nor is it the best model if cultural tolerance and mutual interdependence are desired.

III. Legal Issues Impacting Multicultural Education

Besides the multicultural education issue, there have been subtle and tangential issues in American society recently that have themselves smacked of bias, discrimination, and inequality, especially toward minorities in schools. The following issues/cases are only some of the problems our society has tried to address through the schools and the courts. Each has had either a direct or an indirect impact on minority groups, and many continue as unresolved concern.

A. De Jure and De Facto Segregation

Although schools by law have been ordered to integrate since 1954 in the *Brown v. Board of Education of Topeka* case, *de facto* segregation remains. In 1964 the Supreme Court mandated speedier plans for integration with *Griffin v. County School Board of Prince Edward County* and *Rogers v. Paul*. School districts have made many attempts to obey legal demands and right moral shortcomings (for example, busing, magnet schools, and special voluntary programs), but discrimination, unequal educational opportunity, and the vicious cycle of poverty remain. Gunnar Myrdal's classic thesis entitled *An American Dilemma* was instrumental in showing the discrepancy between the "American creed" of equality and the actual practice of discrimination against minorities. Many credit him for the enactment of civil rights legislation after 1944.[42] This seminal work, however, was not enough to turn discrimination around quickly. The Supreme Court had to rely on federal district courts to enforce desegregation. All too often these lower courts were "part of the social fabric of the local communities and resisted attempts at speedy desegregation."[43] After years of legislation and lawsuits, "white flight" from districts heavily enrolled with minority students continues. Cities like Houston, Boston, New York, Chicago, Dallas, Los Angeles, and San Antonio have all had drastic increases in minority school populations because of white flight. Yet cross-district integration plans, although possible and legally validated by the Supreme Court since the 1950s, have not been implemented. Nobody seems to have a valid answer as to why this has not been used as a way to integrate and supersede white-flight practices. One possible reason for the lack of cross-district integration is the wide difference school districts have in tax bases. The 1987 *Edgewood ISD v. Kirby* case (discussed at a later trial level in chapter 3) may have ended that roadblock.

In *Swann v. Charlotte-Mecklenburg Board of Education* (1967), the Court described three ways in which racial integration could be accomplished: racial quotas, redistricting, and busing. The impact on minorities and white students was significant because it was the first time specific methods were set down and because it forced compliance. In *Milliken v. Brandley* (1974), the Court also concluded that remedial education, retraining of teachers about the special learning needs of minorities, and special counseling directed toward minority students should help eliminate the "continued effects" of segregation in the past. In agreeing to this, the Court finally recognized the need for minority rehabilitation as well as for integration.

Almost one-third of all Hispanic students are in schools with over 90 percent minority students. Although *Keyes v. School District No. 1, Denver, Colorado* (1973) included Hispanics in desegregation plans, the number of segregated Hispanic students has continued to increase since the 1980s.[44] This trend is but another example of how discrimination continues, even though legal precedent outlaws it. State courts have attempted to equalize tax bases so that school districts can pay for facilities, teachers, and materials on a more equitable basis. But loopholes allowing districts to collect and keep monies above the state base permit unequal funding to continue.

San Antonio ISD v. Rodriguez (1973) was an early instance of the Supreme Court's trying to judge the constitutionality of school finance plans. The Court ruled that the school finance plan was constitutional because it did not discriminate against poor and minority students living in poor school districts. The disproportionate amount of money levied on property owners from poor districts was not enough to deny the students their rights under the equal protection clause of the Fourteenth Amendment. *Edgewood ISD v. Kirby* (mentioned previously) was, in essence, a continuation of the original *Rodriguez* case. The district court declared it unconstitutional to permit substantial inequities in funding for public education and directed the state of Texas to develop a more equitable way of distributing funds. A new Texas law has outlined a distribution formula, but it also allows local districts to collect more than the base funding, thereby continuing the unequal distribution of funds for richer districts. This case, however, has led the way for all states to mandate more equitable education, particularly to help minority children living in poor districts.

Forced integration plans have met with limited success. Quite often they have been either circumvented or ignored by local authorities. *Cisneros v. Corpus Christi ISD* (1970) recognized "Mexican-Americans" as an "identified ethnic minority with a past pattern of discrimination." *Texas v. Certain Named and Unnamed Undocumented Alien Children* (1980) decided in favor of alien children. The state of Texas had enacted a statute withholding state funds for children who were not legally admitted into the United States. The Supreme Court ruled that the children had not been guaranteed equal protection, namely an education, and that they should not be denied an education because of the illegal status of their parents. This landmark case guaranteed a minimal public education to all children, regardless of their status as illegal aliens. Each of these cases tried to equalize, improve, and ensure the educational process for minorities. Although the spirit of the law is clear, the enforcement of the law is uneven. Only social demand will ensure that the moral aspects of the laws are, in fact, carried out.

B. Public Law 94–142 and Minorities

Since 1975 the Education for All Handicapped Children Law (PL 94–142) has guaranteed children access to education through the "least restrictive environment" for learning. While committed to the goal, the federal government enacted this law without much in the way of financial support to the schools. Nevertheless, great strides have been made "mainstreaming" exceptional children. Problems remain, however, that extend well beyond bias against the handicapped and over again into ethnic affairs. Minority children constitute the bulk of children diagnosed as "handicapped." Sometimes they are *wrongly labeled* as retarded because of the misuse of standardized and other tests.[45] Some researchers estimate that as many as half of all "retarded" children may be mislabeled.[46] This label often reflects discrimination against minorities. Mislabeled children are often the victims of poverty and lack of a stimulating environment rather than the victims of physical or mental disorders.

There are cases where children have been classified as mentally retarded simply because they could not respond in English to questions asked of them. For example, an Eskimo child was diagnosed as retarded because he did not respond immediately to a teacher's questions. It was later learned that his culture frowned on individual responses to questions as a matter of courtesy. He was taught to bring issues before the group before he formulated an answer.[47] Such cultural differences have often prompted the mislabeling of children. Not only must teachers be much more sensitive to cultural differences, but also testers and testing devices must be more sophisticated in their distinctions.[48] Although experts are getting better at distinguishing between learning disabilities and cultural differences, classroom teachers need to become more aware of the possibility that a diagnosis is often made on the basis of the child's poverty or lack of English language proficiency.

C. Censorship and Minority Inclusion

Although Americans espouse freedom of religion, press, speech, and assembly, historically they have stopped short when it comes to students by censoring texts. Several organizations, from staunch conservatives to radical liberals, yearly publish approved book lists and censored book lists. Every year several states have hearings into textbooks available to the public school market. Discussions of textbook adequacy lead inevitably to questions of course content, such as whether to teach creationism *and* evolution in the schools, or whether *The Catcher in the Rye*, *The Learning Tree*, or *Huckleberry Finn* should be taught since they stereotype minorities and use derogatory expressions. Recent court cases are focusing ever more sharply on the selection procedures used by schools for evaluating the educational merit of books. *Island Schools Free School District No. 26 v. Pico* (1982) was one of the first cases to show this sharpening focus. The Supreme Court ruled against the arbitrary attempt of parents to ban books available to all students. It did, however, indicate that school boards need to provide other options for offended individual students.

In *Grove v. Mead School District No. 354* (1985) the district court ruled that a book like *The Learning Tree*, though potentially offensive to a black family, was still an appropriate book, as long as students were not coerced into reading it and had, in fact, retained a "free exercise" of the right not to read it. In a similar case, *Mozert v. Hawkins County Public Schools* (1985), the district court upheld the right of a school district to use certain textbooks, even though the books may not have reflected the "Christian value system" some parents wanted. These particular parents were upset because the texts encouraged plurality and diversity of thinking, along with an unprecedented multicultural perspective. They feared that the books would cause their children to abandon the values they were trying to instill in them. Because the district did not allow individual students to opt out of the curriculum, the court made the district pay for the private school the students ended up attending. Although both cases are under appeal to the U.S. Supreme Court, they do represent the courts' position on censorship fairly accurately.

At issue in cases like *Island Schools v. Grove* (1980) is how to judge the merit of exclusionary arguments from competing interest groups. This case laid the framework for reasonable censorship of books by recommending the use of experts in the academic field on review panels. The responsibility of such panels is to ensure that books do not discriminate and exclude minorities. America has two hundred years of constitutional history addressing the proper limits of censorship. Deciding what should be censored and on what criteria and guaranteeing representation of all reasonable arguments are matters not easily resolved. A better understanding of minorities in our schools will one day translate into a great advantage in determining solutions to these perennially perplexing constitutional issues.

D. The Dropout: Minorities as At-Risk Students

Most states in America are experiencing an increase in high school dropouts, despite increases in funding, more awareness of the dropout problem, and efforts by urban schools in particular to turn the numbers around. Of particular note is the high number of minorities dropping out of school. In Texas, for example, 42 percent of blacks and almost 50 percent of Hispanics dropped out before graduating from public high school in 1990. Added to this is the realization that blacks and Hispanics constitute almost half the population of students in Texas public schools. Almost every state is in a desperate struggle to keep its minority youth in school. But Texas, California, New York, Florida, and New Mexico represent the most sizable problem, numerically speaking.

Since one in three Americans will be nonwhite by the year 2000, this problem must be addressed now. Attention to the multicultural needs of this student population must be an integral part of any proposed solution.[49] Note, too, that multiculturalism is not just about race or ethnicity; it strives to ensure opportunities for the "have-nots" of society as well as the "haves." Consequently, it is important to remember that one in four American children is born into poverty.[50] More than 37 percent of Hispanic and 43 percent of black children are part of that impoverished group. All children of impoverished homes will face disproportionate challenges in today's public school classroom.[51]

Tracking and Minorities

Although many court cases have involved minorities, one of the more significant was *Hobson v. Hansen* (1985). The Supreme Court ruled that differences in funding in schools and tracking can be construed as discrimination if applied on an unequal basis. Many American school districts have used standardized tests to ability-group children and track them according to test results. Studies by Lloyd Warner, Robert Havighurst, Talcott Parsons, and many others conclude that tracking is discriminatory because it tends to keep low-income and minority students in inferior programs. In short, upper-class students seem "predestined" for success in school, while lower-class and minority students are improperly tracked into vocational programs. Parsons points out that college selection in the 1960s was a sealed verdict by the time children got to junior high school.[52]

An ethical and legal question is involved in using the school as a sorting system for jobs and opportunities. John Goodlad, Ernest Boyer, and Theodore Sizer are three more recent critics of tracking as a practice supporting an unsubstantiated social Darwinism. They conclude that the system is not only unconstitutional, but also ethically unacceptable. Since the tracking system creates ability grouping, it also runs counter to the teacher's professional obligation to encourage cooperative learning on the part of everyone. Traditional multiculturalists have been persistent in their claims that multicultural education aims at the good of the community by promoting cooperative learning, whereas tracking tends to discourage success in group learning at the expense of the individual!

The potential for disaster is there for *all* students—not just minority students or the impoverished ones. In pure numbers, almost as many whites are dropping out of high school as minorities, and many of these children are from the middle and upper socioeconomic strata. Is this because kids are bored with school? Is it because they see no reason to stay in school, given the potential for acquiring money through drug dealing or other illicit activities as so many newspaper editorials suggest? Could it be that many students do not learn basic skills and as a consequence fall behind their peers until they lose hope altogether? Are schools less challenging than before? Are schools so demanding now that minorities have small chance of succeeding? Are schools and teachers ill-equipped to deal with the myriad of problems faced in America's classrooms? The answer to *all* of these questions may be yes. The real fact of the matter is that there is no one solution to the dropout problem.

Some form of multicultural education is needed for all students. If a sense of community, mutual interdependence among groups, shared responsibility, respect for others' personhood and property, and a desire to do the right thing are to be nurtured along with reading ability, math skills, and a knowledge of science, then multicultural education *is a basic*. Minority students are at risk because they are often impoverished, need help in learning English, and have otherwise been disadvantaged by a social system that has not yet fully come to terms with the notion of interdependence and respect for personhood. Our educational system needs drastic revamping in the near future, not because minority students alone need it, but because all students affected by old models of education are inadequately prepared to meet the challenges of the information era. Higher order cognitive skills are needed, and these include an ability to judge, evaluate, and, perhaps most importantly, prioritize social goals.

IV. A New Multiculturalism in American Education: Beyond Assimilationist or Pluralist Notions

Already noted in this chapter are several factors affecting multicultural education in America. "Multiculturalism" as presently practiced has done more to segment the society than meld it into a unit. The *pluribus* in *e pluribus unum* seems to have overridden the *unum* when it comes to socialization in America. Interdependence among groups and respect for the individual are concepts that too often fall before the crush of majority rule.

Historically, new Americans were assimilated and enculturated to fit into the dominant culture of the Anglo-Saxons. To be American was to give up most of one's previous cultural heritage (if not emigrating from northern Europe). Since most immigrants were originally from northern Europe, it was not much to ask. African-Americans were a different story. They were stripped of their heritage, while Mexican-Americans and Native Americans were forced to yield to the majority in other more subtle and varied ways. This type of Americanization into the mythical melting pot created winners and losers. Abject poverty continues to ensure a class of "losers" under the control of establishment-types, the "winners" of today.

More recently, beginning in the 1930s, a pluralistic or ethnocentric position has emerged. Pluralists argue in favor of a plurality of studies, curriculums, and ideologies to be studied by each microculture as a way to garner power and end victimization of earlier discrimination. In advocating these practices, pluralists have begun drawing attention to the concept of interdependence (recall chapter 3). But this advance in social consciousness is not yet appreciated by all sectors of the academic world. College campuses continue to reflect separatism—offering degrees in African-American studies, Hispanic studies, Native American studies, Asian-American studies, and women's studies. "Plurality" has meant separateness. To the extent that these studies are misunderstood or promoted as "we-they" studies, there has also been a predictable backlash leading to "straight pride" groups, "men's studies" and white student unions. Partly tongue-in-cheek, these groups, nonetheless represent critical and contentious hostility to pluralistic studies.[53]

The growth of narrowly focused independent programs on our college campuses has, in some critics' eyes, created a lapse of quality. The lack of required course work or general studies has the *potential* to create a tremendous division between ethnic studies and the rest of the university, but it is not inevitable. In fact, this should be avoided at all costs. It is time educators encourage a *new* multiculturalism in American schools, a transculturalism that promotes ethical principles such as equality, due process, tolerance, and color blindness. In short, it is time for a thoroughly *transcultural approach to multiculturalism*. But, to avoid the confusion that proliferation of jargon creates, we can say more simply, that it is time to learn what it means to join together as an interdependent community.

Chester Finn warns that principles like equality and tolerance are fairly modern and fragile ideas when compared to and set against much older and more primitive forces such as tribalism, prejudice, violence, and ethnocentrism.[54] If the ideals of interdependence and respect for personhood are to survive in America, we will have to educate children differently than in the errant pluralist or forced assimilationist methods of enculturation that have contaminated the educational system in the past.

The assimilationist model for America is no longer meaningful, since as a macroculture America is no longer trying to reduce a wise variety of cultures into the myth known as the melting pot. Neither have mutual interdependence, tolerance, and color blindness followed from previous assimilationist approaches. The need to Americanize new Americans is much more a need to diversify ideas and solutions as interdependent needs arise rather than to treat everyone the same in all cases. Previous pluralist models of multicultural education have tended to exacerbate the problem by encouraging independence of competing groups. Finger pointing, scapegoating, and win-lose mind-sets do not produce a sense of shared responsibility, interdependence, tolerance, or respect for individual personhood. Any study that singles out a group to emphasize that its members should be suspicious of others outside the group and should "win" by showing their superiority over others is not the kind of multicultural education our public schools should promote.[55]

A new multicultural education is in order. Education promoting pluralism should be replaced by education promoting transculturalism—that is to say, a model that ends moral turpitude, and promotes a sense of justice, respect for human dignity and equality, and tolerance or previous cultural difference. Transcultural education should be based on values that are meritorious in any culture worth its salt. Students should understand that there are differences in skin color, foods, dress, religion, and customs that separate us but that there *are* also norms and values that unite us and distinguish us from the rest of the animal kingdom. The assimilationists underestimate the importance of microcultures on a child's early development. So, too, earlier pluralists overestimated the importance of the same microcultures to ethical decision making.[56] For example, identity with a larger group such as one's country and with a smaller group such as one's family is important, but having a *shared* identity of mutual respect on a universal scale is also important. Without a context larger than their own family and culture, students will be unable to evaluate the merits of their own worldview as opposed to that of any other.

At this point it must be reiterated that some cultures *are* better than others. To deny this is to take a relativistic position that ignores the advances humans have made in becoming more *civil-ized* as a species. If we follow the relativist argument, we would have to defend cannibalism, human sacrifice, foot binding of women, fertility rites, juju festivals, or any other cultural trait as much as the heroic feats of Mother Teresa and Martin Luther King, Jr. Some cultures are better than others—not because of how they eat, what they wear, what their ethnic origins are, or how they look, but because of their success in elevating the human spirit. We may certainly disagree about eating preferences on religious or other grounds. Cultures should not be flattered or denigrated on the basis of such trivial matters. On the other hand, they should be evaluated and critiqued for their support and defense of, say, basic human rights. The difference in these levels of evaluation is that the latter deal with universal respect for human dignity.[57]

To summarize, we should study transcultural education as if adopting a moral stance. It is a matter of doing good for others without becoming either patronizing or dogmatic. It is important to be articulate and remain open-minded in cultural matters, while we remain insistent that all persons be accorded equal respect. Most Americans want character education; they admire such things as honesty; respect for private property; taking responsibility for one's actions; fair judgment; tolerance; and respect for family, country, and human dignity. For education to develop such character traits in children, the educational system and our network of cultures must reflect these traits. The schools must each become a microcosm wherein the virtues of mutual interdependence, tolerance, protection of individuals, and universal suffrage are evident virtues.

Transcultural education—if it is to reflect tolerance for the social habits of others and develop a set of deep-rooted moral concerns (as well as a sense of community with all humanity)—should draw attention to the interdependence of us all as a central area of study. Studying cultures as interdependent produces a synergy that creates mutual respect and a win-win psychology that benefits all. Being transcultural means individuals are willing to reject their own cultural bias in favor of one that promotes more universally acceptable values. Interdependent *transcultural* education is a curricular approach for *all* Americans, not just for minorities. The next chapter suggests some models for that accomplishment.

QUESTIONS FOR DISCUSSION

1. What is the difference between enculturation and acculturation? Is there a preference for either of these in American education? Explain your answer.
2. Explain the meaning of the terms *culture* and *ethnism*.
3. Compare the assimilationist and pluralist notions of multicultural education. Why may there be a need for a new definition of multicultural education beyond these two?
4. Compare and contrast the "Americanization" of any two minority groups discussed in this chapter. Which has had more success in this process? Why do you think so?
5. Why is the melting-pot theory a myth?
6. How do the three images or models of our educational system affect how consensus is reached? Explain.
7. Describe how other issues in American education impact multicultural education and ethical decision making.
8. List three court cases that have had an impact on minority education in the last fifty years. Explain their significance.
9. Describe the difference between breadth and depth of consensus. Give two examples of issues with breadth and depth.
10. Discriminate between multicultural and transcultural societies.

NOTES

1. See Alfred Kroeber and Clyde Kluckhohn, *Culture: A Critical Review of Concepts and Definitions* (New York: Vintage Books, 1952).

2. George Theodorson and Achilles Theodorson, *A Modern Dictionary of Sociology* (New York: Barnes Noble, 1969).

3. Norris B. Johnson, "On the Relationship of Anthropology to Multicultural Teaching and Learning," *Journal of Teacher Education* 28 (May/June 1977): 10–15.

4. See D. Gollnick et al., *Multicultural Education in a Pluralistic Society*, 2d ed. (Columbus, Ohio: Merrill Co., 1986). See also V. Parrillo, ed., *Rethinking Today's Minorities* (Westport, Conn.: Greenwood Press, 1991) for further discussion of the changing minority makeup in America.

5. Theodorson, *Modern Dictionary*, 124.

6. See Jean Piaget, *To Understand Is to Invent* (New York: Penguin Books, 1980). See also his basic works on cognitive development.

7. Kroeber and Kluckhohn, *Culture*, 159–68.

8. See Marcus Hansen, *The Immigrants of American History* (Cambridge: Harvard University Press, 1940).

9. Andrew Billingsley, *Black Families in White America* (Englewood Cliffs, N.J.: Prentice-Hall, 1968), chap. 1.

10. Anthony Lewis, "Toward a Second Reconstruction," in *Black History: An Appraisal*, ed. M. Drimmer (New York: Doubleday & Co., 1968), 426.

11. Gerald Gutek, *Education in the United States: An Historical Perspective* (Englewood Cliffs, N.J.: Prentice-Hall, 1986), 137–38.

12. Gilbert Osofsky, *The Burden of Race* (New York: Harper Torchbooks, 1967), 184.

13. Lewis, "Toward a Second Reconstruction," 422.

14. Richard Current et al., *A Survey of American History*, vol 1 (New York: Alfred A. Knopf, 1983), 464–66.

15. See Percy Bates, "Desegregation: Can We Get There from Here?" *Phi Delta Kappa* 72 (September 1990): 8–12.

16. James Comer, "Racism and the Education of Young Children," *Teachers College Record* 90 (Spring 1989): 359. See R. Alba, *Ethnic Identity: The Transformation of White America* (New Haven: Yale University Press, 1991).

17. Joel Spring, *American Education: An Introduction to Social and Political Aspects* (New York: Longman, 1989), 128. See also Kofi Nomotey, ed., *Going to School: The African-American Experience* (Albany, N.Y.: SUNY Press, 1991).

18. Diane Ravitch, *The Revisionists Revised* (New York: Basic Books, 1978), 31.

19. John P. Brown, *Old Frontiers* (New York: Arno Press, 1971), 508.

20. Ibid., 518.

21. For further reading, see Sherry L. Smith, *The View from Officers' Row: Army Perceptions of Western Indians* (Tucson: University of Arizona Press, 1990). For additional information on inequalities in Indian education see U.S. Senate, *Indian Education: A National Tragedy, A National Challenge*. 91st Congress, 1st Session, 1969. Report 91–501.

22. Cited by Karen Winkler, "Bringing American Indians into the Mainstream of Colonial History," *The Chronicle of Higher Education* 36 (June 20, 1990): A3.

23. J. Dodd and S. Ostwald, "Multicultural Implications for Teaching" (Paper presented to the Montana Education Association, October 20, 1989).

---

24. David Weber, *Foreigners in Their Native Land* (Albuquerque: University of New Mexico Press, 1973), 187.

25. Ibid., 223.

26. U.S. Commission on Civil Rights, *Ethnic Isolation of Mexican-Americans in the Southwest*, Study #1 (Washington, D.C.: 1971 Commission Study), 11–12.

27. Harold Hodgkinson, "Texans: The State and Its Education" (Washington, D.C.: Institute for Educational Leadership, American Council of Education, 1986), 11.

28. Lucy Huang, "The Chinese American Family," in *Ethnic Families in America*, ed. C. Mindel and R. Habenstein (New York: Elsevier, 1981), 116–117.

29. A. Kikumura and H. Kitano, "The Japanese American Family," *Ethnic Families in America*, 43–45.

30. James Banks, *Multiethnic Education: Theory and Practice* (Boston: Allyn & Bacon, 1988), 4.

31. Oscar Handlin, *Immigration as a Factor in American History* (Englewood Cliffs, N.J.: Prentice-Hall, 1959), 167–74.

32. Ellwood P. Cubberley, *Public Education in the United States* (New York: Houghton Mifflin, 1934), 745.

33. William E. Drake, *The American School In Transition* (Englewood Cliffs, N.J.: Prentice-Hall, 1955), 555–56.

34. V. Maseman and Y. Iram, "The Right of Education for Multicultural Development: Canada and Israel," in *Human Rights and Education*, ed. N. B. Tarrow (New York: Pergamon Press, 1987), 101. See also B. M. Bullivant, *Race, Ethnicity and Education* (Melbourne: Macmillan, 1981).

35. Banks, *Multiethnic Education*, 28.

36. Dinesh D'Souza, *Illiberal Education: The Politics of Race and Sex on Campus* (New York: Free Press, 1991).

37. More recent research in instruction has shown that most new curricular designs have not been given much of a chance to make a difference, and that the significance of most was not high. Part of this could be attributable to the politicalization of the curriculum rather than to a sincere effort to test the long-term results of innovation in instruction.

38. Gary Clabaugh and Edward Rozycki, *Understanding Schools* (New York: Harper & Row, 1990), 40–45.

39. Mortimer Adler, *The Paideia Proposal: An Educational Manifesto* (New York: Macmillan, 1982), chap. 4.

40. Allan Bloom, *The Closing of the American Mind* (New York: Simon & Schuster, 1987), 336–65.

41. See Theodore Brameld, *Education for the Emerging Age* (New York: Harper & Row, 1950), 21–27.

42. Gunnar Myrdal, *An American Dilemma: The Negro Problem and Modern Democracy* (New York: Harper & Row, 1944), lxx–lxxiii.

43. Joel Spring, *The American School, 1642–1990* (New York: Longman, 1990), 339.

44. Joseph Newman, *America's Teachers* (New York: Longman, 1990), 203.

45. S. A. Kirk and J. Gallagher, *Educating Exceptional Children*, 5th ed. (Boston: Houghton Mifflin, 1989), chap. 1.

46. M. L. Smith, *How Educators Decide Who Is Learning Disabled* (Springfield, Ill.: Charles C. Thomas, 1982).

47. Nathaniel Gage and David Berliner, *Educational Psychology*, 4th ed. (Boston: Houghton Mifflin, 1988), chap. 7.

48. Ibid.

49. Thomas Payzant, "Making a Difference in the Lives of Children: Educational Leadership in the Year 2000," *Basic Educational Issues and Facts 2* (Spring 1987): 1.

50. U.S. Bureau of the Census data, 1986.

51. Ibid.

52. See Robert Havighurst et al., *Growing Up in River City* (New York: John Wiley & Sons, 1962). See also T. Parsons, "The School as a Social System: Some of Its Functions in American Society," in *Society and Education*, ed. R. Havighurst et al. (Boston: Allyn & Bacon, 1967).

53. Chester Finn, "Why Can't Colleges Convey Our Diverse Culture's Unifying Themes?" *The Chronicle of Higher Education* 36 (June 13, 1990): A40. See also American Association of State Colleges and Universities, *The Lurking Evil: Racial and Ethnic Conflict on the College Campus* (Washington, D.C.: U.S. Government Printing Office, 1990).

54. Finn, "Why Can't Colleges," A40.

55. See Geneva Gay et al., eds., *Expressively Black: The Cultural Bias of Ethnic Identity* (New York: Frederick A. Praeger, 1987). See also Geneva Gay, "Achieving Educational Equality Through Curriculum Desegregation," *Phi Delta Kappan* 72 (September 1990): 56–59.

56. Banks, *Multiethnic Education*, 122.

57. Immanuel Kant is usually credited for this notion of moral behavior.

For Further Reading

Multicultural Education Theory/History

Banks, J. *Multiethnic Education: Theory and Practice*. Boston: Allyn & Bacon, 1988.

Bennett, C. I. *Comprehensive Multicultural Education*. Boston: Allyn & Bacon, 1986.

Brown, J. P. *Old Frontiers*. New York: Arno Press, 1971.

Clabaugh, G. and E. Rozycki. *Understanding Schools*. New York: Harper & Row, 1990.

Crawford, J. *Bilingual Education: History, Politics, Theory and Practice*. New York: Crane Publishers, 1989.

Cruickshank, D. *Research That Informs Teacher and Teacher Education*. Bloomington, Ind.: Phi Delta Kappan, 1991.

Cubberley, E. P. *Public Education in the United States*. New York: Houghton Mifflin, 1934.

Current, R. et al. *A Survey of American History*. Vol. 1. New York: Knopf, 1983.

D'Souza, D. *Illiberal Education: The Politics of Race and Sex on Campus*. New York: Free Press, 1991.

Gutek, G. *Education in the United States: An Historical Perspective*. Englewood Cliffs, N.J.: Prentice-Hall, 1986.

Handlin, O. *Immigration as a Factor in American History*. Englewood Cliffs, N.J.: Prentice-Hall, 1959.

Hansen, M. *The Immigrants of American History*. Cambridge: Harvard University Press, 1940.

Hill. H. *Effective Strategies for Teaching Minority Students*. Bloomington, Ind.: Phi Delta Kappa, 1991.

Lewis, A. "Toward a Second Reconstruction," in M. Drimmer, ed., *Black History: An Appraisal*. New York: Doubleday & Co., 1968.

Nathan, J. *Free to Teach: Achieving Equity and Excellence in Schools*. New York: Penguin Press, 1991.

Shade, B. J., ed. *Culture, Style and the Educative Process*. Springfield, Ill.: Charles C. Thomas, 1989.

Tyack, D., ed. *Turning Points in American Educational History*. Waltham, Mass.: Blaisdell Pub. Co., 1967.

Ethnic Studies

Billingsley, A. *Black Families in White America*. Englewood Cliffs, N.J.: Prentice-Hall, 1968.

Kallen, H. *Cultural Pluralism and the American Ideal*. Philadelphia: University of Pennsylvania Press, 1956.

Myrdal, G. *An American Dilemma: The Negro Problem and Modern Democracy*. New York: Harper & Row, 1944.

Newman, J. *America's Teachers*. New York: Longman, 1990.

Percell, C. *Education and Inequality: A Theoretical and Empirical Synthesis*. New York: Free Press, 1977.

Rattery, J. *Center Shift: An African-Centered Approach for the Multicultural Curriculum*. Washington, D.C.: Institute for Independent Education, 1990.

Weber, D. *Foreigners in Their Native Land*. Albuquerque: University of New Mexico Press, 1973.

Acultural Theorists

Adler, M. *The Paideia Proposal: An Educational Manifesto*. New York: Macmillan, 1982.

Bloom, A. *The Closing of the American Mind*. New York: Simon & Schuster, 1987.

Finn, C. *We Must Take Charge*. New York: Free Press, 1991.

Chapter Five

Teaching in a Multicultural and Multiracial Society

OBJECTIVES:

After studying this chapter you will be able to:

1. Explain problems facing multicultural education in American public schools.
2. Recognize curricular inconsistencies in our schools against multicultural education, like testing, the use of "core" courses, and minority-inclusion programs.
3. Understand how norm-referenced tests and criterion-referenced tests affect minority students.
4. Analyze and discuss the strengths and weaknesses of the curriculum guidelines suggested in the chapter.
5. Understand the different uses of bilingual and ESL teaching, and how they may still be biased.
6. Discuss the need for consistency between theory and practice in teaching.
7. Explain the meaning of bias and racism.
8. Explain how teachers can be aware of personal, institutional, curricular, and administrative bias and racism.
9. Understand why multicultural education needs local support for it to work.

I. Misconceptions and Inconsistencies in Multicultural Teaching

A. The Historical Precedent

Teaching in a modern society like America would in itself be a challenge, without adding its cultural and ethnic diversity to the list of elements affecting learning. Teachers do more than just teach subject matter or present facts for students to remember. Some of their more critical duties are to ensure an equitable and safe environment for learning (free from violence, discrimination, drugs, and academic impotence) and to help acculturate and enculturate children into the community (while developing character, a sense of fair play, and a willingness to cooperate interdependently with others). These in themselves are no small tasks!

In a republican form of democracy, participation by *all* citizens is the keystone. When the National Commission on Excellence in Education submitted its now famous *A Nation at Risk* report in 1983, it suggested that America was at risk because its citizenry was not participating in the democratic process. The commission declared that few high school graduates had sufficient skills even to recognize the danger presented by an uneducated public. We were, in essence, at risk because we did not possess the necessary foundation of a democracy, namely, an informed, educated public, capable of making well-reasoned choices.[1] Aristotle in *the Politics* mentioned an educated citizenry as a necessary ingredient for any successful democracy. All subcultures must take part in democratic life—the society cannot afford to waste anyone's valuable talent.

More recently, President George Bush's *America 2000* educational strategy, *A Nation Prepared* written by the Carnegie Taskforce on the Teaching Profession, and *A Profile of American Youth* compiled by the U.S. Department of Education all aspire to produce a better informed citizenry, capable of competing in the international job market. The bottom line in all of these reports suggests America will decline in productivity unless its schools improve achievement scores.[2] Although this economic motive for improved education is quite popular today, it misses the mark when it assumes all Americans will be guaranteed equity of opportunity. Minorities continue to fail in school because of unequal educational practices.

Since Americans now represent many more culturally and ethnically diverse backgrounds than at the turn of the century, our schools are now the one common social institution assigned the duty of preparing these children for democratic responsibility. Historically, preparing minorities for American life has meant that all students become "Americans" of the establishment ilk and give up most of their previous culture to fit into the macroculture. This practice continues, because those in authority still do not appreciate the loss of human capital it causes and the discrimination it represents. Minority students themselves want to belong to the mainstream. Their parents are often in favor of this assimilation, in hopes their children will have better prospects for success than they had. Both are often willing to accept new cultural perspectives without understanding that such acceptance actually discriminates against them, rather than accommodates them.

America's public school children are far from being monocultural, but in some ways the public schools teach as if they *do* have (or aspire to have) only one culture. Most of the effort in multicultural education is to fit minorities into the majority culture, without understanding that the majority needs to be acculturated as well. As discussion in chapter 3 implied and chapter 4 made evident, the predominant assimilationist model of multicultural education attempts to enculturate minority children without trying to acculturate *all* America's children into a transcultural society.[3] Despite this glaring drawback, the assimilationist model is *still* the main form of multicultural education in public education. Cultures are dynamic entities, requiring their members to adapt to changing values, conventions, and environments. James Banks, a prominent researcher in multicultural studies, argues that we have in the past thirty years merely added new kinds of multicultural education, such as the pluralist model and the multiethnic models.[4] Now all of them exist as a hodgepodge of multicultural ideas, thereby confusing the issue as to what multicultural education means and what goals it should have.

The first part of this chapter is designed to show some examples of inconsistencies in our educational goals that affect present multicultural education objectives; the second section will discuss some critical problems for teachers teaching in a multicultural society. The second section will also discuss the need for consistency in theory and practice in multicultural teaching and the use of local and regional resources.

B. Four Curricular Inconsistencies Affecting Multicultural Education

To emphasize the inconsistencies of present theory and actual practice in American public education, consider four ways our schools try to equalize education for all: (1) they use standardized tests to measure success in student learning, regardless of the cultural background of students; (2) they utilize "core" courses that are fact-oriented and supposedly unbiased because they promote general studies; (3) they practice "minority-inclusion" programs that demonstrate ethnic and cultural accomplishments with events like Black History Week and Fiestas Patrias Day as examples of the culture; and (4) they provide bilingual education or English-as-a-second-language (ESL) programs for non-English-speaking students. Why is it, then, that 42 percent of Native Americans, 39.9 percent of Hispanics, 24.4 percent of blacks, and 9.6 percent of Asians/Pacific Islanders dropped out of America's public schools compared with 14.3 percent of whites in 1988?[5] A closer analysis of what the schools propose as equal opportunity and what is actually happening to minorities is warranted.

Testing

Most educators are aware of the cultural bias in IQ tests. Much research has been done and much literature has been written on the "nature-nurture" controversy in the process of trying to determine *potential* for learning. There is no argument that inheritance (nature) and environment (nurture) are the two most important factors affecting a person's performance in learning. The disagreement is over how much each affects learning. The estimates of the ratio between heredity and environment range from as high as 90 percent heredity and 10 percent environment, to 40 percent heredity and 60 percent environment. Although Stephen J. Gould suggests any such estimate of a percentage at this juncture is premature, other psychologists and educational theorists do claim to have the "right" proportion.[6]

One extreme (often called the Jensenist view) argues that almost all a person's potential is based on genes, or what the person inherits from his or her parents.[7] These researchers fall into the high-level category of hereditary percentages. They believe environment has almost no influence on a person's potential to learn; hence, there are theoretically *races* with better gene pools than others. Since whites and Asians tend to do better on IQ tests than blacks or Hispanics, the Jensenists argue that these gene pools must be better suited for academic pursuits. They conclude that blacks and other races do not fare better in our schools because of their racial gene pool. To them academic success is just a fact of "nature." To most researchers this view is blatantly racist, particularly when it is used as a justification for lower achievement and for unequal educational opportunity for minority school children. Cultural and economic differences have significant influence on student school performance as chapters 3 and 4 have demonstrated.

The other end of the continuum, the "nurture" enthusiasts, characterized by psychologist Alfred Binet, proposes that environment is a very significant factor in intelligence potential. These theorists argue that a nurturing home life and a safe, diverse learning environment at an early age can have a significant effect on potential. Studies of various ethnic groups have shown that children can improve their IQ scores as much as twenty points with better learning environments and instruction. Twenty points can be a significant difference in measuring a child's potential. For example, children could be categorized as "slow" with a 75 IQ, but almost at the mean level (one hundred points) with twenty points added to their score. Although educators, psychologists, biologists, and others do not agree on the percentages between environment and heredity, they all concede that environment is a factor in learning potential.

Ulric Neisser, Richard Wagner, and Robert Sterinberg have concluded that a tremendous bias in IQ tests exists because of the *one* answer and *one* thinking strategy the questions seek. Their research suggests IQ scores of minorities would be significantly higher if "real-world" questions were asked.[8] The results of the most recent research suggest that it is quite difficult to remove all bias from tests, and that they leave something to be desired as absolute standards of student potential or achievement.

One principal reason IQ tests are especially biased is because *cultures determine the definition of intelligence.* In studies between North Americans and the Kpele tribe in Africa, the Africans sorted an arbitrary set of objects by function (bone/dog, saw/building, wrench/car), while the Americans sorted the same group of objects by classification or taxonomy (living/dead, machines/instruments, animate/inanimate). When the Kpele were asked to sort the way "unintelligent" people of their tribe sort things, they began to arrange the objects taxonomically. Kpele simply thought that a categorization of objects by classification was useless and impractical. The lesson to be learned from this research is to recognize that much of demonstrated intelligence is culturally determined and that IQ tests reflect culture at least as much as potential when testing minority children.[9]

IQ tests are not the only form of standardized tests with built-in cultural biases. Norm-referenced and criterion-referenced tests are also biased, and minority children are being unfairly evaluated on the same criteria as the majority in almost every part of the country. The effects of IQ bias compounded with the effects of biased standardized tests place minority students at a severe disadvantage. Tests are indeed helpful in determining relative *knowledge* levels of minority children, whether they are norm-referenced (based on average scores of similarly aged and similarly taught students) or are criterion-referenced (based on a standard of knowledge and accomplishment). But educators must be careful when trying to measure "norms" or when arbitrarily referring to criterion-referenced tests as if they were unbiased. On the other hand, the tests are not the "enemy" of minority or majority children. Rather the real issues may be, What are the tests measuring? How are they measuring it? and What is to be gained by making such measurements in the first place?

In the case of norm-referenced tests, minorities have traditionally fared worse than whites. It is not hard to figure out why. These tests measure the score of an individual against all other individuals who take the test in the norming population. Since most of the students taking this type of test are establishment children, the tests are written in the language and culture most representative of that group. It follows in this country, then, that whites will generally do better in norm-referenced testing. This kind of test is culturally biased because of language and thought processes expected of the majority of test takers. Norm-referenced tests are designed to prescribe a hierarchical classification of respondents for use in quotas or for setting numerical limits on qualified candidates. Minority students have a much higher likelihood of scoring on the lower end of the hierarchy because of their limited access to the establishment's high culture. Minority students are placed or advised into general, vocational, or technical tracks in schools, not because they are incapable of doing college-preparatory work, but because they have fared predictably worse in biased norm-referenced tests.

Psychologists warn that standardized norm-referenced tests are discriminatory because they measure much more than competence in content areas. They measure student adaption to a predetermined, hidden curriculum of conformity based on the predominant culture's belief system. Such tests do not eliminate cultural bias in the questions, nor do they attempt to. Rather, they reflect the establishment's commitment to an assimilationist philosophy. They do not do a good job of making allowances for how students from other ethnic groups interpret questions or the meaning behind the answer. Neither do they consider how the values inherent in language usage may skew the results among minority groups.[10] Remember, the tests evaluate student responsiveness in relation to all other students of the same age and grade. This gives those with greatest access to the majority culture a distinct advantage. Differences in cultural interpretation are not important considerations in norm-referenced measurements of *school* success. But is school success all that matters in educational terms?

Criterion-referenced measurement seems less discriminatory against minorities because the tests measure students by comparing them to an "absolute" standard of quality. But even with such absolute standards there is cultural bias in both the questions asked and the answers expected. As already noted, cultures determine their own standards for intelligence. No psychometricians are so skilled that they can evade their own cultural pasts when constructing tests. Table 5.1 is a simple comparison and contrast between norm-referenced and criterion-referenced tests. Of particular note are the implications these tests have on minorities and on the American macroculture. Both types of tests are, at times, more or less discriminatory.[11]

Table 5.1

Comparison and Contrast of Norm-referenced and Criterion-referenced Tests in Relation to Minorities in America

Test Type	Norm-referenced	Criterion-referenced
Goals/Purposes	Create classifications of students, compare relative knowledge of students, create a hierarchy to be used for quotas or rewards	Determine "absolute" knowledge of students, classify students in terms of "mastery" or competencies, estimate specific knowledge of students and where they are having problems
Possible "Strengths"	Useful when ranking students is necessary, can create competition among students and cooperation between student and teacher, encourages conformity to teacher or curricular expectations	Can create an accurate measurement of whether a student knows the answer to specific questions, useful in measuring student progress in content knowledge, can encourage cooperation among students, encourage conformity to measurable objectives, help define levels of learning and is good for self-paced learning, can help designate where a student is having problems so remediation can be effective
Possible "Weaknesses"	Creates relative hierarchies, does not measure absolute knowledge of students, has only a relative value of comparison, can encourage competition among students to an unacceptable level, assumes education should be the unit of discrimination for "haves" and "have-nots," hides teacher and curricular inadequacies as they relate to life skills or problem solving	Assumes the absolute knowledge base has something to do with success in life, does not give a comparative analysis of students, becomes answer-centered in its definition of learning, does not always measure depth of understanding on the part of the student, tends to define education in factual or measurable terms

Table 5.1

Continued

Implications to Minorities	Tends to classify students and track them, evaluates students on a more longitudinal scale (assumes they have been using same language and cultural belief system throughout life), does not make use of cooperative skills, produces a quota system that generally places minorities in the bottom of the hierarchical scale, lowers motivation because of built-in cultural bias, creates a polarization of "winners" and "losers" between groups	Gives minorities more of a chance to become proficient, allows for more cooperative learning (often a cultural trait of minorities), does not have quotas that generally discriminate against minorities, can classify students as "backward" or "remedial" because of cultural differences, can hide discriminatory behavior in teachers against minority students, assumes the goals are not discriminatory against minorities because the curriculum is seen as merely transmission of facts

The task here is to recognize the strengths and weaknesses of these two types of tests and try to eliminate the cultural and ethnic bias each exhibits. A more obvious limit is the definition of education each induces. Suffice to say that the tests discriminate against minorities and assault both the concept and implementation of multicultural education.

Core Curriculum

The second inconsistency is the use of a "core" curriculum. The "core" is assumed to be an identifiable knowledge acquisition that should be mandatory for all children. Advocates of this position argue that subjects like science and math have no cultural bias and that these are merely basic elements of knowledge to be taught. This is just not the case. Science has its assumptions based on conventions decided by the dominant scientific community. Typically, the communities of scientists and scholars alike base a large portion of research and scholarly conventions on a language and paradigm (set of constructs, beliefs, and rules) originating in a conceptual and sometimes geographically localized intellectual culture. Science and scholarly pursuits generally exhibit cultural bias. Imre Lakatos In *Proofs and Refutations* shows this to be true even in mathematics. In any case, to understand a discipline requires some knowledge of the culture in which it evolved. All knowledge is evolved in cultural context.[12]

Willard V.O. Quine poses another explanation as to the structure of scientific knowledge. He believes:

The totality of our so-called knowledge or beliefs, from the most casual matters of geography and history to the profoundest law of atomic physics or even pure mathematics and logic, is a man-made fabric which impinges upon experience only along the edges. Or, to change the figure, total science is like a field of force whose boundary conditions are experience.[13]

In Quine's interpretation, there is a "worldview" of science or any other subject, but individual and cultural interpretations (based on our experiences) create a difference of opinion of how to use the worldview in various circumstances. In other words, cultures do influence conceptual frameworks.

Curricula in American schools continue to be fact-oriented or answer-centered, as if all that should be known is what various authorities and empirical knowledge declare or imply. The fact that knowledge has a built-in cultural interpretation is not easily perceived among the lay community, nor is it adequately understood by curriculum experts or teachers. Minority students do not share the same background knowledge of the world as the establishment's "experts" understand it. When talking about the core curriculum in American education, we must be careful to recognize "hidden curricula" (implied or assumed educational goals) of the dominant culture. A core curriculum supposing education to be largely a transmission of facts does a disservice to the society it serves. It is unacceptable because (1) it assumes everybody has the same interpretation culturally, and (2) it neglects the transitory nature of knowledge.

Added to the core-course dilemma is the different meaning of what is, in fact, core to the curriculum. Various learning tracks have different core courses, undermining the reason to have them at all. For instance, children in the "vocational track" (VT) in high school take business English rather than the English literature in the college-preparatory track. Similarly, VT students might take business math rather than algebra or geometry, or wood shop or typing rather than a language. They may even have more study periods or free periods than normally afforded college-bound students. As mentioned in both chapters 3 and 4, minority children are especially vulnerable to this unequal treatment because they are put into the vocational track much too early. It is understandable why these students do not fare as well in either norm-referenced or criterion-referenced tests. They simply do not get the same preparation. The children are economically and socially tracked for the rest of their lives, all because they did not show the same level of progress early enough. The vicious cycle of poverty and corresponding lack of opportunity for minorities continue despite economic support nationally and reactive alternatives locally.[14] A reassessment of the meaning and application of so-called core courses is needed.

Minority Inclusion

A third misconception about our curricula in America's schools is the value of events like Black History Week, Chinese New Year parades, or Cinco de Mayo festivals. These are often soft attempts at satisfying state requirements for minority inclusion and multicultural education. Minority inclusion can be defined as the recognition and appreciation of a microculture through the use of special recognition days, months, or celebrations. Minorities are given a designated time to express their own ethnicity and cultural beliefs. Cultural differences are emphasized, along with the contributions the minority has made. If the purpose is to accommodate pluralities and awaken society to appreciate other cultures, this is not the way to do it. Norman Drachler, as early as 1973, wanted to get beyond this kind of paternalism. He states:

We ought to be beyond the stage where we devote a week to "Black History.". . .
Our American history and literature courses need not be a telephone directory of

ethnic contributions, but they should be representative of *all* Americans who have played a role in American society and contributed to the dynamics of the development.[15]

To devote one week to black contributions, Asians, Native Americans, or any other subgroup is placing the contributions of these groups into a "footnote" of American history, thereby reducing the importance and the value of these groups in the overall accomplishment of the macroculture. In many ways minority inclusion alienates students from both their microculture (ethnic identity) and their macroculture (being an American). The school curriculum should emphasize both the microculture and the macroculture so children are not divided between love and devotion to family and devotion to country. Presently, minority children are caught between these two forces in their lives.

Harry Rivlin in *Cultural Pluralism in Education* writes:

No child should have to feel that he must reject his parents' culture to be accepted. Indeed, his chances of adjusting successfully to his school, to his community, and to the larger society are enhanced if he is not encumbered by a feeling of shame and inferiority because he was not born into another family and another culture.[16]

Children need to understand that families are an integral part of American life. In addition, children should understand that diversity of interest and human freedoms are guaranteed and protected by the American Constitution. Our schools today, however, do not promote appreciation and respect for both diversity *and* unity. Teachers have been asked to fill in the minority contributions the textbooks and curriculum guides often neglect. This is a difficult task when the teachers themselves have been educated by the same texts and curriculum guides and are primarily members of the established majority.[17]

Schools continue what John Ogbu calls "a subtle mechanism of inferior education . . . a caste between races."[18] That is, through differential educational arrangements, the schools continue to program minorities for life in the lowest socioeconomic classes. Although programs like VISTA, federally sponsored school lunch programs, Title VII, and Title I are designed to remove hindrances at the local level, schools still encourage discrimination, albeit subtly. There is reason for hope on the local level, however. Efforts from the private sector like the School-to-Work Action Project (SWAP) in Denver, the Stay-in-School Task Force in Dalton, Georgia, and the Adopt-A-Student program in Atlanta are successful initiatives that are helping at-risk children.[19] The Effective Schools research project, outcome-based education, and programs in states like Oregon, Washington, and Florida are designed to improve overall achievement, accountability, and teacher expectation. But, again, these programs handle the problem of minority achievement with more intense remediation and mastery learning (reflecting establishment values), rather than with a transcultural perspective of interdependence, mutual respect, and tolerance.[20] These efforts deserve recognition, but they are either too few, or they are not really oriented toward minorities. They are themselves in danger of being a new form of minority inclusion.

Bilingual/ESL Education: Problems and Promises

Mandated special education for children speaking a language other than English at home is a relatively recent occurrence. *Lau v. Nichols* (1974), mentioned in the last chapter, mandated "special educational programs" for Asian children, but not necessarily bilingual programs. The 1968 Bilingual Education Act, or Public Law 90–247, is the primary legislation used to provide special help to Asian and Hispanic children (as long as there are enough children in a particular language to constitute a class). Although bilingual teaching is not mandated by this act, it is one of the two most common models used to help these children. The other model teaches all non-English-speaking children in the same class regardless of their native language. The native home language is used only in English instruction. This English-as-a-second-language (ESL) instructional method is designed to enculturate the students and continue their education without losing the momentum of learning they have already developed in their native tongue. Since 7.9 million school-aged children speak a language other than English at home, the need for bilingual and ESL classes is evident.[21]

There are important differences between these approaches. The ESL approach is more direct in its attempt to teach the English language. Furthermore, it requires fewer teachers with foreign-language fluency. It seems to work quite well with children of migrant workers who frequently move from school to school, or when the home language is a combination or conglomeration of English and another language. Children who speak some English are categorized as limited English proficient (LEP). In Texas, for example, the language often spoken by Hispanics is "Tex-Mex," a combination of English, several dialects of Spanish, and possibly even Amerindian. ESL also seems to work with children speaking the dialect that has come to be called black English.[22] ESL is particularly effective when there are several children who speak different languages, but not enough to constitute a full bilingual class. For instance, twenty-one languages other than English were spoken by children attending Houston public schools in 1991. It would be unfeasible to establish bilingual classes for all of these languages.

Bilingual programs, in contrast to ESL, are designed to teach the structure and foundation of the native language before teaching the child English. The assumption in this approach is that children need to learn their first language and all the *cultural* meaning that goes with it before being enculturated into the mainstream. In this way, or so it is argued, the student retains cultural pride, heritage, and familial values while at the same time learning American history, heritage, and values. Table 5.2 represents the difference between ESL and bilingual education, each having assets and liabilities that need to be considered before being used.[23]

Table 5.2

A Preliminary Comparison Between ESL and Bilingual Teaching Methodologies

Bilingual Teaching	ESL Teaching
Takes full advantage of knowledge, values, and language already learned from another culture.	Forsakes part of culture, language, and ethnic background in favor of or immersion into new culture more quickly.
Relies on research supporting the learning of one language before learning another. Relies strongly on the development of the native language.	Argues that native language is often not a formal language, and that it is better to learn the official language as early as possible.
Requires many years of instruction in two languages and is a relatively slow process.	Requires only partial instruction in native language until basic rules in English are learned. Is fast and gives more immediate results for the effort.
Requires many teachers proficient in native languages and in all subject areas.	Requires fewer teachers in native language because English is the only subject being taught in a bilingual setting.
Builds good self-concept and motivation because of the integrative nature of the curriculum with the native culture *and* the new culture.	Side effects include an inability to easily resolve conflicts between familial and macrocultural values, beliefs, and meanings. A sense of shame, a loss of motivation, parental conflict, and frustration could result, causing high dropout.
More costly because of the need for specialized instruction and more costly preparation of teachers.	More cost effective because there is minimal use of additional specialized instruction. Children from several cultures can be placed in the same class.
Does not work well if child moves residence often, but can take advantage of parental help with schoolwork at home.	Provides a more stable transition if child moves quite often, but cannot rely on much parental help because of language barrier.
Defines multicultural education as truly multicultural, bilingual, and more multiethnic. Transculturation initiated.	Defines multicultural education in the traditional assimilationist model.
Longitudinal results are a bilingual, bicultural student who has experience accommodating other cultures and other ways of learning.	Longitudinal result is a person partially assimilated into the macroculture, with little acculturation occurring.

At first glance, the long-term benefits of bilingual education seem clear. Children become proficient in two languages and are capable of taking the perspectives of other cultures. They are not required to immediately sacrifice native languages, cultures, and values in order to fit into the macroculture. Many minority parents, however, have not wanted their children in bilingual programs because they fear the children will be denied access to substantive educational fare. Some parents have argued that it is better to teach children in English to ensure fluency in the predominant language. In short, bilingual programs, although they take much more time and effort, are not always perceived even by *minorities* as *the* answer to ensuring equal educational opportunity for their children.

Some critics argue that bilingual education tends to produce a "bilingual bureaucracy," separating children even more from the mainstream culture than what was originally intended.[24] These critics propose that bilingual education, like many other programs designed to protect and serve minorities, has actually been politicized to the point that a whole new bureaucracy has grown to protect itself rather than the students.

Expense, qualified faculty, flexibility, and minimal commitment to language proficiency and special programs are the reasons why ESL programs outnumber bilingual programs today. However, the price paid for using ESL programs can be quite high in the long run. ESL represents an assimilationist ideology. Consequently, students in ESL programs risk loss of cultural identity, loss of motivation, and the lack of minority community support. All of these losses increase potential minority dropout rates.

The limited definition of multicultural education used in ESL programs takes on the look of assimilation rather than enculturation and acculturation. Historically, ESL programs were started in states as merely interim measures until enough bilingual teachers were trained, or they were started to deal with LEP students who had at least some knowledge of English. Since public schools and colleges no longer require a second language for graduation, the pool of qualified language specialists as prospective teachers is limited. ESL teaching, rather than merely a stop gap measure, is becoming the established practice because of lower cost and lack of qualified language-proficient teachers. Although recruitment efforts for minority and bilingual teachers have increased, there is little improvement in the relative number of these teachers in the nation's teaching corps. In 1985 the estimates were that almost three-fourths of non-English-speaking children were not getting any language training at all. When they did, some teachers complained that the programs were actually holding children's progress back when they reentered regular classrooms.[25]

Conservatives like educators John Silber, Allan Bloom, and Senator S.I. Hayakawa have labeled any minority language instruction as "inferior" and unfair to the children. Bloom, for instance, argues that multiculturalism waters down academic pursuit to a level that makes it impossible for students to have good standards for judgment.[26] Hayakawa describes multiculturalism (and bilingual education) as a "force that imperils the future of the country." He concludes that it tends to divide us and make us rivals for power and, furthermore, does nothing to increase the amount of what is learned.[27] All of these views argue for a return to universal standards in education, a common curriculum, and total-immersion English programs for minorities. This adds up to another version of assimilation, asking minorities to learn about traditional American values without asking establishment-types to learn about the values of other cultures.

A strong possibility looms that by sheer default the majority of minority non-English-speaking children will be taught by ESL or even regular teachers in the near future. If this does occur, then these children will not receive a multicultural education. Instead, they will have settled on them a monocultural education depriving them and the nation of the students' previous cultural heritages. Drastic changes in the ESL program and its methodologies are needed if this trend is to be changed.

In summary, testing, core curriculums, minority-inclusion practices, and ESL programs are just four examples of how schools' efforts to help minorities have gone awry. The next section of this chapter will discuss how teachers can effectively address the gaps between multicultural educational theory and practice.

II. Theory and Practice in Multicultural Teaching

While the previous section dealt primarily with curricular and testing flaws, this section is designed to help teachers recognize bias in American curricula; understand racism, ethnic bias, and other types of cultural inequity; and develop plans in order to close the gap between theory and practice in multicultural teaching.

A. A Definition of Terms

Many people use the term *racism* with abandon. The term is most usefully defined as discrimination, or favoritism, for or against a group or groups categorized or delineated by racial origin. It is a set of attitudes, beliefs, or behaviors that one's own race is superior to others. *Bias* is further defined as an unreflective inclination of mind or temperament—a bent or prejudice for or against something.

Schools face many types of racism. Some of these reveal themselves in institutional structures, while others are inherent in the curricula. Some are inherent in various informal social and individual arrangements and considerations made by school officials. For example, institutional racism, as described by Ogbu, is revealed in the amount of money that is spent in predominantly black schools for teachers, libraries, supplies, counselors, and ancillary equipment.[28] Curricular racism, on the other hand, may not always be so evident. Having children read *The Adventures of Huckleberry Finn* without discussing how blacks are depicted in the novel usually reflects a curricular prejudice, though it could also be an instructional (teacher-based) prejudice. Instructional discrimination (both social and individual) is the most subtle of all. For example, a teacher may assume that Asian children will do well in math or that Hispanic children will not do as well as Asians. When teachers, consciously or unconsciously, spend more or less time with a given group of children because of stereotypical images of them, the teachers harbor a clear form of racism. Similarly, if the time spent or not spent with these children creates a negative self-image of minorities, then individual performance will again suffer.

Individual racism and social racism are difficult to overcome. Teachers, administrators, students, and parents each have their own stereotypes of races and biases. Each group tends to bring these into the educational setting, thereby affecting it in profound ways. Both Robert Merton in his seminal work *Social Theory and Structure* and Jennie Oakes in *Keeping Track: How Schools Structure Inequality* document the problem of teacher expectation and bias and the way these influence student success. For example, in oft-repeated Pygmalion-type experiments, teachers are told that various groups are "slow" and "accelerated" or "smart" and "dumb." The results are predictable. Regardless of IQ scores, race, ethnic origin, or previous success in school, the group labeled "accelerated" does well, and the "slow" group does not. Teacher influence and expectation create success as much as individual student competence.[29] Racism, cultural or ethnic bias, and other forms of discrimination contaminate student performance and achievement. Consequently, teachers owe it to both students and the community at large to eliminate instructional and curricular bias in the schools. As will be made clear in chapter 6, this principle is central to the individual ethical code of every *professional* teacher.

B. Racism, Bias, and Discrimination in Curricula, Teaching, and Educational Institutions

Schools can only do so much in dealing with issues of racial discrimination. The ultimate resolution requires national emphasis in and outside academic settings. What teachers *can* do, however, is recognize racial bias and discrimination when they occur in the curriculum, in their students, in administrators, in other teachers, and even in themselves. Whenever and wherever bias and discrimination are identified, steps must be taken to eliminate them.

Textual/Curricular Racism and Bias

Teachers often do not have the opportunity to choose their own textbooks. Many states have elaborate textbook adoption procedures, and the quality of the adoption process varies greatly from state to state and from district to district. Too often book companies try to sell their books with "eye appeal" and graphics rather than with intellectual or genuinely pedagogical content. Teachers must serve as additional buffers by identifying bias and racism in texts and acting to correct bias wherever it occurs. This is done by supplementally instructing the class about bias and/or reporting concerns about the bias in a textbook to the proper textbook adoption committee.

Some of the more common forms of instructional and curricular racism or bias include (1) stereotyping of groups, (2) selective inclusion or exclusion of factual information, (3) prioritizing impacts of groups, (4) linguistic narrowness, and (5) cultural imbalance.[30] Each practice contributes in its own way to the problem of bias and discrimination. An illustration of each will be helpful in recognizing the widespread aspect of this problem in instruction and curricular models still being used.

Blatant examples of *stereotyping* include referring to blacks as "lazy," "musical," or "uneducated"; Native Americans as "savages" or the "vanishing breed"; women as "consumers" and men as "producers"; and Asians as "good in math," "cooks," or "launderers." More subtle forms of stereotyping are terms like "those people," the "unwashed masses," or "our legacy," as if certain groups were and always will be a burden. Separation of one group from another does more than merely show similarities and differences; it can be a way of discriminating against them. (You will have a chance to check your own preconceptions of ethnic groups later in this chapter and again in chapter 7.)

Selective inclusion—or exclusion of accomplishments or contributions of minorities—is yet another form of bias. Examples of this are found in the writing of American history whenever Native Americans are treated as only a sidelight or as a nuisance, or whenever the "winning" of the West is portrayed as fighting back the "red scourge." An even worse exclusion would be to depict westward expansion as a trek into a wilderness that nobody owned. Because Native Americans live with nature rather than trying to conquer it, they are seen by many to be a lost civilization that has left nothing substantial or permanent to study and admire. This kind of exclusion and bias must be eliminated in texts and curricula.

An example of *prioritizing impacts* would be to include minorities as footnotes in the mainstream of history rather than as an integral part of it. Excluding broken treaties, wars, and injustices like slavery is just another form of bias and racism. Placing the development of the repeating rifle above the importance of friendly Mexicans and Native Americans in westward expansion is an example of misplaced impact. While some Indians and Mexicans were hostile to new immigration, many more were tolerant, and even helpful.

Linguistic narrowness is using a language in ways that are biased toward a minority group. For example, to depict American Indians as "roving" or "migrant" suggests they have no purpose for land other than hunting. It belittles the lifestyle of the first Americans and also distorts the importance of land and its overall meaning in their lives. To use the language of other cultures to narrow meaning is another form of bias and racism. For instance, terms like *ghetto, barrio,* or *tent city* are sometimes used to describe groups and their habitats, but these are more than just descriptive phrases about homes. They are narrowing in their depiction of the cultures in general—often in derogatory ways.[31] The use of other languages can be helpful in describing different meanings a culture might convey, but it also can lead to stereotyping and overgeneralizations. Using only English to describe other cultures and beliefs can also create misconceptions and even distortions of other cultures. Languages themselves are not evil or bad, but they can label groups in derogatory or misrepresentational ways. Teachers must be alert to such injustices.

Cultural imbalance occurs when an establishment culture recognizes only the accomplishments and contributions of the majority, without recognizing the contributions of minorities.

Instructional and Institutional Bias

It takes practice, sensitivity, and dedication from teachers to correct or supplement curricular materials that are biased. It takes even more skill to recognize bias and racism in their own teaching and personal perspectives. People have many reasons why they are personally biased or prejudiced. Personal biases will show up in individual teaching practices as well as in efforts at administrative guidance. Bias is not always shown in what people say and do. It also shows up in what they do not say or do not do. The checklist in table 5.3 illustrates the kinds of questions teachers should ask themselves to avoid personal biases in their instruction. The checklist is not complete and can serve only as a starting point for self-evaluation and evaluation of school practices.[32]

Table 5.3

An Initial Illustrative Checklist for Bias and Racism in Teaching and Administration

Teaching

Do I spend too much time acknowledging, talking, questioning, or favoring a particular group in my class? Which ones? Why?

Do I neglect or overlook certain children in my classes? Which ones? Why?

Do I feel superior or inferior to any groups in my class?

Do I have specific children I treat as "pets," "favorites," "troublemakers," or "dummies"? What are the criteria I use?

Are there cultural "enclaves" in my classroom? Do minorities interact with me and other students? How?

Do I tolerate biased, racist, or bigoted behavior in students?

Are there different rules for different classes I teach? Why?

Do I include supplemental examples of minority accomplishments as an integral part of American life?

Am I always justifying my authority to students in class? Do I feel I have to control certain students or groups? Why?

Do I encourage other teachers to observe my teaching and critique me for not only style but also bias or unequal treatment of students?

Are minority children doing worse overall in my classes when it comes to grades?

Are parents from minorities able to talk to me and help in the child's education?

Do I tend to ignore or skip over controversial issues in my courses?

How do I answer student questions when they may have racial or biased overtones?

Do I integrate knowledge gained in my class with other interpretations of everyday-life experience and their cultural origins?

Do I check texts for racism and bias? Do I report discrepancies or try in some other way to correct them?

Do I use the ideas of as many children as possible in my teaching? Do I try to include all children in the discussions?

Testing

Are all my test questions answer-centered?

Am I expecting some students to fail my tests?

Are my tests designed to grade on a curve? Do mostly minorities end up on the bottom of the curve? Why?

Is there cultural bias in the way I ask questions or expect answers?

Do I evaluate students for diversity and alternative thinking, when appropriate?

Do I spend almost all of my time teaching to standards?

Do I have tutorial programs for those not doing well? Are they well attended?

Do I have preconceived notions of how individual students will do on my tests?

Table 5.3

Do I disregard the background of my students and test just for content knowledge?

Do I use tests for disciplinary purposes against minorities or the students who do not show fast progress? Do I give pop quizzes or unannounced tests when classes misbehave? Are the minority students the ones who do badly in these tests?

Do I make sure tests have reliability and validity?

Administration

Does the school reflect institutional bias and racism with fewer facilities and materials and less support for programs comprised of mostly minorities?

Do administrators reflect a professional attitude and behavior toward all students? Is there a mechanism for grievance about racial, cultural, and gender inequities at my school?

Do I hear racist, ethnic, or gender-based remarks in the teachers' lounge or among teachers? Do I say something to them about it?

Are gangs, segregated activities, and a lack of school spirit prevalent in my school? Why?

Are administrators concerned about reducing inequities and bias? How?

Do I report curriculum bias to my curriculum specialists or principal? Are there procedures for this?

Are there minority teachers and administrators in my school? Do they adequately represent the student population in my school? How?

Does the administration welcome comments and criticisms?

Giving the "right" or "wrong" answers to these questions does not guarantee freedom from bias or deliberate bias on the part of the teacher. For example, if most of the students doing badly on a graded test are minorities, it could mean they did not understand the questions or concepts being used. Racism may not have been intended at all. It is not the act or result itself that constitutes racism or bias. But it is always important for teachers to question the rationales and motivations in their teaching. If a teacher designs a test to purposely place minorities at the bottom of the performance curve, this *is* clearly biased and racist practice. Anyone representing the profession of teaching must avoid this sort of behavior.

The first step in eliminating bias and racism is to *want* to eliminate it. Teachers, administrators, and parents must all do their part in this process, but the real work starts with you . . . now! Our schools should be exemplars in the resolution of racist practice, but, admittedly, total success in eliminating the problem will come only if society follows suit. Only then will racism and bigotry become a thing of the past rather than a foreboding of an immoral future.

C. Addressing the Gap Between Theory and Practice in Multicultural Teaching

The following problem areas in multicultural education leave tremendous gaps between theory (intended goals) and practice (what actually happens in American public schools). If we are to produce *true* transcultural education as a unifying theme for American's future, teachers must address these problems.

Each problem, as it is described, is a simplified portrayal of the predicament, but it is also a starting point for discussion and improvement. There are no simple solutions to these problems. If they were simple, the problems would have already been solved. Consistency in multicultural teaching theory and practice requires teachers, administrators, and curriculum experts to be committed to the principles of mutual interdependence among groups and respect for individual personhood. It also requires an understanding of agreed-to goals and plans, as well as an understanding of how to accomplish them. These problems must awaken teachers to the need to be more professional in adopting transcultural teaching strategies—strategies that will make a difference between giving lip service to equality, justice, and due process, and actually leading the way to their realization. Suggested "problem focuses" are included as a way to kick off the discussion. The focuses are not intended as *the* answer to issues presented, but only to suggest some promising ways to think about the topics.

Problem #1: Real Educational Equality of Opportunity Is Needed.

Americans say they want equal educational opportunity for all children. Still, they do not make enough allowances for the effects of poverty, ethnic differences in learning and language development, and the fact that bias and discrimination continue to fester between microcultures and the macroculture. On the one hand, multicultural education aspires to bring all "into the fold," but, instead, it often isolates, separates, and nullifies. *Problem Focus:* More time, effort, and resources will have to be afforded at-risk students. America and all it stands for are at risk because students are at risk. How will teachers begin to remedy this problem?

Problem #2: "Success" in Education Is Too Narrowly Defined.

"Success in education is based primarily on a preselected, content-based standard reflecting not only Western culture, but also the current predilection for scientific knowledge. SAT's, college boards, other standardized test scores, and class standing in high school are biased in favor of the establishment's high culture. Educators should develop testing instruments that reduce cultural bias and cultural exclusion. Furthermore, educators should find ways to measure skills other than the ability to accumulate unrelated bits of knowledge."[33] *Problem Focus:* Assessment, and not testing, is the issue. We want to assess how well students are learning things worth learning, and not just test for behavior easy to measure. Educational ideals must drive efforts at assessment and not the other way around. For example, other appropriate skills to measure could include cooperation skills, leadership qualities, alternative thinking strategies, and artistic flair. As a teacher, how would you go about identifying what ought to be learned, and how well it is being learned? How would you test for artistic flair, leadership, and alternative thinking? Do other cultures rely on cooperative skills? How?

Problem #3: Multicultural Education Should Not Be for Minority Students Alone.

Multicultural education is now taught as if it were almost exclusively for minorities. This attitude is reminiscent of the British Empire's imperialism—military and governmental bureaucracies assumed a "white man's burden" in protecting Britain's colonies, while at the same time exploiting them. The assumption behind multicultural education seems to be that minority children not only need to be enculturated and assimilated, but also kept separate from the larger American culture. Furthermore, there is little thought that the larger establishment culture needs to be acculturated to the world of minority cultures. The dangers in this way of thinking are that the larger culture loses opportunities for growth and productive change, while the minority cultures lose their sense of identity and importance to the world. Using an isolationist approach of cultural pluralism to counter the one-way enculturation creates suspicion, doubt, "win-lose" or "us-them" polarization, hate, and envy. Rather than unifying our culture, pluralist programs fragment school society into castes or partisan systems. To avoid this, multicultural education must evolve into a transcultural education for all. *Problem Focus*: Consider requiring all students to study a second language. Develop integrative curricula in multicultural education rather than "inclusion" programs that promote separatism and castes. Insist on multicultural approaches in textbooks and curriculum guides. As an individual teacher, what can you do to make your class a *transcultural* environment?

Problem #4: Special Programs Also Discriminate.

Bilingual education, ESL programs, mainstreaming, Head Start, remedial courses, and other special programs, although well intentioned, sometimes create divisions, discriminatory environments, and separatism of their own. Children may be unfairly classified, tracked too early, and, even worse yet, misdiagnosed. *Problem Focus*: Teachers must be aware of bias in IQ tests, norm-referenced tests, criterion-referenced tests, and curricular designs that place students in special programs. Teachers must encourage the development of curricula that ensure all students will take courses reflecting transcultural diversity. What should such courses look like? How would you go about teaching such a course in, say, literature, health, science, mathematics, or social studies?

Problem #5: Plurality and Diversity in Thinking Are Discouraged.

Although our society expects students to learn how to resolve conflicts, recognize inconsistencies, test hypotheses, make value decisions, and right injustices, very little time if any is spent in our public schools helping students practice these skills. Although character development is an expectation of our schools, the curricula, teaching methodologies, and expected standards in tests do not reflect these goals. *Problem Focus*: Integrate curriculum goals, core courses, and assessment practices to evaluate student skills in divergent thinking. Develop cognitive objectives stressing analysis, synthesis, and evaluation rather than basic knowledge.[34] Require students to practice cooperation and unbiased assessment of problems. Recognizing that individuals cannot make decisions wholly free from their culture, upbringing, and other external influences, how would you help children become less subjective? How would you encourage children to reach intersubjective agreement on controversial issues?

Problem #6: Present Purposes and Meanings of Multicultural Education Are Lacking.

Multicultural education should not be a political expediency, a legal strategy, or an answer to the problem of built-in discrimination and bias. Nor should it be a way to merely fit minorities into the American mainstream so they will be economic "assets" rather than "liabilities." It should not just be a listing of legal precedents that have been ruled on, or a strategy to "keep the lid on" social injustices. Rather, it should unify people with common goals, purposes, and ideals. Continued politicalization and legalization of "multicultural education" have weakened it to the point that it rarely accomplishes anything more than learning the English language and a minimal knowledge of a locally recognized high culture. *Problem Focus*: Require students to compare and contrast cultural perspectives; develop a global sense of problems; and develop cross-cultural competencies (see chapter 7). Require *all* students to think about their own ethnic and cultural backgrounds. Have them discuss the interface between their own and other "American" cultures. What would it take for a teacher to develop a worldview in students, without any particular bias? How can a teacher help students develop a transcultural perspective?

Problem #7: The Moral Basis in Present Multicultural Education Is Lacking.

Multicultural education must concentrate on unifying rather than dividing Americans. This requires an end to the divisiveness, polarization, and "we-they" mentality that have plagued the schools in the past forty years. Using a moral basis in the study of cultures (as the unifying themes of our common humanness) would be a helpful way to integrate skill in making moral choices. It would also be useful to help students discriminate between high and low cultural achievement and recognize how each culture has contributed to human progress. *Problem Focus*: Use case studies to help students make judgments of fairness, justice, due process, and "rightness." Teachers must also help students discriminate among cultures in their treatment of humankind. How would you show students that while cultural determinants may specify what we see as relevant in a certain scenario, respect for personhood seems to be a transcultural moral consideration?

Problem #8: Multicultural Education Is Too Politicized and Inflexible.

Multicultural education has faced varying levels of support or nonsupport, interpretation and misinterpretation, depending on the political climate in Washington, D.C. and in the state capitals. The results of this political waffling are predictable. Administrators and teachers have reduced multicultural education to a level of mere "compliance." That is, they do what they have to do legally to survive. Few seem to view multicultural education as an opportunity to move forward. Long-term goals and impacts have not been realized because of the year-to-year changes in funding, transient support, and ill-formed philosophies. Much of the research and program development thus far has been directed toward initial implementation rather than toward learner needs and characteristics. Flexible instructional formats to capture the spirit rather than the letter of the law and systematic assessment of individual teacher's sensitivity to multicultural issues should be encouraged. *Problem Focus:* A long-term national policy for multicultural education should be developed. Federal and state funding should support long-term goals. Teachers must be convinced of the merit of long-range transcultural policy. How could you convince your colleagues that teachers ought to be able to reach consensus regarding multicultural education?

From Social Compliance to Social Responsibility

The rationale for having assimilation, immersion, minority-inclusion, or enculturation programs has typically been to make minorities conform. There has been little interest in fostering a dynamic interdependence between minorities and the establishment. We have viewed our schools as purveyors of social compliance, rather than social responsibility. In particular, schools have set out to retool minorities into roles that preserve and support the establishment. In chapter 4 the school-as-job-finder model was described as the predominant model for education in America today. The rationale for this kind of schooling is to support industrial needs and economic demands, regardless of culture. This approach fails to recognize the importance of schools as places where communal cooperation is gained and *exchanged*. Too much time has been wasted by educators fine-tuning the curricula of yesteryear, reworking outmoded instructional training programs, and currying favor with politically persuasive groups. The time has come for a rebirth of social responsibility as a major goal in education.

Multicultural education faces the same plight as most of our American education. Personal experience, cultural background, and the ability to evaluate what has been learned have been lost in the race to establish accountable, standardized criteria for measuring "learning." Assessment and testing instruments now determine what we teach, and not the other way around! Teaching cultural understanding has become a subject to be tested—just like everything else. As a consequence, multicultural education is in danger of losing its dynamism, its signifying purpose, and its meaning. Teaching for testing *is* teaching without meaning. It leaves nearly everyone without a sense of history, pride, dignity, or belongingness.

Education is a social invention. Among other things, it incorporates students into an integrative whole. Although conformity and subservience may have been some of its goals in the recent past, the nation can no longer afford such an egocentric luxury. All students need to acquire life concepts such as the meaning of democratic action, justice, equality or opportunity, and individual human dignity. These are not learned as "subjects." Rather, they are learned in concert with others. The "rightness" or "wrongness" of a person's actions is not the same thing as knowing that crayfish molt or Goths roamed Europe. The value of a culture is not just knowing its peculiarities of dress or diet, but rather how it promotes the human endeavor to improve life. The two-way, integrative, and cross-cultural nature of transcultural education is the ideal medium for such understanding.

Social responsibility is an elusive and difficult concept to learn. It is, in part, based on circumstances, but also reflects a moral commitment to do the right thing. It demands cooperation, but also respects the individual's right to be different. It presupposes a search for the truth, but also an understanding that humans are fallible in their interpretations. Education has not done well lately in promoting life concepts. One of the major reasons why is that it has lost a sense of purpose. It now adheres to static and uniform notions of learning and knowledge rather than to dynamic ones. Transcultural education can help right the course of American education. Teaching transcultural education is like teaching ecology—it loses its value and meaning if taught in the abstract. Subjects like these two must produce personal plans of action, addressing real needs. The alternative is a society unprepared to make ethical choices.

Filling the Theory-into-Practice Gap with Local Support

Many national organizations have been in favor of multicultural education in this century. Almost every professional education organization recognizes the importance of and need for multicultural education. LULAC and the NAACP were pioneer advocates of minority education and continue to extol the virtue of multicultural approaches to teaching in our public schools. The federal government and the courts have legislated and ruled extensively to improve minority education through multicultural methods of instruction. Yet with all of these higher level efforts, implementation (and consequently the success of the program) has been left to local authorities and districts. Without local support, multicultural programs will suffer, or even die.

One of the strengths of multicultural education is the realization that children first develop a sense of worth and personhood from their native cultures (microcultures). Parents are invaluable in a child's overall development in and outside of school because they, above all others, can integrate home life with the curriculum of the schools. But recent studies have revealed a growing cultural shock between teachers and students. The low number of minority teachers and the growing number of minority students have widened the gap between theory and practice. Added to this is the lack of knowledge teachers have of minorities in America.[35] If the gap is prevalent between teachers and students, it is also getting wider between teachers and parents.

There used to be ways minority neighborhoods prepared their children for public schools. Before the age of bilingual, ESL, or multicultural education, Hispanic children in America were helped in neighborhood schools called *escuelitas* or "little schools." Starting around age four, the children learned English and spelling and reading in their native tongue as an informal "head start" for the time when they entered public school. These informal classes were often taught by English-speaking parents of the neighborhood as a local response to a community need. This community-supported education proved invaluable for Hispanic children trying to enter a school that had no consideration for other cultures. Asian and African-American communities had similar community programs. The key to a successful program in multicultural education is strong commitment from the community and strong administrative/teacher support. Without that support, especially from parents, the experiment has little chance of success.

Recent movements toward site-based management or school-based management, although not a panacea, promise to improve both the planning and the implementation phases of educational goals, including the development of transcultural education. Site-based management gives administrators control of their own schools, allowing them freedom to hire, fire, augment, and subsidize when and where needed. Site-based management also allows parents to actively choose particular schools and educational tracks for their children. There may be abuses of this choice, but they can be minimalized if administrators are given freedom to organize schools in equitable ways. Multicultural education would get additional support and would benefit because parents would already be actively involved in their children's education. A more active role by parents, and particularly minority parents, would be a boon to minority children and the nation at large.

If administrators have more flexibility, so would the teachers. One of the largest complaints by teachers about present school practices is the inflexibility of educational plans and the lack of initiative afforded them. If more broad-based curricula were developed, teachers could spend more time with community support programs and parents. As it is now, teachers must spend an extraordinary amount of time filling out mounds of paperwork to ensure that each child's educational program complies with various regulations. Broad-based curricula suggest that more time could be spent with individual plans and their implementation rather than with the present inflexible evaluation and assessment criteria used in most states. Minorities would be better served if the educational system were flexible enough to individualize and integrate learning goals, while at the same time developing tolerance and respect for personhood in all students.

The most radical changes in education will take place at the local level. Each community, if given choices, will figure out for itself what measures will improve learning and educational design. Local assistance from businesses, professional organizations, and community service organizations will be necessary to ensure success. Adopt-a-student and adopt-a-school programs are springing up in almost every major city in America. These and many more incentive programs to keep students learning are a necessary part for turning around the failure rate of students at risk.

In summary, with parental and administrative support, teachers can turn schools into transcultural social laboratories—places where they can take advantage of culture-specific learning models when possible. Teachers and parents together will develop cooperation skills and skills in making moral, economic, and public social choices. Only then will society succeed in maintain the opposing forces of unity *and* diversity so necessary to the American way of life.

Questions for Discussion

1. Describe four curricular inconsistencies in American schools that adversely affect multicultural education. How do they do so?
2. How are IQ tests culturally biased?
3. Can you defend the proposition that criterion-referenced tests are less discriminatory against minorities than norm-referenced tests? Why or why not?

4. Core courses can become culturally bound. How does this happen? Give two examples.
5. Compare and contrast bilingual teaching to ESL teaching pursuant to motivation, time needed to teach, and cost. Which is more responsive to LEP children? Why?
6. Define racism and bias.
7. What are five ways personal bias/racism can be recognized in your own teaching?
8. List and describe five problems in multicultural education that need correction. In what ways could they be corrected?
9. What curricular improvements could be made with multicultural education? Explain them.

NOTES

1. National Commission on Excellence in Education, *A Nation at Risk* (Washington, D.C.: U.S. Government Printing Office, 1983).
2. See Lamar Alexander, *America 2000: An Educational Strategy* (Washington, D.C.: U.S. Department of Education, 1991). See also Carnegie Taskforce on the Teaching Profession, *A Nation Prepared: Teachers for the 21st Century* (New York: Carnegie Forum on Education and the Economy, 1986). See also H. Daly and J. Cobb, Jr., *For the Common Good: Redirecting the Economy Toward Community, the Environment and a Sustainable Future* (Boston: Beacon Press, 1989) for an opposing view to the economic motive for education.
3. See Terry Dean, "Multicultural Classrooms, Monocultural Teachers," *College Composition and Communication* 40 (February 1989): 23–37. See also Diane Ravitch, "Diversity and Democracy: Multicultural Education in America," *American Educator* 14(Spring 1990).
4. James Banks, *Multiethnic Education: Theory and Practice* (Boston: Allyn & Bacon, 1988), 115–16.
5. Byron N. Kunisawa, "A Nation in Crisis: The Dropout Dilemma," *NEA Today,* (January 1988): 62–64.
6. Stephen J. Gould, *The Mismeasure of Man* (New York: W.W. Norton, 1985). See also A.G. Dworkin and N. Black, *The IQ Controversy* (New York: Pantheon Books, 1981), 410–546.
7. Arthur R. Jensen, "How Much Can We Boost IQ and Scholastic Achievement?" *Harvard Educational Review* 39 (Spring 1969): 100–108.
8. See Ulric Neisser, "General, Academic, and Artificial Intelligence," in *The Nature of Intelligence*, Lauren Resnick ed. (Hillsdale, N.J.: Erlbaum, 1976). See also Robert Sternberg and Richard Wagner, eds., *Practical Intelligence* (Cambridge: Cambridge University Press, 1986).
9. Nathaniel Gage and David Berliner, *Educational Psychology*, 4th ed. (Boston: Houghton Mifflin, 1988), 55.
10. Ibid., 574.

11. See J.C. Clift and B. Irmie, *Assessing Students, Appraising Teaching* (New York: John Wiley & Sons, 1981) for a more in-depth assessment of pros and cons of each kind of test without reference to culture.

12. See Thomas S. Kuhn, *The Structure of Scientific Revolution* (Chicago: University of Chicago Press, 1962), 2–5, for an explanation of science as a series of shifting paradigms, each complete. See also Imre Lakatos, *Proofs and Refutations* (London: Cambridge University Press, 1976) and the writings of Nelson Goodman.

13. Willard V.O. Quine, "Two Dogmas of Empiricism," *From Logical Point of View* (New York: Harper & Row, 1961), 42.

14. See Mortimer Adler, *The Paideia Proposal: An Educational Manifesto* (New York: Macmillan, 1982). Adler has asked for a common curriculum for all students and the elimination of tracking in high school.

15. Norman Drachler, "A Rationale for a Pluralistic Society," in *Eliminating Ethnic Bias in Instructional Materials,* ed. Maxine Dunfee (Washington, D.C.: Association for Supervision and Curriculum Development, 1974), 5.

16. M. Stent, W. Hazard, and H. Rivlin, eds., *Cultural Pluralism in Education: A Mandate for Change* (New York: Appleton-Century-Crofts, 1973), viii.

17. Lamar Miller, "Evidence of Ethnic Bias in Instructional Materials," *Eliminating Ethnic Bias in Instructional Materials,* 13. See also Christine Sleeter, "Multicultural Education as a Form of Resistance to Oppression," *Journal of Education* 171 (Fall 1989): 51–71.

18. John Ogbu, *Minority Education and Caste* (New York: Academic Press, 1978), 103–4. See also M. Tran, "Building Cross-Cultural Bridges," *Social Education* 54 (April 1990).

19. Andrea Bermudez, "Examining Institutional Barriers of Language Minority Students," *Educational Issues of Language Minority Students* 4 (1989): 33.

20. See Joan D. Abrams, "Making Outcome-Based Education Work," *Educational Leadership* 43 (September 1985): 30–32. Madeline Hunter's mastery approach is similar in that she emphasizes grade-level achievement, regardless of student population. See also Donald Cruickshank, *Research That Informs Teachers and Teacher Education* (Bloomington, Ind.: Phi Delta Kappa, 1991) for a more extensive list of outcomes-based education used by schools.

21. D. Waggoner, "Estimates of the Need for Bilingual Education," *IDRA Newsletter,* September 1986, 5.

22. *Martin Luther King Elementary School Children v. Ann Arbor School District (1979) recognized black English as a separate dialect.*

23. See C. Ovando and V. Collier, *Bilingual and ESL Classrooms* (New York: McGraw-Hill, 1985), 24–46, for a more in-depth analysis of the two approaches.

24. See Rosalie P. Porter, *Forked Tongue: The Politics of Bilingual Education* (New York: Basic Books, 1991).

25. Cynthia Gorney, "The Bilingual Education Battle," *Washington Post National Weekly Edition,* July 9, 1985, 7.

26. Allan Bloom, *The Closing of the American Mind* (New York: Simon & Schuster, 1987), 227–45. See also John Silber, *Straight Shooting* (New York: Harper & Row, 1989), 25.

27. S.I. Hayakawa, "Make English Official: One Common Language Makes Our Nation Work," *The Executive Educator* 9 (Spring 1987): 36.

28. Ogbu, *Minority Education and Caste*, 101–104.

29. See Jennie Oakes, *Keeping Track: How Schools Structure Inequality* (New Haven: Yale University Press, 1985). See also Ray C. Rist, "Student Social Class and Teacher Expectation: The Self-Fulfilling Prophecy in Ghetto Education," *Harvard Educational Review* 40 (August 1970): 411–50. See also J. Nathan, *Free to Teach* (New York: Pilgrim Press, 1991).

30. M. P. Sadker and D. Sadker, *Teachers, Schools, and Society* (New York: Random House, 1988), 229–31. See also Del Stover, "The New Racism," *American School Board Journal* 177 (June 1990): 14–18.

31. See Myra and David Sadker, *Teachers, Schools, and Society*, 229–31, for additional samples of bias in the curriculum. See also *Eliminating Ethnic Bias*.

32. See also Thomas Good and Jere Brophy for several works on teacher preparation.

33. See Jeannette Abi-Nader, "Creating a Vision of the Future," *Phi Delta Kappan* 72 (March 1991): 546–49.

34. See Benjamin Bloom's treatise on educational objectives in the cognitive domain in Benjamin Bloom, ed., *Taxonomy of Educational Objectives, Handbook 1: Cognitive Domain* (New York: David McKay, 1956).

35. Anthony G. Dworkin, *Teacher Burnout in the Public Schools: Structural Causes and Consequences for Children* (Albany, N.Y.: SUNY Press, 1987), chap. 1.

For Further Reading

Multicultural Teaching

Banks, J. *Multiethnic Education: Theory and Practice.* Boston: Allyn & Bacon, 1988.

Banks, J. *Teaching Strategies for Ethnic Studies.* Boston: Allyn & Bacon, 1987.

Barron, M.L., ed. *American Cultural Minorities: A Textbook of Readings in Intergroup Relations.* New York: Alfred A. Knopf, 1962.

Clift, J. C., and B. Irmie. *Assessing Students, Appraising Teaching.* New York: John Wiley & Sons, 1981.

Fuchs, L. *The American Kaleidoscope: Race, Ethnicity, and the Civic Culture.* Middletown, Conn.: Wesleyan University Press, 1991.

Grungeon, E., and P. Woods. *Educating All.* New York: Routledge & Kegan Paul, 1990.

Ovando, C., and V. Collier. *Bilingual and ESL Classrooms.* New York: McGraw-Hill, 1985.

Sleeter, L.E. *Empowerment Through Multicultural Education.* Albany, N.Y.: SUNY Press, 1991.

Stent, M. et al., eds. *Cultural Pluralism in Education: A Mandate for Change.* New York: Appleton-Century-Crofts, 1973.

Taba, H. et al. *Intergroup Education in Public Schools*. Washington, D.C.: American Council of Education, 1952.

Weis, L., ed. *Race, Class, and Gender in American Education*. Albany, N.Y.: SUNY Press, 1988.

Testing/Bias/Inequalities in Schools

Dunfee, M., ed. *Eliminating Ethnic Bias in Instructional Materials*. Washington, D.C.: Association for Supervision and Curriculum Development, 1974.

Dworkin, A.G. *Teaching Burnout in the Public Schools: Structural Causes and Consequences for Children*. Albany, N.Y.: SUNY Press, 1987.

Hammill, J. *Ethno-Logic*. Urbana, Ill.: University of Chicago Press, 1990.

Nomotey, K. *Going to School: The African-American Experience*. Albany, N.Y.: SUNY Press, 1991.

Oakes, J. *Keeping Track: How Schools Structure Inequality*. New Haven: Yale University Press, 1985.

Ogbu, J. *Minority Education and Caste*. New York: Academic Press, 1978.

Ogburn, W. *Social Change*. New York: Delta Books, 1964.

Wilson, W.J. *The Truly Disadvantaged*. Chicago: University of Chicago Press, 1987.

Chapter Six

Professionalism in Teaching

OBJECTIVES:

After studying this chapter you will be able to:

1. Define the term *profession*.
2. Outline general criteria for a profession.
3. Explain why teaching is a profession.
4. Explain why some people do not consider teaching a profession.
5. Identify the special and unique responsibilities teaching implies.
6. Differentiate between current sociological definitions and a more traditional definition of a profession.
7. Differentiate between a profession and professional performance.
8. Explain why teachers must emphasize education rather than training.
9. Recognize strengths and weaknesses of codes of ethics.
10. Discuss how the future of American education may require new thinking about the teaching profession.

I. What Constitutes the Profession of Teaching?

A. A Definition of a Profession

To truly be a profession, a job must have duties and responsibilities that are distinct from other callings and that all mature adults are expected to honor. A simple definition for the term *profession* is an occupation that properly involves a liberal education or its equivalent and mental rather than manual labor. Professions adhere to specific moral and specialized responsibilities in serving the public. Three of the most revered and time-tested vocations, sometimes called the "learned professions," are the clergy, the law, and medicine. These professions have unique and special responsibilities to the public and to their clients. Despite recent criticism about their motives, they are revered because they (1) profess these special responsibilities, (2) require years of education and practice to acquire the necessary expertise, and (3) perform a *vital* service, presumably, as evidenced by their high station in societies.

Doctors are duty bound to treat the sick and the injured. Lawyers are duty bound to prosecute cases on behalf of their clients, including individuals, corporations, and governments. In like manner, the clergy tend to the spiritual needs of the faithful and the physical needs of the less fortunate. Each profession, as a community within the larger community, is expected to serve the needs of its clients regardless of income, status, or racial origin. Teaching, too, has a rich tradition of service. Always

Table 6.1

Public Rating of Eleven Top Careers/Professions, 1984

Occupation	Value to Society	Prestige/Status
Physicians	2	1
Clergy	1	2
Bankers	7	3
Judges	6 (tied)	4 (tied)
Lawyers	6 (tied)	4 (tied)
Public School Principals	4	5
Public School Teachers	3	6
Funeral Directors	5	7
Local Politicians	8	8
Advertising Practitioners	10	9
Realtors	9	10

Source: S. Elam, "The Gallup/Phi Delta Kappa Poll," © 1989 Phi Delta Kappan, Inc.

implicitly and sometimes explicitly, the teaching profession insists on a moral pledge from teachers to prepare children for participation in the democratic process of citizenship. Schools are the starting point for students to develop the habit of learning and other adult responsibilities. Of specific note is the teacher's obligation to aid students in understanding the concepts of mutual interdependence, equal opportunity, tolerance, and respect for human dignity. It is in the classroom and in the schools where children exercise their understanding of these concepts.

Teaching is as important, historic, and responsible to its public as the three "learned professions." As table 6.1 demonstrates, teaching is highly regarded by the American public. Preparing children to be constructive members of the community is an essential service. Even so, the table also reveals that teaching does not receive an equally high rating in terms of prestige. In fact, those in teaching face widespread repudiation and criticism from the public about their lack of professionalism. Does teaching lack something the other professions have? Are teachers still professionals, or have they become mere bureaucrats doing others' bidding? Teachers are not widely accepted as professionals. Rather, they are labeled semiprofessionals, bureaucratic functionaries, trainers, or technicians.[1] Part of this inconsistency starts with the varied definitions and criteria people use for a profession.

B. Criteria for a Profession

The following characteristics of a profession are useful for deciding whether or not teaching is a profession. When the learned professions first evolved, there were no students of (rather than in) the professions. A person's education in these professions was either self-taught or an apprenticeship with those who were in the profession. Hence, there were no tidy categories of being debated showing how the practitioners of these occupations constituted a class of servants wholly different from perhaps, and superior to, all other job holders. Nevertheless, professionals from the earliest times in Greece, Israel, China, and Africa were all regarded as special and, in important ways, different from everyone else. Thus, the most traditional notion of professionalism, free from all the scholarly accouterments, reads something like this:

> A professional is *most centrally* one who has undertaken, with a select group of others, a special set of moral obligations in service to the community. Less centrally, the professional is duty bound to acquire a specified set of skills and knowledge.

The American Association of College Teachers of Education (AACTE) lists twelve criteria for a profession that warrant review. In its opinion, a profession:

1. Provides an essential service to society
2. Is concerned with an essential part of life
3. Possesses a body of knowledge needed for practice in the skill
4. Decides about clients based on the most valid knowledge available
5. Is founded on basic knowledge from which it develops its own knowledge and skills
6. Is organized into associations and is given broad autonomy to license, limit membership, and police its own
7. Agrees to performance standards
8. Goes through protracted and monitored preparation
9. Elicits a high level of public trust for performance

10. Has a strong service motivation and lifetime commitment to competence
11. Gives its members authority to practice
12. Has relative freedom from direct supervision and takes responsibility for its actions[2]

Some of these characteristics do obviously apply to teachers. Others do not. This can be said for almost all professions; hence, no profession meets *all* the criteria mentioned. At first glance, it may seem that there is a glaring omission, namely, the lack of specialized moral responsibilities. In fact, this concern is reflected in a limited way in the AACTE's item 7. Couching the moral element in such sterile language may cause moral responsibilities to be easily overlooked. Let's hope that is not the case.

Sociological Descriptions of a Profession

According to sociological descriptions, a profession can be generally described as a social classification and categorization based on occupational duties, social status, and perceived importance to the society it serves. Sociologist Joseph Newman profiles a profession as having three characteristics: (1) performance of a unique service; (2) a defined body of knowledge; and (3) autonomy.[3] With only these three criteria we could wrongly classify plumbers, crop dusters, computer programmers, or mechanics as professionals. This sociological definition is lacking in many of the ACCTE criteria, but also in one key criterion—the special moral responsibility and concern for the individual and society that professionals must have. Wholly lacking in most sociological definitions of a profession is the need for an ethical bent, a moral commitment, a shared moral consensus and obligation, and an altruistic sense for "the other."[4] Table 6.2 outlines most of the similarities and differences between sociological, the AACTE, and traditional definitions of a profession.

Abraham Flexner as early as 1915 described a profession as an "intellectual activity based on a particular knowledge base rather than a routine"; it was "practical rather than academic or theoretical, internally organized and motivated by the betterment of society."[5] Flexner's definition is a bit more traditional (based on high goals and principles of conduct and ethical behavior) than current sociological definitions (based on some occupational or class systemization). Flexner's early work showed a need for a set of ethical standards based on service to the *client* rather than to just the society or organization.[6] So, a professional must pay tribute to *client*, *society*, and *profession*.

While many jobs have some of the listed characteristics and criteria for a profession under one or more of the foregoing taxonomies, some of the notions of a profession are more central and specialized. In other words, *not all are of equal weight.* A biologist, through his or her own research, may know about the workings of a human heart much better than even a physician, for example, but the physician has a *special* obligation to treat a person keeling over and clutching his chest at a cocktail party. Through the Hippocratic oath, a doctor pledges to heal and serve whenever possible. Although the biologist may know even more than the doctor about what just occurred, he or she has no *special* duty to assist the heart-stricken person. In a similar vein, teachers also have a special set of duties to educate students fairly and efficiently—all the while role-modeling the highest moral interest and courage in the classroom. Although the teacher's special duties are different from those of a doctor or a lawyer, they are no less unique and no less important. Critics such as John Goodlad and Roger Soder have lambasted educators for being unprofessional, but their charges are based on the difference between what teachers prescribe as professional

Table 6.2

A Comparison and Contrast of Sociological, AACTE, and Traditional Definitions of a Profession

Sociological Definitions	Traditional Definitions	AACTE Definitions
1. Provides a unique service	1. Is a vital service	1. Provides essential service to society
2. Based on occupational requirements	2. Relies on a code of ethics/conduct	2. Assumes a code of conduct
3. Social status of occupation categorized	3. Status based on occupational duties	3. Status based on occupational duties
4. Tends to neglect higher moral commitment	4. Includes higher moral commitment	4. Strong service motivation and lifetime commitment
5. Autonomous rule required	5. Autonomous rule required	5. Autonomous rule required
6. Specialized knowledge required	6. Specialized knowledge requires long years of study and practice	6. Requires specialized knowledge and protracted preparation and education
7. Requires some type of licensing	7. Requires credentials	7. Requires licensing and degrees
8. Training-oriented	8. Special responsibilities and intents are known and sworn to	8. Requires membership in professional organization

(i.e., duty, service, moral responsibility, autonomy) and what society prescribes as professional (i.e., limited membership, high status, absolute control of profession). The difference in the two perspectives does complicate the discussion of teacher professionalism, but it does not distract from the fact that teaching is a profession.[7]

Sociological definitions, although they lack higher goals and morality, do not diminish the inclusion of teachers as professionals. Teachers have a time-honored role they and they alone have held along with preaching, doctoring, and lawyering. Teaching is not just a job. It is a way of life that exists exclusively to bring about the betterment of society and individuals. Sociologists would have us believe that any specialized and credentialed service is a profession. Teachers and other time-honored professionals know that this is not enough. Professionals have a special obligation to want to do the right thing for humanity.

C. Profession Versus Professional Performance

There is a difference between defining a profession and evaluating the performance of those within the profession. Many doctors, lawyers, and teachers call themselves "professionals," but they fail the litmus test when meeting their professional responsibilities. They are *in a profession*, but they do not *act professionally*. When a lawyer divulges a protected trust, that lawyer acts unprofessionally. The existence of unprofessional lawyers is a tragedy, but it does not suggest that the ideal of the profession no longer exists or no longer defines the purpose of the profession.

This is similarly true in teaching. If a teacher is evaluated only by what appears in a departmental curriculum outline and a set of lesson plans, the professional nature of teaching is in jeopardy. It is inappropriate to suggest to a teacher that there is no room for students to further analyze, synthesize, or modify what might be detailed on coursewide standardized tests. Teachers are professionals and as such should be allowed to exercise some control over what is learned and how it is learned. Teachers, and not department heads or curricular theorists, are charged with presenting what David Purpel calls "models, theories, and schemata that give order and meaning to otherwise random observation."[8] The teacher's goal, then, is to help his or her students understand the world in which they live and the world in which they will grow. Few outsiders know the subject matter better than a truly professional teacher, and nobody knows that particular set of students better than the teacher. Indeed, we could argue that professional responsibility requires that teachers question anything antithetical to serious educational pursuit, including narrow and trivial instructional goals. Recent discussions about national teaching standards by such organizations as the National Board of Professional Teaching Standards and the Holmes Group are examples of how teachers, although represented in these groups, lose effective control of the criteria for their own profession.[9]

Secondary Meanings of the Term *Professional*

Plumbers, actors, rock stars, and athletes often call themselves professionals, but nobody considers any of these in the same category as doctors, lawyers, or teachers. They are not professional by either moral commitment or acquired expertise. This notion of "professionalism" is a *secondary* meaning, indicating merely that they are not amateurs. They are paid for their performance. References to this definition of a professional in discussions of professionalism only impair sincere efforts of delineating professional duties and responsibilities. This confusion should be avoided when describing the teaching (or any other) profession.

Businesses, bureaucracies, and service organizations often distinguish "executive-types" from "workers," using decision charts, titles, rankings, and type of work expected as indicative of professionalism. General job descriptions and hierarchical designs may be convenient for classification and categorization of people for sociological and organizational purposes, but they also have the twofold effect of (1) diluting, oversimplifying, or missing altogether the special charges professionals are obliged to obey, and (2) equating decision-making power with professionalism. Neither power, status, nor other forms of social ranking have any necessary connection with professionalism. Maybe this is one reason there is so much confusion in public education today about professionalism.

Administrators are distinguished from teachers on flowcharts, in the exercise of power, and in salary, but that does not make them more professional than teachers. It does not even mean they are professionals. As noted in the case of business people, power, money, and status do not identify the school administrator as a professional. If a school administrator has a claim to professionalism, it is as *an educator*. In terms of professional status, the administrator is no different than the classroom teacher.

We may argue that there are many more professions besides the four already mentioned (such as architecture and engineering), but these pale in comparison with the learned professions in terms of responsibility and special obligations. These "newer" professions, as A. M. Carr-Sanders categorizes them, or "semiprofessions" as Amitai Etzioni delineates them, have taken great strides to warrant professional status, but they will not be given the same regard as the learned professions. As important as engineers and architects are, they do not have *special and unique* obligations to the public and to their clients that drive them forward beyond all other interests. They do not take the same moral stance to enlighten, protect, fairly judge, and serve others as do the learned professions.[10] Society holds them accountable for following protocols ensuring public safety, but little else.

D. Teaching: The Profession

From the earliest descriptions of the profession, teachers were required to be someone whom students could emulate. Teachers were expected to role-model an array of admirable traits. Furthermore, anyone presuming to assume the mantle of mentorship was thereby duty bound to serve as role model. In the search for truth, fair judgment, and knowledge, teachers were expected to be the exemplars of their society. The "good life" evolved only in those intellectually able and psychologically prepared for serious study. These characteristics were virtues to be acquired not solely through teaching, but rather through proper associations. Virtue, as Socrates explained it, is a by-product of the student-teacher relationship, and not a direct consequence of the act of teaching.

The expected behavior of teachers has not changed much in two-and-a-half millennia. Teaching remains a highly moralistic enterprise designed to impart knowledge and promote the search for truth throughout life. A teacher's search for truth extends from mundane and practical types of understanding—such as "A teacher should not smile until Christmas" (an oft-quoted tenet of classroom discipline taught to prospective teachers)—to the most complicated—such as the search for the smallest particle in nature. Achieving self-actualization within and through a system of mutual interdependence is an end-product of this search for truth. Teachers historically have led the way in the search for truth, every bit as much as they have talked about truths the establishment regards as uncontroversial. Surely, teachers can never show the way in practical, theoretical, and moral reasoning if they are not active and exemplary participants in these activities themselves. Teachers are not so much the guardians of knowledge as they are the agents of knowledge attainment and appreciation. These capacities were and are central to a teacher's role in a society.

Precedents of Teaching in American History

Early American history might have something to do with the current suspicion that teaching is not professional. In colonial times, educators were found almost anywhere. They were sometimes plucked from the ranks of the clergy. Some European immigrants with a bachelor's degree sold themselves into teaching in order to get passage to America as indentured servants. Many teachers were even recruited from the ranks of the same grammar schools from which they came. Despite the oft-publicized Massachusetts Bay Colony model that mandated universal primary education, many colonies had no such requirement or inclination to educate their youth. Universal schooling was not formalized and widespread until the late nineteenth century. There was little demand for qualified teachers with formal preparation directed exclusively toward teaching. As a consequence, there was no professional organization; no effort to articulate an ethical code; nor was there any specialized training until the nineteenth century.

In 1823 the Reverend Samuel Hall started a normal school in Vermont, and Horace Mann started one in Massachusetts in 1839. Normal schools were for the specific purpose of preparing teachers. These early attempts to improve teaching practice and preparation are notable, but teaching was, in economic parlance, a "buyer's market." Before schooling became mandatory, teaching was largely considered an informal, temporary calling until a person found a well-paying job or reached another social stratum.

This type of historical beginning in the teaching profession speaks volumes to even the most untrained professional ear. While the learned professions had comparatively early professional organization and development (for obvious reasons of public safety and protection from unscrupulous practitioners), the teaching profession had no such urgency to be controlled and organized (even though two thousand years earlier Plato had warned of the need for such in the *Protagoras*). Schooling in America was considered a mere civilizing influence in a life dedicated to mostly manual or repetitive labor.

The Horatio Alger Myth in Educational History

The Horatio Alger myth (a person can be a success without an education) is yet another nineteenth-century remnant of America's educational chronicles. Alger, an author of considerable popularity in the 1880s, was famous for his poignant stories of street waifs named "Ragged Dick" and "Mark, the Match Boy" who through hard work became noble creatures.[11] These mythical children became folk heroes because they shunned formal schooling in favor of hard work. Schooling, in Alger's portrayal, was bogged down in triviality. In a country wide open for exploration and development, education was viewed as unnecessary. The Horatio Alger myth implied that all a person needed in America was a strong back and a will to succeed. Those few teachers who did exist were often depicted as inhumane harpies (such as Ichabod Crane) forcing their wills on poor, unprotected children. Contemporaries often thought that a teacher's job was not to teach practical knowledge of marketable skills, but rather to teach knowledge useless to all but the most urbane dilettante. This characterization, although unfair, still infects the minds of the American public. Such depictions agitate against the public's vision of teaching as a profession.

It is up to teachers to change this image by taking a proactive role in the development, assessment, and enactment of educational goals. The perceived role of teacher as trainer, mere disciplinarian, or expert conditioner must be replaced with roles requiring students to think, assess, tolerate, and value. The Horatio Alger portrayal is only one of the many myths about the role and importance of teachers that has to be turned around by professional action and dedication.

Despite criticism and chiding for *not* being or acting professional, those in—and those aspiring to be in—the profession of teaching can view with pride the accomplishments, dedication, and service teachers have given to humanity over the years. Many of the greatest minds have come from the ranks of teachers. What other profession can point to such notables as Comenius, Plato, Socrates, Aristotle, Aquinas, Robert Hutchins, Confucius, Hegel, Pestalozzi, G. W. Carver, Montessori, Bethune, and Wittgenstein, just to name a few? These people were great scholars and thinkers, but they were also *teachers*. Their contributions to the betterment of humanity are no less notable than, say, the contributions of the discoverers of the polio vaccine, the designers of the modern computer, or the drafters of the American Constitution. Thus, in short order, even the most casual perusal of educational history leads us to conclude that teaching not only is a profession, but also is quite possibly the single profession of such honored champions. Ambivalence such as the public is experiencing toward the profession will never alter the fact that in its heritage, teaching need not be inferior to any calling. *Teaching is in every sense of the word a profession.* The current diminished status of teachers exists, not because teaching is no longer a profession, but rather because governmental structures and regulations place teachers in compromising relationships with both the community and their respective disciplines.

Despite continued intrusions by government and unwarranted criticism by self-appointed critics, teachers continue their work with aplomb. Teachers continue their work with a devotion to duty matching that of the three learned professions. It is up to teachers to both professionally *perform* and further *specify* the goals of the teaching profession so that future generations of teachers and the public will better understand this calling and benefit.

In *A Nation Prepared*, the Carnegie Taskforce on the Teaching Profession recommended that teachers press for a national certification procedure. This recommendation resulted in the formation of the National Board of Professional Teaching Standards. Those within and outside the profession see board certification as a way of ensuring national recognition of professional status for teachers.[12] The board certification test, like any paper-and-pencil test, has its limits when evaluating competency. It may, however, be one way to judge content knowledge and knowledge of learning and instructional theory for future teachers. Not all states are willing to cede their credentialing power to a national board, and, indeed, there has been strong opposition to it from many quarters. As a profession, teachers must get involved intimately in this discussion. Historically, such certification would be a milestone for teaching. Teaching professionals would be compelled to enter the discussion of the profession's competencies, or face the consequences of an outside agency's dictating policy and competencies to them.

Teaching Is Not a Semiprofession

Sociologists such as Carr-Sanders suggest that teaching is a "semiprofession" because it has no "theoretical principles" of its own and relies on "technical skill rather than professional practice."[13] It may be true that teachers "borrow" knowledge from other fields—such as psychology, philosophy, and all the various subject disciplines—but they also have their own theoretical principles in curricular design, development, and evaluation. Teachers are not technicians doling out verbatim what they have been given. They, instead, weigh, judge, analyze, and evaluate curricula, students, and their own teaching practices. They engender their own curricula, teaching strategies, and instructional tools, based on sound and unique theoretical principles. If critics like Carr-Sanders would take the time to notice, for example, they would see that law is heavily influenced by social science research (for example, *Brown v. Board of Education of Topeka*); medicine borrows from biology, chemistry, and pharmacology; and the clergy rely on philosophy and psychology. Professional knowledge, although distinct, is also founded in a myriad of disciplines.

As for "professional practice" in teaching, supervised internships, practice teaching, improvement workshops, and tenure/promotion guidelines are all procedures for ensuring the expert use of professional skill. Indeed, merit pay systems founded on yearly evaluations are effective ways to test some professional skills. For Carr-Sanders to argue that there are no special skills or knowledge to gain before teaching is to assume that a person only needs common sense to teach. All of us have degrees of communication skill, but we do not all have the expertise to teach. Prolonged practice and a commitment to find and present the truth remain prerequisites to the teaching profession.

Teachers, like all professionals, must take a moral posture—a desire to do the right thing despite its popularity or whether it meets social criticism well. As Kevin Ryan has put it, "Nothing can be more dangerous than having our children taught by moral eunuchs."[14] The profession of teaching is not a semiprofession because it goes beyond the basic moral conventions of society and assumes the special trust society gives it. Historically, no profession has taken up this cloak of responsibility any better.

Teaching and Limited Membership, Power, and Control

There is little doubt teachers have less control of their own profession than, say, doctors and lawyers. It might seem at first glance that teachers suffer a diminished professional role compared with these professions because they do not limit membership or control admission criteria as selectively. That may be the case, but the moral appeal of the teaching profession may draw far greater numbers than the moral appeal of law and medicine. Lawyers help the guilty as much as the innocent. Doctors sometimes cause pain and death while trying to cure people. In contrast, good *teaching* makes everyone better as a result—both directly and indirectly. Some lucky few may never need a doctor or a lawyer, but everyone needs teachers. By sheer numbers alone, teachers provide society a more constant and visible service.

Despite its importance, the teaching profession gets only infrequent positive deference from political leaders and other establishment-types. In stark contrast, the American Medical Association and the American Bar Association have tremendous political power. It is deceptive, however, to place blame on uncaring politicos and unscrupulous agencies as if only "big money" talks. True, teachers are paid much less than other professionals, but their numbers do count. The political difference lies in the fact that organizations like the AMA and ABA require members to pay heavy dues for membership and that such organizations also exercise tight control of their constituents. Teachers pay no such exorbitant fee for political support; nor do their professional societies have such absolute control. Teachers do wield political power, and for good or for bad they are able to discern the profession's direction free from an organization's strict control. More often than not, the political power of doctors and lawyers is short-lived and issue-driven.

Moral Accounting

Rather than focusing on professional responsibility, most of the discussion about teaching among teacher educators and student teachers seems to center around topics like the limits of a student's attention span, the optimal time for review of key ideas, or the best way to handle inappropriate behavior. Although much time is spent on topics like these, a sense of moral accounting is always expected of teachers. The moral obligation, special commitments, and social responsibility remain permanent regardless of the curricula, content, measurable outcomes expected, or other technical aspects of information exchange. The real question should not be whether teachers walk through a prescribed routine, but whether they have a common sense of moral

Table 6.3

Representative "Goods" Required of Teaching

a. Learning
b. Respect for personhood
c. Appreciation for a transcultural community and sensitivity
d. Commitment to expand intellectual horizons in themselves and in their students
e. The search for truth
f. Equality of opportunity, fairness, justice, and freedom of expression
g. Honesty and respect for another's property
h. Mutual interdependence and a global perspective

purpose. With this knowledge teachers must make some of the most difficult but necessary decisions about education. Some decisions will not be popular; others will even be in direct conflict with what may be in vogue. But nobody promises teachers an easy time when it comes to teaching. These kinds of decisions and responsibilities are what makes teaching a profession and not just a job.

Although teachers face tremendous pressures from all sides of society (and sometimes fail in their efforts), they must take the position of a moralist and always do things out of moral principle and not convenience. Table 6.3 lists some of the "goods" of teaching—acceptable to any teacher. These goods are exemplary of the kinds of moral goods teachers should require of their children. These goods are not all-inclusive, but they do represent the moral accounting teachers must make in their classrooms. They are *special duties* teachers accept as professionals. While others may decry these virtues, they are a way of life for teachers.

E. Codes of Ethics—Strengths and Weaknesses

Although codes of ethics are not the only way to understand a profession, they do perform an important role in suggesting the contours of professional behavior and goals in general. Most "codes" for teachers are similar in nature.

They require teachers to be responsive to students, colleagues, employers, community, and discipline. In one way or another they declare that teachers should honor learning as an unequivocal good in and of itself.

Although far from being codes, teaching contracts serve as the standard safeguard against inappropriate teaching practice today. Because teachers are not required to live by a formally articulated professional code, a rudimentary code of conduct is often part of the contract. As a minimum, these contracts describe what constitutes "improper" or "immoral" behavior of teachers, but they leave it up to school boards or district officials and ultimately the courts to decide if such behaviors occur.

Early teaching contracts were quite limiting for teachers. It was not uncommon for women to swear that they would not get married during the school year; that they would not be seen in the company of unmarried men; that they would wear at least two petticoats under their dresses; that their dresses would not be above the ankle in length; that they would clean, sweep, and dust the schoolroom every day; and that they would get at least eight hours of sleep a night.[15] These restrictions, taken from a

1915 South Carolina school board contract, were obviously for female teachers. Men had much fewer restrictions. Humorous as this contract sounds now, its purpose was to ensure against early resignation, dereliction of duty, or improper manner. It is unnecessary and in some cases illegal to require such strictures of teachers today.

There are marked differences between a contract and a code of ethics. Contracts specify behaviors and limits of authority, whereas codes identify areas of moral responsibility. Codes are a type of social contract between a person and his or her colleagues as well as a promissory note to society. Codes outline rules of conduct and responsibility. They are also a credo—an affirmation of the individual's sense of responsibility to clients, the profession, and the public alike.

Professional organizations like the National Education Association (NEA) the American Federation of Teachers (AFT), and Phi Delta Kappa (PDK, a professional fraternity in education) all have codes of ethics, bills of rights, or human rights creeds that denote and outline behavior expected of their members. Table 6.4 contains the preamble of the NEA Code of Ethics.

The NEA Code of Ethics, simply paraphrased, expects each teacher to believe in the dignity and worth of every human being, pursue truth, provide equal educational opportunity, and "nurture democratic principles."[16] Additionally, Principle I of the NEA code requires teachers to: (1) commit to "the stimulation of inquiry," (2) allow free expression of students, (3) promote free exchange of ideas, (4) provide equal access, (5) show no favoritism, (6) not use their position for private gain, and (7) "protect from conditions harmful to the student."[17] Principle II of the code requires truth in declarations about qualifications and expertise and advances the profession by encouraging all members to enforce the rules for teaching preparation and teaching practice.[18]

Table 6.4

Preamble, NEA Code of Ethics

The educator, believing in the worth and dignity of each human being, recognizes the supreme importance of the pursuit of truth, devotion to excellence, and the nurture of democratic principles. Essential to these goals is the protection of freedom to learn and to teach and the guarantee of equal educational opportunity for all. The educator accepts the responsibility to adhere to the highest ethical standards.

The educator recognizes the magnitude of the responsibility inherent in the teaching process. The desire for the respect and confidence of one's colleagues, of students, of parents, and of the members of the community provides the incentive to attain and maintain the highest possible degree of ethical conduct. The Code of Ethics of the Education Profession indicates the aspirations of all educators and provides standards by which to judge conduct.

The remedies specified by the NEA and/or its affiliates for the violation of any provisions of this Code shall be exclusive and no such provision shall be enforceable in any form other than one specifically designated by the NEA or its affiliates.

The AFT Bill of Rights (not shown) outlines the entitlements teachers should have as professionals. A summary of these rights includes the right to have an opinion, to have freedom of religion, to teach without political interference, to be paid adequately for services, to have materials adequate for teaching, and to have a trial by peers when accused of misconduct.[19] While it is not specifically stated, teachers must also ensure these rights for their colleagues. Although not strictly a code of ethics, the intent of the AFT Bill of Rights has ethical implications.

The Phi Delta Kappa Human Rights Creed in Education, table 6.5, is more specific about the duty of teachers to endorse and advance the rights the republican form of democracy affords. Although this is not an all-encompassing list of rights, it is a good indication of what a professional organization in education expects of its members. As with the AFT Bill of Rights, there is an expectation that teachers be afforded the same rights as their students and fellow citizens. An additional duty requires that teachers act to engage the respect of the community at large for these same rights.

A bill of rights or a code of ethics might be a precondition for a profession, but it is insufficient for ensuring that all members act in a professional manner. No code in the world can guarantee absolute compliance to its spirit or detail all the behaviors it implicitly addresses. What a code or bill of rights does, however, is provide guidance for those wanting to do the right thing in the exercise of their professional expertise. Table 6.6 provides some strengths and weaknesses of codes of conduct/ethics that may be useful for further discussion.

Codes of conduct are no better than their adherents and the intent of the group. Merely having a code of conduct is not the answer to ethical teaching practice.

Table 6.5

Phi Delta Kappa Human Rights Creed in Education

As an educator in a democratic society, concerned with the human rights of people everywhere, I will exemplify in my behavior a commitment to these rights. Knowing that educators and the educative process must make a significant contribution toward ensuring these rights for all people, I will translate my belief in basic human rights into daily practice. I believe in the right of every person and in his concomitant responsibility:

1. To equal opportunity in education, housing, employment, the exercise of franchise, and representation in government
2. Of due process and equal protection under the law
3. Of freedom of speech and of the press
4. To dissent
5. To freedom of or from religion
6. To privacy
7. To be different
8. Of freedom from self-incrimination
9. To trial by jury of actual peers
10. To security of person and property
11. To petition and redress of grievances
12. To freedom of assembly

Table 6.6

Strengths and Weaknesses of a Code of Ethics/Conduct

Strengths	Weaknesses
1. Summarizes "norms" of behavior for members	1. Can be taken too literally
2. Provides guidance as to parameters of responsibility	2. Does not guarantee ethical behavior of members
3. Is useful for initial discussion and resolution of problems	3. Can actually discriminate against people if misconstrued or misinterpreted
4. Is a statement of intent and universality of purpose	4. Is useless unless accompanied with a "spirit" of morality (wanting to do the right thing)
5. Protects and serves society	5. Can be limiting as to wider responsibility the code suggests
6. Denotes special and unique responsibilities and guidelines of the profession	6. Is meaningless unless earnestly policed by its own profession

Individuals rather than codes make a profession responsible to the public. Codes do, however, serve an important purpose in that they are a useful set of rules for conduct and service to society. They are a written declaration of *intent* and a helpful *guide* to use when confronted with decisions involving conduct. Without them, we have little idea of the special responsibilities and aims of the profession or its declared purposes.

Ironically, American education has little chance of improving unless teachers assume professional responsibility and adopt a moral stance.[20] They must resist the assignment of "semiprofessional" to what they do and reject as equally demeaning descriptions such as "trainer," "technician," and "functionary." Teachers are TEACHERS and proud of it, proud of their colleagues in history from Socrates, Christ, Buddha, and Confucius to Marva Collins and Jaime Escalante. The term *teacher* denotes professional. A teacher's credo should be found in his or her code of ethics and not just implied in a performance contract. A teacher must produce an educated person rather than a super-industrialized, economically viable end-product that does well on standardized tests. Historical models of "good" teaching advancing sameness, routine, predictability, and trainability are no longer commensurate with feasible goals of education. Although the present industrial-era model of American education (school as job finder) has placed industrial needs above human needs, educators must get beyond this model. New "goods" as outlined in table 6.3 must replace the industrial-era "goods."

Talcott Parsons in 1959 suggested that society use teachers as socializers and schools as places where children learn to accept and maintain the goals, values, and roles society expects.[21] This assimilationist concept may have worked when cultures were similar, but it does not take full advantage of the potential contributions of all Americans today. It does not promote equal opportunity, justice, stimulation of inquiry, or free exchange of ideas. Like teachers of millenniums past, today's teachers must continue to aim at higher goals. The new education must reflect a code of teaching ethics that fosters tolerance, plurality, diversity, respect for personhood, and a sense of mutual interdependence as essential to the socialization process that will improve American society.

II. The Future of Education and the Profession

A. Some Trends and Prospects

For years Americans have seen and read about the need for improved education. Reports such as *A Nation at Risk* and *A Nation Prepared*, the *America 2000* strategy, and a number of other suggestions were mentioned in chapters 4 and 5. Professional organizations like the NEA, the AFT, and PDK suggest that public education is failing to meet present and future needs. As a result, the nation itself is in peril. Alarming statistics like a high school graduation rate of 68 percent in Texas (and even lower in several other states) and 74 percent nationwide have shaken the nation's pride and economic future. The prospect of losing three thousand children from America's high schools every day is chilling, tragic, and frightening.[22] The need to improve public education is a given. But the prospect for improved results in education seems grim in light of other social problems needing attention.

Texas, California, New York, and Florida—four of the most populous at-risk states—face a citizenry with very poor prospects for employment in the new millennium. These states are by no means alone in their battle against illiteracy. Fully 45 percent of black children and 39 percent of Hispanic children in America are among those classified as poverty-stricken, and the figure for all children living in poverty has increased to 21 percent.[23] Is there no recognition that those most risking failure in schools come from minority homes? These same homes are also, by and large, poverty-stricken homes. There is a strong correlation between education level attained, status, and economic income level. The National Center for Educational Statistics places only 7 percent of high school dropouts in high income families, 11 percent in the high-middle class, 13 percent in the low-middle class, and 22 percent in the lower class.[24] Although there are higher dropout rates in the lower classes, the crisis is growing at *all* levels. Access to the establishment is thereby systematically reduced as the number of dropouts increases with each new generation.

The professional teacher stands alone as the one force most concerned with reversing this trend. David Halverstam in his book *The Next Century* suggests that America seems paralyzed in the face of what would be for most countries threatening news. Halverstam claims America has picked up many bad habits in the last quarter-century, including a general lack of concern for education.[25] He suggests America reassess its inflated view of its world role and assume a more global perspective. In his eyes, the "American century" is now over. It is time to retool for a truly educated public. As controversial as this book is, it does point to the need for very different educational goals for America.

Illiteracy in America is widespread. Almost one in five Americans cannot read, write, or perform mathematical skills well enough to be a productive, self-sufficient member of the work force.[26] The ultimate economic and social cost, should this continue, is catastrophic. In 1988 Marvin Cetron, a well-known futurist, predicted that by the year 2000 about 95 percent of American jobs will need some degree of skill in "generating, processing, retrieving, or distributing information."[27] Cetron adds that more than half of the new jobs will require a college education or its equivalent. Our knowledge base will quadruple every ten years as, understandably, communications and information transfer will be the major employer. Yet only one in five high school juniors in 1988 "could write a comprehensible note applying for a summer job," and less than one-third of high school seniors knew within fifty years when the Civil War was fought.[28] Other more alarming examples published by the National Endowment for the Humanities in 1989 point decidedly to a weak knowledge of history, geography, and literature by high school and college *graduates*. Besides the few armchair critics and journalists who have brought this plight to our attention, only teachers seem to recognize how desperate the situation really is.

In February 1990 the National Governors' Association (NGA) adopted a set of national goals for public education. Included in these twenty-first-century goals are: (1) every high school will have a graduation rate of 90 percent, (2) America's children will be "first in the world in mathematics and science achievement," (3) every adult will be literate, and (4) every school in America will be drug and violence free.[29] Laudable as these goals are, they are formidable goals for our schools. Our students continue to perform badly in tests in mathematics, science, and language skills compared with students in other industrialized nations. Teachers are working toward solutions, but they cannot work miracles in the wake of intrusive public policy and irresponsible media.

Social Trends

Is the educational system in a crisis? Is the nation at risk? Many fear the answer to both questions is yes. Even if the answer is yes, that does not solely implicate teachers in the impending tragedy. As American life models more and more closely what is on television and in the movies, the closer it moves toward chaos and away from enlightened communal effort. The United Way, for example, recently predicted that if trends continue, one in three Americans will have a drug problem during his or her lifetime.[30] Already researchers have found that 56 percent of American students who graduated from high school in 1987 began using alcohol and 29 percent began using drugs before the tenth grade.[31] Eleven percent of all thirteen-to-seventeen-year-olds in the country had been arrested in 1987.[32] Almost one in seven American children is born to a teenage mother, and more than half of those mothers never finish high school. Figure 6.1 presents social, economic, demographic, and educational trends that suggest a radically changing society. Although these social ills may seem to have little to do with literacy rates or school success, they are all part of the social setting for students and teachers. Education does not occur in a vacuum. The task of the teacher is enormous. Teachers have not caused these problems, but teachers seem to be all society has to try to counteract them.

Social Impacts on Education

James Ketelson, former CEO of Tenneco, estimates that the total lifetime earnings lost by those Americans not having a high school diploma from the class of 1984

A. Demographic Trends of Children*

Present (1987)

- 76% White
- 14% Black
- 9% Hispanic
- 1% Other
- 20% Born out of wedlock
- 66% Live with both parents
- 40% Only child
- 57% Have working mother
- 50% Will experience divorce in family by age 18
- 20% Considered poor
- 2 million *reported* maltreatment cases

Future (2000)

- 72% White
- 15% Black
- 12% Hispanic
- 1% Other
- Trend upward
- Trend downward
- Trend upward
- Trend upward
- Trend slightly upward
- Trend upward
- Trend upward

B. Economic Factors

1. Present Postindustrial Era

- 3% Of the population produces all the food for the country
- 16% Move every year
- 68% Work in services
- 15–20% Jobs require a college education
- U.S. government owes $2,600 to every American
- 1 in 4 jobs relies on foreign markets
- "Strategic Planning" is only 2-4 years long

2. Twenty-First-Century Economics Forecast

- 30% Jobs rely on foreign markets
- 23% Jobs will need a college education, but all will require preparation beyond high school
- 1.5% Jobs in agriculture
- 80% Jobs in services
- All job descriptions will change every 7 years
- Majority of new jobs in companies of less than 20 workers

3. Changing Occupations**

Declining	Growing
Chemical, Electrical Products, Railroad, Petroleum, Steno, Mining, Shoe Manufacture	Legal Assistant, Publishing, Medical assistant, Computer Repair, Programmers, Systems Analysis, Sales, Travel, Food Service, Cashiers, Residential Care, Managers, Engineering, Scientists, Nursing

C. Social Factors

- Average home has TV on 7 hours a day
- Half of America's children will live in family settings alternate to nuclear family by 2000
- Average American reads one book cover to cover in entire lifetime after formal schooling
- Most-read publication is *TV Guide*
- The speed of communication has increased 1 million times in last 100 years
- 1 in 3 Americans will have a drug problem in his/her lifetime
- Knowledge has increased 4 times in last 10 years

*Source: U.S. Bureau of the Census, *Statistical Abstract of the United States: 1988* (108th edition.) Washington, D.C., 1987.
**Source: U.S. Department of Labor, *Workforce 2000: Work and Workers for the 21st Century* (Washington D.C.: U.S. Government Printing Office, 1987).

Figure 6.1 Trends, Factors, and Events Potentially Effecting Education for 21st Century America

alone amounts to $228 billion. The added cost to the community in lost tax reve-
nues, welfare payments, and other social services is another $100 billion.[33] These are
unacceptable figures by any social standard.

Social problems have always spilled into the classrooms, whether they be mani-
fested in violence, drug abuse, dropout rates, truancy, low achievement levels, vandal-
ism, racism, or a plethora of other possible events experienced in the educational
system. Indeed, schools are often lambasted for society's problems when they are not
totally to blame. For example, low achievement, low graduation rates, and student
apathy about school are "educational" problems, but parent apathy, the drug subculture, and frustration about social mobility most certainly contribute massively to these
so-called educational problems!

Teachers need to stand tall as professionals, no matter what conditions from outside the school influence students. Through conspicuous demonstration of their own
sense of professionalism, teachers can begin to show the rest of society that the teaching PROFESSION needs the respect and support of society if it is to become an appropriate counterbalance to the trends described here.

America *is* a multicultural society. The nation cannot afford to allow one-third of
its population—the minorities that constitute the bulk of America's nonestablish-
ment-types—to continue to fail establishment-oriented education. Our racial, cultural,
and ethnic interdependence requires us to act in responsible ways when it comes to
equal opportunity and access to educational facilities. The profession requires educators to advance the potential of America by advancing the abilities of all Americans.

B. A Need for Restructure in Education

At present, the educational system continues to discriminate against minority cultures. Fully half of America's Hispanics and 40 percent of its blacks continue to have
trouble in school, as dropout rates demonstrate. To be truly professional, individual
teachers must act to ensure unbiased and multicultural participation in local classrooms. Course objectives must become flexible enough to allow for plurality and diversity of thinking while still requiring attention to rigor in problem solving as the
discipline demands. If America wants full citizen participation and tolerance, interdependence and communal cooperation, it must allow teachers to practice these intellectual and moral virtues.

Site-Based Management

Site-based management, decentralized planning, and other instructional models oriented toward personalized education are coming into vogue. These structural changes
are being tested in several states, and early results seem to suggest that the more decentralized plans and objectives are, the better they are for the students.[34] The theory
behind site-based management is to assign decision making to the lowest level possible, but still have common educational objectives for the district and state.[35] The
learning environment, too, is more local or individualized requiring less supervisory
paperwork and thus giving teachers more time with the students. The localization of
educational practice also allows more flexibility in teaching and curricular design.
Administrators are able to spend money where it most serves the special needs of
each student and the community. Parents find that they, too, have more opportunity
for communication with school officials and, in some cases, for selection of schools.

In this ideal world, teachers would have more opportunity to practice the professional responsibility they are duty bound to uphold.[36]

Decentralization and individualization, however, are not panaceas to America's educational problems. Decentralization is an administrative tactic that allows for the exercise of more teacher prerogative than is now being allowed. Individualization can be as discriminatory and biased as any other curricular design. The real work, as usual, remains with the professionally inspired career teacher. Schooling and schooling strategies are quite different from teaching and teaching strategies. At best, the former allows for the latter. Schooling should *not* be equated with education. Education is a preparation for lifelong learning. It is not the sum of all learning a person will get in life. As simple as this may sound, and indeed as often as we have heard it, institution-alized American education does not yet seem to understand this distinction. Rather, institutional education has been all too eager to settle for credentialing students with degrees and credits and making sure they pass standardized tests. The professional teacher wants much, much more for students.

Thinking Ahead

Professional teachers, by their very nature, are concerned with desirabilities in the face of all possible adversity. They want to help people decide what *should* be, not just what is. In short, the professional teacher's approach is inherently value-laden. It forces the professional to ask the question, What ought to happen? A lesson teachers can learn from futurists is to be concerned about trends, possibilities, and desirabilities to help society envision a more desirable future. Studying the effects of curriculums, management plans, computer-assisted instruction, busing, and a myriad of other social trends and possibilities must be as much the job of teachers as writing lesson plans. As professionals, they must maintain both a moral stance and the stance of a moralist as they direct students toward their own and society's future benefit. By training and by default teachers alone are the experts in preparing students for life in the future.

Pyrrhic Victories in Education

King Pyrrhus in the third century B.C. won a great Greek victory against the Romans, but he did so at a terrible cost to his army. He has been quoted as saying, "Another such victory would undo us." We in education are facing much the same dilemma. Budget cuts, accountability legislation, and outright interference from the courts and agencies both within and outside of traditional educational lines have wreaked havoc on the profession. Any teacher resistance to mandated change in education is con-strued as "stonewalling" and being (of all things!) "unprofessional." Past Secretary of Education William Bennett was even guilty of this attitude at times. He proposed that accountability in teaching (in the form of standardized test scores) is the answer to most educational problems He identified the symptoms easily enough, but he erred when trying to diagnose the disease. He stated, "There are greater, more certain and more immediate penalties in this country for serving up a single rotten hamburger than for furnishing a thousand school children with a rotten education."[37] What Ben-nett said is true enough, but he was wrong in his suggestion that teachers have been responsible for serving children an inferior education.

Such sensationalism confuses the issues and the groups trying to inspire and im-prove the profession. Bennett's suggestion that accountability of teachers, rewards for good principals and teachers, improved student performance on standard exams, and par-ental choice of public or private school (with tax breaks) will end most of America's educational woes just does not recognize all the other forces influencing education.[38] He would have better served education if he had joined hands with teaching professionals and attacked the media, parental apathy, and unwieldy government agencies.

Having no power, little say-so, and limited resources, teacher-educators continue to be blamed for failed plans of improvement they had no part in originating. While extolling the importance of the teacher, the states shackle classroom teachers with curricula that are politically expedient. Teachers are asked to socialize students; educate for AIDS; mainstream; integrate; prepare students for a job; propagandize against alcohol, drug use, sexual promiscuity, smoking, and a dozen other societal "don'ts"; enforce dress codes; reduce teen pregnancy; and ready students for citizenship. There has been no sign of prioritizing these "additional" goals for teachers, nor of making them educational goals rather than mere programs of behavioral control. Like King Pyrrhus, educators are left with only a few weapons to deal with a myriad of social problems.

The Promise of Wisdom

Lynne Cheney, a champion of humanities in the classroom, concludes, "In our schools today we run the danger of unwittingly proscribing our heritage."[39] The number of high-risk, disadvantaged kids is growing, fewer children speak English as a first language, high dropout rates of more than 30 percent continue, and curriculum content continues to swing from one extreme (content) to another (process). American children continue to trail other Western nations by every academic measure.[40]Teachers, and not just William Bennett, could have told the public that pouring money into education will not guarantee success. But just as Napoleon saw opportunity in the chaos of battle, it is still the responsibility of educators—the true experts—to move toward desirable ends for education. The alternative is a society we did not plan, anticipate, or desire.

The challenge to educate American youth is an awesome responsibility. Handing it to teachers and saying "Do it!" is unfair and counterproductive. They, of course, must do their part, but the advent of truly lifelong learning is yet to be realized. Teacher-educators can do their part in widening the scope and definition of education beyond mere accumulation of data, but in the next twenty years different skills and criteria will be needed by the "classroom" teacher. The future of American society *does* rest with teachers. They must unify the educational effort in ways that improve the human condition. As teachers they must not just be good teachers. Rather, they must also be good thinkers. Wisdom is promised by professional educators, but it only comes when teachers assume the responsibility the profession demands.

As America moves into the new century, the era portends both promise *and* catastrophe. Table 6.7 summarizes the transition schools must undergo in the next several decades.[41] Whether these suggestions are exactly right or timely is not that important. What is important is to preserve the spirit of hope and to nurture new ideas to meet new challenges. One thing all critics of education seem to be saying is that present educational models are failing. It impinges on professional educators, therefore, to change failure into success by getting into the discussion about where education should be going.

Table 6.7

The Changing Character of American Public Education

Present	Future
1. Industrial-era paradigm	1. Information-era paradigm
2. Monocultural	2. Transcultural
3. Answer-centered	3. Problem-centered
4. Competitive structure	4. Cooperative structure
5. Extrinsic motivation	5. Intrinsic motivation
6. Age-specific	6. Cross-generational
7. Nine-month operation	7. Year-round operation
8. Lockstep sequence of coursework	8. Developmental sequencing and based on interests
9. Past and present-oriented curriculum	9. Future-oriented curriculum
10. Local and national in scope	10. Global in scope
11. Time-specified and location-bound	11. Time and location free
12. Uses teaching machines	12. Uses human/machine partnerships
13. Preselected content and goals	13. Participant-controlled curriculum

In summary, professional educators have a challenging career in front of them. Their charge is an awesome responsibility. Many of the suggested directions for education will require a teaching force capable of not only transmitting what is known, but also helping others recognize the need for cooperation, mutual respect, and interdependence. Practice in resolution of problems, the search for intersubjective agreement, and proactive (rather than reactive) decision making becomes the foundation for the new professional curriculum in education.

In Retrospect

Throughout this book three themes have become increasingly more evident. First is the idea of respect for personhood. If there exist moral rules universally compelling to the species, surely this must be one. People are reluctant to treat one of their own abusively. Moral theorists from Immanuel Kant to John Rawls—and more recently Thomas Nagel, Derek Parfit, Amartya Sen, and Charles Taylor—all recognize the importance on a grand scale of avoiding victimizing anyone. Tribal societies were offended by the arbitrary abuse of their own members, and more recently the notion of "one of our own" continues to extend over outward on a much broader scale. If moral theorists can convince humanity of the need, respect for personhood will one day include all of humankind.

A second theme of this book is mutual interdependence. As mutual respect and interdependence extend ever outward from loved ones, to neighbors, to fellow citizens, then to other participants in a vaguely defined, shared macroculture, and ultimately to the species at large, so, too, does the voice of conscience and cultural tolerance. As the family of humankind expands, the close quarters confining the species become more evident.

Competition among groups remains as active as ever, but isolationism is no longer an option. People must address one another as individuals and as groups, and only tolerance for acquired differences can make this a satisfying prospect.[42] Respect for personhood, for others of one's own kind, becomes at this level respect and tolerance for the contributions of other cultures. No longer can other cultures be feared or avoided or studied as some sort of humanoid-like object of curiosity. Spaceship earth is forcing all groups to interact far more frequently than at anytime past. The risk of catastrophe is great if these interactions occur in ways that are ruthless or otherwise too aggressive. More and more cultures are finding that the frequency of interactions forces more tolerant attitudes upon all.

The best interactions occur among those cultures that have become truly interdependent, one on the other. Nowhere is this more visible than in the evolving European Economic Community (EEC). Proximity of interests has forced longtime foes and economic rivals to become interdependent. As the interdependency among the cooperating nations increases, so will the sense of interdependency. As interdependency increases, so will respect of one interdependent nation for another. Ultimately, cooperation among interdependent nations will be valued far more than competition. Indeed, it is the EEC's internal interdependency that will make it a competitively successful organization against the rest of the economic world. As Robert Axelrod's studies with individuals show, in the game of winners versus losers that the world plays economically, cooperation benefits all players far more than cut-throat competition. As the value of interdependency becomes more broadly appreciated by all in the world, better survival of the species will be secured.

The third theme is that teachers can advance the cause of interdependency by creating a transcultural environment in their classrooms. Transculturalism insists not on the obliteration of cultural boundaries, nor on the persistence of cultural separation—it insists on tolerance for all cultures—and more. Transculturalism, as defined here, insists on respect for all cultures to the extent that each culture can be a resource from which individuals can borrow to make their own lives and their own communities better. This cross-cultural *interchange*, rather than domination, is the keystone to true human improvement. The quest to make human life better in ever-more expansive efforts is the natural extension of respect for personhood advocated by so many moral theorists today. It remains the principal moral imperative of the teaching profession.

In many ways the historian may well be tempted to conclude that today's moral theorists have finally begun to catch up with the key element in the teaching profession's most motivating moral commitment—to respect the personhood of all students as ends rather than means and to encourage others to do so too. In this it can be seen that moral philosophy; social, legal, and political theory; and multiculturalism all cross paths ultimately in the *practice* of teaching. Given the underlying philosophy of these seemingly disparate areas, we can almost feel now the truth of John Dewey's dictum, "Philosophy is a theory of education in its most general phases." Professional teachers give philosophy life, and life enlightenment. They provide the forum for the continued deliberation necessary for human improvement. They must never shirk this, the most central of all their professional duties.

QUESTIONS FOR DISCUSSION

1. What constitutes a profession? What are some of the criteria professions use?
2. Why is teaching not considered a profession by some people? What criteria do they use?
3. Is teaching a profession? Explain.
4. What are the unique and special responsibilities educators have to their clients and to the public?
5. Explain the difference between training and education. Why does the profession of teaching advocate education rather than training as the goal of public schools?
6. What are strengths and weaknesses of codes of ethics? List and explain five ethical principles educators must defend.
7. How might schools in the future be organized? What kind of instruction and knowledge will they promote? Why?
8. What is the Horatio Alger myth? How does it affect social views of teaching?
9. How are employment contracts for teachers different from codes of ethics? Are there similarities?
10. How might education in the future be different from the present? Explain the possible role of teachers in that change.

NOTES

1. See Donald Myers, *Teacher Power—Professionalization and Collective Bargaining* (Lexington, Mass.: Lexington Books, 1973).
2. R. Howsom, et al., *Educating a Profession* (Washington, D.C.: American Association of College Teachers of Education, 1976), 6–7.
3. Joseph Newman, *America's Teachers* (New York: Longman, 1990), 91.
4. Abraham Flexner, "Is Social Work a Profession?" *Proceedings of the National Conference on Charities and Correction* (Chicago: Hildmann Printing, 1915), 26–28.
5. Ibid.
6. See Joel Spring, *American Education: An Introduction to Social and Political Aspects* (New York: Longman, 1989), 47.
7. John Goodlad and Roger Soder, et al., *The Moral Dimension of Teaching* (San Francisco: Jossey-Bass, 1990), 53–56.
8. David Purpel, *The Moral & Spiritual Crisis in Education* (Granby, Mass.: Bergin & Garvey, 1989), p. 60.
9. See *Toward High and Rigorous Standards for the Teaching Profession* (Detroit: National Board of Professional Teaching Standards, 1991).
10. A. M. Carr-Sanders, "Metropolitan Conditions and Traditional Professional Relationships," in *The Metropolis in Modern Life*, ed. R. Fisher (New York: Doubleday & Co., 1955), 278–86. See also Amitai Etzioni, ed., *The*

Semi-Professions & Their Organization: Teachers, Nurses, Social Workers (New York: Free Press, 1969), v–ix.

11. See Horatio Alger, Jr., *Struggling Upward and Other Works* (New York: Bonanza Books, 1923). See also Alger, *Ragged Dick and Mark, the Match Boy* (New York: Collier, 1962).

12. Carnegie Taskforce on the Teaching Profession, *A Nation Prepared: Teachers for the 21st Century* (New York: Carnegie Forum on Education and the Economy, 1986), 3–31. See also L. Weis et al., eds., *Crisis in Teaching: Perspectives on Current Reforms* (Albany, N.Y.: SUNY Press, 1989). See also Martin Haberman, "Licensing Teachers: Lessons from Other Professions," *Phi Delta Kappan* (June 1986): 719–22.

13. Carr-Sanders, "Metropolitan Conditions," 279–83.

14. Kevin Ryan, "Teacher Education and Moral Education," *Journal of Teacher Education* 35 (September 1988): 20.

15. Examples of such contracts are of public record in states like South Carolina, North Carolina, Texas, and Illinois and in most of the West. As late as 1940 many southern states still required similar contracts from teachers.

16. NEA Code of Ethics (Washington, D.C.: National Education Association, 1986), 1.

17. Ibid., 2.

18. Ibid., 3.

19. These are a summary of rights from the AFT Bill of Rights and are not intended to be a literal description of all the rights of teachers.

20. Paul A. Wagner, "The Idea of a Moral Person," *Journal of Thought* 22 (Fall 1980): 24–33.

21. Talcott Parsons, "The Social Class as a Social System: Some of its Functions in American Society," *Harvard Educational Review* 29 (Fall 1959): 297–309.

22. Esther Ferguson, "We Lost 3000 Kids Today," *Parade Magazine*, April 12, 1987, 8.

23. Texas State Board of Education, "Quality, Equity, Accountability: TSBE Long-Range Plan for Public Education," Austin, November 1990, 10.

24. National Center for Educational Statistics, "Percentage of High School Drop-Outs and SES," *Annual Report* (Washington, D.C.: NCES, 1985).

25. David Halverstam, *The Next Century: A Crow's Nest Critique of the United States* (New York: William Morrow, 1991), 86–121.

26. Ibid., 15.

27. Marvin Cetron, "Class of 2000," *The Futurist* 22 (November/December 1988): 9.

28. Ibid.

29. National Governors' Association, "National Goals for Education," (Washington, D.C.: U.S. Government Printing Office, 1990).

30. United Way Strategic Institute, "Emerging Trends," 1988.

31. Texas State Board of Education, "Quality, Equity, Accountability," 11.

32. Ibid.

33. James L. Ketelson, "A University for the 21st Century," *Houston Post*, August 5, 1990, C1.

34. States like Kentucky, Tennessee, Florida, and Texas are trying out pilot programs in site-based management. About twenty-two states have the idea on their agendas for the next ten years.

35. Edward Pauly, *The Classroom Crucible* (New York: Basic Books, 1991). Pauly argues that teachers must be allowed to set their own policies. An advocate of site-based management, Pauly sees this approach as a necessary step in recognizing teachers' professional authority in public.

36. Chester E. Finn, *We Must Take Charge* (New York: Free Press, 1991). Finn argues for the need to divest authority with education. With this increased *recognition* of the teacher's professionalism, there will be legitimate demands by the public that student performance increase.

37. William Bennett, speech to the National Press Club, Washington, D.C., September 8, 1987.

38. Ibid.

39. Lynne Cheney, "In American Memory: A Report on the Humanities in the Nation's Public Schools" (Washington, D.C.: Office of Publications, National Endowment for the Humanities, 1987), 4.

40. Several studies by the National Endowment for the Humanities, the Educational Testing Service, and others have shown that American education lags behind most First-World countries in science and math.

41. See J. Bowman, F. Kierstead, C. Dede, and J. Pulliam, *The Far Side of the Future* (Washington, D.C.: Education Section, World Future Society, 1978), 78–84. See also the writings of Draper Kauffmann, Robert Theobald, James Botkin, Marvin Cetron, Harold Shane, and John McHale.

42. R. N. Bellah, et al., *The Good Society* (New York: Alfred A. Knopf, 1991). This is evidently the product of our collective search for moral conscience in the 1990s—or is the author's claim.

For Further Reading

Teacher Rights/Student Rights

Bennett, K. P., and M. LaCompte. *How Schools Work*. New York: Longman, 1990.

Bullough, R. V. *First-Year Teacher: A Case Study*. New York: Teachers College Press, 1989.

Corwin, R. *A Sociology of Education: Emerging Pattern of Class, Status and Power*. New York: Appleton-Century-Crofts, 1965.

Donley, M. D., Jr. *Power to the Teacher*. Bloomington, Ind.: Indiana University Press, 1976.

Fisher, L., and D. Schimmell. *The Civil Rights of Teachers*. New York: Harper & Row, 1973.

The Teaching Profession

Holmes Group Report, *Tomorrow's Teachers*. East Lansing, Mich.: Holmes Group, 1986.

Howey, R. K., and N. Zimpher. *Profiles of Preservice Teacher Education*. Albany, N.Y.: SUNY Press, 1989.

Howsom, R. et al. *Educating a Profession*. Washington, D.C.: American Association of College Teachers of Education, 1976.

Lieberman, M. ed. *Building a Professional Culture in Schools*. New York: Teachers College Press, 1988.

_____. *Education as a Profession*. New York: Prentice-Hall, 1956.

Macroff, G. *The Empowerment of Teachers*. New York: Teachers College Press, 1988.

Myers, D. *Teacher Power—Professionalization and Collective Bargaining*. Lexington, Mass: Lexington Books, 1973.

Pulliam, J. *History of Education in America*. Columbus, Ohio: Merrill Co., 1991.

Purpel, D. *The Moral & Spiritual Crisis in Education*. Granby, Mass.: Bergin & Garvey, 1989.

Visions of Reform: Implications for the Teaching Profession. Washington, D.C.: Association of Teacher Education, 1986.

Educational Futures

Bowman, J., and J. Pulliam. *Educational Futures: In Pursuance of Survival*. Norman, Okla.: University of Oklahoma Press, 1973.

Gabor, D. *Inventing the Future*. New York: Alfred A. Knopf, 1964.

Kauffman, D. *Teaching the Future*. Palm Springs, Calif.: ETC Publishers, 1976.

Kierstead, F. et al., eds. *Educational Futures: Sourcebook I*. Washington, D.C.: World Future Society, 1979.

Shane, H. *The Educational Significance of the Future*. Bloomington, Ind.: Phi Delta Kappa, 1973.

CHAPTER SEVEN

Theory into Practice

OBJECTIVES:

After studying this chapter you will be able to:

1. Recognize cultural traits of groups within and outside American society.
2. Delineate your own cultural preferences and biases.
3. Develop an in-depth analysis of cultures, showing high-culture contributions and low-culture contributions to the world.
4. Practice ethical decision making as a teacher faced with everyday educational dilemmas.

Throughout this book concerns for practical teaching strategies have been integrated with concerns central to teaching professionalism in a multicultural society. Both have been kept within the limits of what can be expected in the career practice of individual teachers. Pursuant to this general goal the first chapter began by showing that it is unreasonable to argue that morals are relative extensions of culture. In addition, chapter 1 noted empirical evidence (from the work of psychologist Lawrence Kohlberg and economist Richard Dawkins, to sociobiologists Philip Kitcher and Robert Trivers) showing that there seems to be a deep structure to moral experience.[1]

Indeed, universal understanding of the term *moral person* is alluded to in the writings of philosophers as widely diverse (in time and culture) as Aristotle, Alasdair MacIntyre, and Charles Taylor (to name but a very few). Each argues that central to every human's quest to achieve something of the "good life" is an attempt to find universal "goods." Of course, the *interpretation* of this deep structure occurs in the context of specific cultures, subcultures, and families. Thus, while a deep structure may be operative, its realization in a given situation will reflect the interpretation of all these communal influences.

Since professional teachers freely encumber themselves with special professional duties, it is evident that they are also committed to living life as moral persons. To understand what that means, the teacher must understand what it means to possess a moral stance as well as the stance of a moralist. As you will recall, moral persons *care* about doing good and remember well that humans are fallible in their moral thinking. Moral persons do not merely follow impulse when thinking about moral matters.

They arrive at rules to live by until good reason shows that such rules, as they stand, are unwarranted. Such rules always produce some benefit, while victimizing no one.

You learned in chapters 2 and 3 that as agents of society, teachers are expected to explain, demonstrate, and otherwise show students what the duties of citizenship are under the implied social contract. Public school students do not need to know all the teacher has learned about Aristotle, Thomas Hobbes, John Rawls, or any other social theorist, but they do need to get the idea that both individuals and societies thrive when three conditions are met. First, there must be a pervasive attitude of respect for each and every individual in the community. Second, there must be a similarly pervasive attitude of respect for the various cultures, subcultures, socio-economic classes, and gender differences that influence collective development. Third, contrary to Hobbes's suspicions or the separatist leanings of some pluralists, communities do not succeed when cooperation is motivated solely by fear of what might happen if cooperation breaks down.

Discussion in chapters 4 and 5 reminded us it is through learning to *depend* on one another that we develop trust and respect for others' willingness to work with us in communal fashion.[2] Mutual interdependence is the social condition ensuring that whatever cultural, gender, or economic features may distinguish us from one another, a cooperative sense of shared purpose will bring us together into one macrocommunity. The United States has not always been successful in fulfilling this condition. In fact, the Civil War, the civil rights movement, and the women's movement are but three conspicuous examples of how America has wrestled with this issue. And, much to the detriment of the teaching profession, teachers have not only been unsuccessful in leading us to a better world, but also all too often they have accepted the political expediency or status quo, thereby abrogating their professional responsibilities to student and community alike.[3]

America is more a polyglomerate culture than ever before in its history. Any teacher who does not recognize the need for a new and very special approach to multicultural education is either naive or merely unprofessional. This need cannot be left for legislators to negotiate. It is a professional matter demanding attention by teachers. Too much has already been politicized in American education. For example, the New York State Department of Education recently proposed a new multicultural curriculum for all public school students.[4] Former Harvard Dean of Education Diane Ravitch, President Lynne Cheney of the National Endowment for the Humanities, and others express concern that in its heavy-handed way New York may have gone too far, substituting a hostile, separatist education, void of the achievements of Western culture, for one that is more evenly balanced.[5] Whether separatism will occur remains to be seen. Without a doubt, however, it is the classroom teacher who will implement any mandated program, and hence it is the classroom teacher's commitment that will secure success. With this in mind, legislators and other outside critics must stop trying to tie the hands of professional teachers or engaging in efforts to deprive teachers of their responsibility.

The consensual assent of teachers is critical to the success of any educational program. Not only should policymakers seek to secure teacher support, but also they should allow teachers to assume their proper role as creators of curriculum and designers of appropriate methodology. Through teacher preparation courses such as the one for which this book is designed, teachers are again gaining a collective sense of empowerment and purpose. Teachers who study at length their own professional ethics recognize that they serve students whose community horizons are multicultural and that these horizons should evolve into a transcultural perspective. American students can no longer be assimilated into a tidy set of mores prescriptive of one distinct culture, nor can a nation this size afford the luxury of curricular programs that produce jealousy, hostility, or any other form of uncooperative separation. American students must know something about all the cultures and groups that influence their own and other nations. American students must become increasingly transcultural in their perspectives, and the way this will happen is through teachers who themselves have developed a transcultural perspective.

In what follows, you are presented with several exercises that will begin to prepare you for the field of teaching *as a genuine professional*. The first two exercises direct your attention to the sorts of things you need to know in order to see the world through a transcultural perspective. A series of case studies will then present you with examples of the everyday moral problems likely to strike any teacher charged with managing a diverse and often divisive student body. Hostile or uncooperative parents, unsympathetic supervisors, discipline-specific demands for maintaining high standards, and collegial relationships with other professionals are only a few of the issues teachers face, but they represent the moral dilemmas professionals must address. A final exercise will guide you in professional goal setting.

I. Cultural Studies Survey

Professors of anthropology and sociology spend their lives studying one small aspect of a given culture. So what follows is not an attempt to make you an expert in the cultures studied. Rather, the intent is that through the following Multicultural Investigative Survey (MIS) assignment you will become at least somewhat conversant with the high culture and ordinary cultural conventions of a given ethnic group. The assignment asks you do to some research and subsequently to make some personal judgments about the heroes, achievements, and preoccupations of a given ethnic group. Use the format for the MIS shown in figure 7.1.

Now it may be that you are a member of one of the ethnic groups you are asked to study. As a consequence you may find that your judgment on certain matters varies considerably from the judgment of individuals outside your microculture. Thus, to help you and your classmates appreciate how varied your ideas are from one another, you are asked to answer each question, first, as you would expect an American belonging to the ethnic group to answer (whether or not you are a native of that group) and, then, as you would expect a person originating from that culture (living outside America) to answer the same question. It is expected that you and your colleagues will begin to learn a great deal about various cultures and that you will want to learn more. With your curiosity thus piqued, you should find yourselves drawn into compelling discussions with one another as you try to sort out reasons why your collective responses exhibit whatever variety you find. As these discussions move toward conclusion each day, you will find yourself building an appropriate transcultural knowledge base.

Part I. (Culture Listed Here)

	A How a member of the microculture would answer.	**B** What a member from the culture of origin would answer.
Favorite Athlete	_____	_____
Artist (Performing)	_____	_____
Artist (Fine)	_____	_____
Artist (Literary)	_____	_____
Celebrity	_____	_____
Entrepreneur	_____	_____
Humanist	_____	_____
Mathematician	_____	_____
Military Leader	_____	_____
Moral Leader	_____	_____
Philosopher	_____	_____
Political Leader	_____	_____
Religious Leader	_____	_____
Scientist (Biomedical)	_____	_____
Scientist (Chemistry)	_____	_____
Scientist (Physicist)	_____	_____
Scientist (Social)	_____	_____

Figure 7.1 Wagner-Kierstead Multicultural Investigative Survey Sample Form

	A	B
	How a member of the microculture would answer.	What a member from the culture of origin would answer.
Favorite Pastime	_____	_____
Favorite Type of Music	_____	_____
Favorite Type of Culinary Item	_____	_____
Favorite Opera or Musical Production	_____	_____
Favorite Art Form	_____	_____
Favorite Theater Production	_____	_____
Favorite Sporting Event	_____	_____
Greatest Vice	_____	_____
Major Economic Resource	_____	_____
Major Religion	_____	_____
Most Important University	_____	_____
Most Common Occupation	_____	_____

Part II. (Culture Listed Here)

1. Describe the standard of living of the group: _____
   _____
   _____

2. Describe social/family structures: _____
   _____
   _____

3. Describe political/economic orientation: _____
   _____
   _____

4. Describe how religion affects everyday life of the people: _____
   _____
   _____

5. Describe the orientation of the people to education: _____
   _____

6. Describe any special characteristics of the culture: _____
   _____

Figure 7.1—*Continued*

7. Describe culture-specific gender differences: _____
_____
_____

8. Describe the prospects for this group to act cooperatively with others: _____
_____
_____

Figure 7.1—*Continued*

The cultures you are asked to address are by necessity limited in number. Thus, one last MIS exercise is left for you to do on a culture of your choice that is not included in the collection of worksheets. Since this set of assignments is quite challenging, you should attempt to fill out no more than two worksheets in any given week. A worksheet will be filled out for each of the following cultures, and others your instructor may assign: A. Arab-American, B. Central American, C. African-American, D. Eastern European-American, E. Western European-American, F. Indian-American, G. Chinese-American, H. Other Asian-American, I. South American/Other Hispanic-American, J. Native American, K. Mexican-American, L. Jewish-American, M. Other.

As a way of helping you along in the exercise, imagine you are describing I. (South American). Under favorite athlete, you may think that people of South American ancestry now residing in the United States would name Roberto Clemente. You believe that he was the first truly great baseball player to come from Latin America and that this would be a primary concern of Americans from South America filling in column A. Under column B you list Pele, the soccer player. Pele is famous in America, but you think his fame is far greater for those living in South America.

As you garner your information about these cultures and share your knowledge with your classmates, you should discover the great diversity each culture has. For instance, to pick just one African political leader is difficult. Nelson Mandela may be a favorite of many African-Americans, but white Americans may find that the Reverend Jesse Jackson comes more quickly to mind. It will become obvious that the more you know of cultures, the harder it is to generalize about them. For example, to say that all African-Americans are generally the same is a naive assumption.

The second point of this exercise is to help you realize the difference between high culture (what is universally acclaimed and contributory to humankind by a culture, i.e., music, art, knowledge, etc.) and low culture (preferred differences that make no significant contribution to humanity in general). Chapter 2 described high culture and low culture in more detail. The intent of the survey is to help you learn more about the high culture of other groups. Whether a person eats spaghetti or egg noodles, wears a serape or a sweater, may be more tied to geography than to any contribution to humanity. As interesting as these low-culture differences are, they are not what is most important about that particular culture. The survey goes beyond the mere mention of diet, clothing, and favorite activities into the more significant realms of recognized belief systems, people from the culture who contributed to humanity in general, and the culture's sense of what is important in life. With that knowledge, you as a teacher can assist students in the search for an ever-evolving, transcultural perspective of mutual respect, mutual interdependence, tolerance, and moral responsibility.

II. Cultural Perception Survey

At this point, you should know far more about the various cultures than you did a few weeks ago. You no doubt found yourself digging through almanacs and reference books of various sorts and soliciting opinions from others. In short, your *intellectual preparation* for adopting a transcultural perspective has now been solidly established. You will find this next exercise far less taxing in terms of the research required, but you may find that in a different way it is equally anxiety producing. In this assignment you are asked to complete the Cultural Value Survey (CVS) as shown in figure 7.2. You will read a statement and then indicate to what degree people in the ethnic group described are in agreement or disagreement with the proposition. Subsequently, you will again consider the same proposition and then answer it as you think a member outside of that ethnic group would answer it.

If taken in earnest, this assignment might make you feel anxious and maybe even a little perplexed at times. That is always a possibility when we risk taking a stand on an attitude we believe a certain group has. There are no right or wrong answers to any of these statements. You are not being asked how YOU feel, only *how you think the American culture at large feels* and *how the group in question feels*. The groups you survey should be the same groups you used for the MIS. Your instructor may also want to use others.

When you have completed this assignment, your instructor may want class members to compare their responses. Then you and your classmates can begin discussing why people seem to have certain attitudinal perspectives of various ethnic groups. When you have completed this second assignment, you will find your transcultural perspective genuinely exhibits more breadth and a more modest depth about cultures than it had before. You will know something about the various cultures, and you will have an idea of some of the perceptions people hold toward various groups within our evolving mutually interdependent society.

You might find you are surprised (or even shocked?) by how you or others respond to the CVS. The importance of this survey is its attempt to show that all of us have some preconceived notions about various subcultures and the biases we suspect others harbor toward them. To have no opinion is but another way of showing our particular bent toward others. The survey is not designed to polarize people, but rather, to bring to the surface impressions we all have about other various subcultures within the American community. If you choose not to reveal your own perceptions about others, this is perfectly acceptable. However, should you decide to refrain from participating, you will miss out on a rare opportunity to share with others your own "hidden curriculum." This exercise is not meant to embarrass you, but to help you learn about your own perceptions. The trust you will need and will develop during this sharing opportunity will instill in you a feeling of community for your peers in this class and, ultimately, for the larger educational community. One of the special things about teachers is their willingness to share ideas in a courageous and professional manner.

1.   The (ethnic subculture here) community believes its members are:

Compassionate

/_____/_____/_____/_____/
Strongly   Disagree   No Different   Agree   Strongly
Disagree   from Other   Agree
                                   Groups

Intelligent

/_____/_____/_____/_____/
Strongly   Disagree   No Different   Agree   Strongly
Disagree   from Other   Agree
                                   Groups

Athletic

/_____/_____/_____/_____/
Strongly   Disagree   No Different   Agree   Strongly
Disagree   from Other   Agree
                                   Groups

Politically powerful

/_____/_____/_____/_____/
Strongly   Disagree   No Different   Agree   Strongly
Disagree   from Other   Agree
                                   Groups

Strongly entrenched in the establishment

/_____/_____/_____/_____/
Strongly   Disagree   No Different   Agree   Strongly
Disagree   from Other   Agree
                                   Groups

Strongly committed to education

/_____/_____/_____/_____/
Strongly   Disagree   No Different   Agree   Strongly
Disagree   from Other   Agree
                                   Groups

Biased toward other ethnic groups

/_____/_____/_____/_____/
Strongly   Disagree   No Different   Agree   Strongly
Disagree   from Other   Agree
                                   Groups

Strong contributors in solving the world's problems

/_____/_____/_____/_____/
Strongly   Disagree   No Different   Agree   Strongly
Disagree   from Other   Agree
                                   Groups

Virtuous

/_____/_____/_____/_____/
Strongly   Disagree   No Different   Agree   Strongly
Disagree   from Other   Agree
                                   Groups

Figure 7.2 **Wagner-Kierstead Cultural Value Survey Form**

2. The rest of the American culture believes the (ethnic subculture here) is:

Compassionate

/_____/_____/_____/_____/
Strongly   Disagree   No Different   Agree   Strongly
Disagree   from Other   Agree
                                  Groups

Intelligent

/_____/_____/_____/_____/
Strongly   Disagree   No Different   Agree   Strongly
Disagree   from Other   Agree
                                  Groups

Athletic

/_____/_____/_____/_____/
Strongly   Disagree   No Different   Agree   Strongly
Disagree   from Other   Agree
                                  Groups

Politically powerful

/_____/_____/_____/_____/
Strongly   Disagree   No Different   Agree   Strongly
Disagree   from Other   Agree
                                  Groups

Strongly entrenched in the establishment

/_____/_____/_____/_____/
Strongly   Disagree   No Different   Agree   Strongly
Disagree   from Other   Agree
                                  Groups

Strongly committed to education

/_____/_____/_____/_____/
Strongly   Disagree   No Different   Agree   Strongly
Disagree   from Other   Agree
                                  Groups

Biased toward other ethnic groups

/_____/_____/_____/_____/
Strongly   Disagree   No Different   Agree   Strongly
Disagree   from Other   Agree
                                  Groups

A strong contributor in solving the world's problems

/_____/_____/_____/_____/
Strongly   Disagree   No Different   Agree   Strongly
Disagree   from Other   Agree
                                  Groups

Virtuous

/_____/_____/_____/_____/
Strongly   Disagree   No Different   Agree   Strongly
Disagree   from Other   Agree
                                  Groups

Figure 7.2—Continued

III. Acting Professional: Case Studies

As noted earlier, being professional requires much more than just knowing things. It requires more than just holding certain attitudes. For most of the past two-and-a-half millennia social theorists would have said it requires "virtue." Many fear "virtue talk" may be antiquated in today's world of fast pace, immediacy, and behavioral response. Philosophers such as Charles Taylor, Alystare McIntyre, and Robert Nozick remind their readers that the quest for virtue is never "antiquated"—that kind of search is always in vogue. Nevertheless, in today's world in discussing what it takes to *be* professional, the language best suited to addressing such questions is generally couched in a language of action. The aspiring professional wants to know, What should I *do*, or refrain from *doing*, in order to *act* professionally?

Just as no code of professional ethics can answer all ethical questions, neither can one textbook (no matter how large or cleverly written!) You have read about the moral world generally and the fact that teachers have special duties by dint of their profession. You know that among these duties are the acquisition of a transcultural perspective, respect for person and culture, commitment to the ideal of mutual interdependence, and a dedication to advancing the intellectual horizons of every student. In line with all this, you have participated in some exercises aimed at developing a more transcultural perspective. Now, turn your attention to cases similar to ones you most likely will face in your first year or two of teaching, and routinely thereafter.

No one can anticipate all the cases you will confront, nor can you be *absolutely sure* the advice you receive in any given case will be RIGHT! Consequently, the best that can be done is to present you with a few typical cases, remind you to refer to the elements of ethical analysis provided in chapter 2, and invite you to begin thinking.

Use the ivory-tower seclusion your class provides to take some risks and to work out your solutions publically, noting all possible consequences. People often deride the "impractical" and "idealistic" atmosphere of the university classroom, but it has some real advantages. The decisions you make here will harm no one. You can falter, be indecisive, lapse into confusion, and even exercise poor judgment. Your errors, however, will be errors of spirit and intellect with no immediate consequence to the real world. Make your deliberations and errors here and now in the protected environment of the ivory tower. In a few short months, when presented with equally difficult cases, your decisions will have immediate effect on your own life and the lives of others. At that point there will be little opportunity to rethink your decisions, systematically run down a checklist, consult your colleagues about various courses of action, and, most importantly, rely on words of wisdom from your professor at critical points of public reflection.

Subsequent to the first two cases you will find court decisions addressing precisely the facts of each case respectively. This is not to mislead you into thinking that the courts are always right, for surely they are not. Rather, the point is to show you how close your own thinking comes to at least one well-informed group in society, namely, jurists. Furthermore, as the elements of ethical analysis note, where law is available it ought to be considered since it does reflect the judgment of those who hold the sovereignty of state. In the additional cases, you will be solely on your own. After each case a short set of questions suggests some subtle considerations you should have addressed but nothing more will be offered by way of THE ANSWER.

Case #1   A Student Search and Seizure

While on hall duty, Mrs. Jones, a high school gym teacher, finds two girls smoking in the lavatory. Such behavior violates school rules and is certainly wrong for two fifteen-year-old sophomores. Juanita admits to smoking and is ready for her punishment. Mary says that she did not smoke at all and that it is all Juanita's fault. Mrs. Jones demands to see the inside of both girls' purses. When Mary opens her purse, a pack of cigarettes is right on top, in plain sight. At the same time, Mrs. Jones also sees cigarette wrapping papers, a glass pipe, and a butane lighter. Suspecting that there may be more than cigarettes in the purse, Mrs. Jones takes both girls to the assistant principal, Mrs. Moore.

Mrs. Moore asks both girls if they smoked in the lavatory. Juanita admits her crime. Mary denies it. Mrs. Jones tells Mrs. Moore that she saw a glass pipe, cigarette papers, and a lighter in Mary's purse. Mrs. Moore opens Mary's purse and finds marijuana, a large amount of money, and a notebook with names of "buyers" and "contacts" listed. She telephones Mary's parents and the police. Mrs. Moore then takes Mrs. Jones aside and tells her that she should say she saw the marijuana when the purse was first opened. Mrs. Jones feels uneasy about lying to the police and to Mary's parents, even though Mrs. Moore says it is her *duty* to get such students out of the school and protect the others.

What would you do if you were Mrs. Jones? Are Mary's rights being violated? Is it right to lie if it will help convict a guilty person? Is it reasonable search and seizure to look further into Mary's purse for drugs when drug paraphernalia are evident? What responsibility does Mrs. Jones have to the school and community? Take time to think over answers.

These facts are taken from an actual Supreme Court case. In *New Jersey v. T.L.O.* (1985), the Court ruled that the student (T.L.O.) was given Fourth Amendment rights because reasonable search and seizure was accomplished. School officials are "sovereign authorities" and assume many duties in loco parentis. But students are still entitled to privacy and security against *arbitrary* invasions by "government" officials. The state argued that students have no need to bring personal items to school; hence, it is proper to search and seize anything owned by students that may disrupt or endanger the school. The Supreme Court ruled that students *did* have the right to bring personal effects like diaries, letters, grooming items, clothes, and equipment to school; hence, their right to privacy must be preserved as much as possible.

The Court recognized that the school has a special need to protect students and keep order. Therefore, flexibility in the rules is allowed when the situation warrants. School officials have the right to search and seize without a search warrant. But there must be "reasonable cause" for the search. The Court concluded that reasonableness of a search occurs when (1) the action is justified at its inception (there are reasonable grounds for the search at the time), and (2) the circumstances warrant the search (i.e., a possible danger to others exists). In an attempt to give school authorities maneuvering room to provide safety and order, but also to protect student rights as much as possible, the Supreme Court acted to ensure a balance between student right of privacy and needed order in a school setting.

What about Mrs. Jones lying? If no legal precedent is involved, are there any conditions that would excuse her behavior?[6] Mrs. Jones did have the right to reasonably search for cigarettes and in the search is entitled to seize other illegal and dangerous items as the situation warrants. If, however, the girls were just walking down the hallway, or were in a smoke-filled lavatory, that would not be sufficient reason to search their property. School officials no longer have the right to act wholly in loco parentis.

Tinker v. Des Moines (1969) made this clear earlier. On moral grounds, does not respect for students' evolving personhood place teachers under a moral obligation to respect some student privacy? What are the limits to this obligation?

Case #2:   Grooming Gripes

Johnny Madison comes his first day of school with *very* long hair. As a matter of fact, his hair is such that it is the talk of the school. Johnny is a member of your first-grade class. Many of the children are snickering and pointing at him and making him the brunt of a number of vicious verbal attacks about his looks. Johnny, a Native American, is defensive about his hair. Part of his cultural heritage is for males to wear their hair long. His mother has put his hair in a ponytail, but the other children pull it and ostracize him from the group. You fear there may be fighting soon.

There is a school regulation against long hair for boys. Do you tell Johnny to get his hair cut? Do you let the situation linger until it dies down or someone gets hurt? Are you, as a teacher, obliged to insist on compliance with school rules? What are the moral limits on your duty to respect Johnny's cultural heritage? Think about your response to this case before reading further.

Again, this case has some legal precedents, but they are not consistent. Many states have held that schools do not have the right to regulate students' hairstyles (Oklahoma, Oregon, and Alaska are three). (*District #8 Seiling v. Swanson* (1973), *Neuhaus v. Federico* (1973), and *Beeze v. Smith* (1972) are all such cases. In contrast, Texas and Mississippi courts have upheld the use of haircut regulations for males. *Mercer v. North Forest School District* [1976] and *Trent v. Perritt* [1975] are such cases).

The Supreme Court has not addressed the issue per se, but the U.S. Court of Appeals did rule in *Davenport v. Randolph Co. School Board of Education* (1984) that grooming regulations are valid for schools, as long as they are not racist or do not discriminate against certain groups. In the story of Johnny Madison, the rule does seem discriminatory against a particular group, Native Americans. What *should* the court rule if this case came to court? Remember the nature of legal thinking. In the cases cited here, a jurist would refer to the one with the most recent date. On constitutional matters, federal courts have priority over state courts.

As a teacher, you have several responsibilities. Must you take measures to help children understand different cultural and religious beliefs? Discrimination against races or ethnic groups cannot be tolerated. Individual rights and tolerance for personhood are key elements to be taught and role-modeled by teachers. Name-calling, ostracism, abuse, exclusion, or any other prejudicial behavior by students against another person(s) should not be tolerated.

What if Johnny were not a Native American? What if he were a federal court judge's son who, rebellious against his mother, decides he likes long hair? Would enforcement of school policy still be discriminatory? What would you *do* as the boy's teacher?

Everyday Cases of Teaching

The best way to learn about professionalism is to practice it. Here are some additional practice cases for your deliberation. These cases may or may not have relevant legal precedents. Several are everyday occurrences—others are not. Each, however, is well within the range of moral decisions teachers face. Subsequent to your decisions, discuss your reasoning with your colleagues. While moral commitment is an individual attitude, professional ethics is, in part, a matter of *acting* in concert with other professionals. Learning to address the moral issues of teaching requires that you develop great subtlety of mind. With the elements of ethical analysis deep in your memory, you should reflect about the most sublime features of the case at hand, all to ensure that what you do is right and defensible within your professional community.

Case #3:   Popularity or Impropriety?

Mr. Wilson is a sixth-year English high school teacher. His friend Mr. Hernandez teaches history. Mr. Hernandez has quite an eye for the ladies, it seems. All the women teachers at the school seem to enjoy his company. Occasionally, on the way home from work, Mr. Wilson and Mr. Hernandez stop for coffee at a popular restaurant. Mr. Hernandez flirts with all the waitresses. They seem to like him and are flattered by his attention.

Lately, Mr. Wilson has been hearing rumors that Mr. Hernandez has been dating some of his students. Mr. Wilson, fearful for his friend, asks Mr. Hernandez about it. Mr. Hernandez jokes about it as if the whole idea were ridiculous, but he doesn't deny the allegation outright!

One day, Beverly Delgado, one of Mr. Wilson's best students, and the principal's daughter, asks to speak to him in private. Beverly tells Mr. Wilson she has been having an affair with a teacher. At first, it was just meaningless fun for both of them, but now Beverly fears being hurt because of her strong feelings. Beverly won't reveal who the teacher is, but says he isn't one of her instructors this term. At that moment, Mr. Hernandez walks by and seems to make a point of saying hello to Beverly. After he passes, Beverly looks at Mr. Wilson and tears well up in her eyes. She runs down the hallway and into the lavatory.

Mr. Hernandez is the only Hispanic teacher at the school. In fact, there are few minority teachers in the school district at all. Mr. Hernandez is quite a handsome fellow and at twenty-five is the talk of all the high school coeds. What should Mr. Wilson do? Does he owe any special duties to Mr. Hernandez as his friend or as his colleague? Does Mr. Wilson owe it to the profession to weed out unprofessional teachers? Should Mr. Wilson undertake to act in Beverly's behalf in this matter? Should Mr. Wilson confide in Beverly's father, the principal? Should other teachers or the school counselor know? Is it possible Mr. Hernandez could be the victim of prejudicial treatment? If so, is it because he's handsome? A minority? Do teachers have to protect students from worldly and imprudent teachers? Is Beverly just infatuated with Mr. Hernandez, thinking that something exists when it doesn't? What does Mr. Wilson actually know about the situation? Should he investigate further? If you were Mr. Wilson, what would you do?

Case #4:   Grading Differences

Mary Markham has been a teacher at Foley High School for sixteen years. At the end of last year, she was appointed chair of the mathematics department. There are eight teachers in the department. For years the teachers have shared teaching the introductory algebra course. In this way all teachers get a chance to teach an introductory course, maintaining their math and pedagogical skills in several areas. The idea is to keep renewed vigor in the course and enhance faculty interaction. But the course has become a bit of a problem for Mrs. Markham.

The five sections of introductory algebra have very different student success rates. Mr. Johnson's class has a high number of As and Bs with few Cs, Ds, and Fs. He argues that students should be evaluated on progress, and not just on what they know. If a student tries hard in Mr. Johnson's class, he or she gets extra credit.

Ms. Adams's two classes have a fairly even distribution of grades. In fact, Ms. Adams prides herself on a bell-curve distribution. In her words, Ms. Adams believes "most students are average." After nine years of teaching all kinds of math, she is certain that a bell curve is warranted. "After all," she states, "that's what society wants. People want to know who's better than someone else."

Mr. Joseph, a teacher for twelve years, has taken another tack. In his grading, he doesn't care whether everybody gets an A or everybody gets an F. He has outlined strict measurable standards and grades accordingly. When 60 percent of his class got Ds and Fs the first grading period, parents and students protested that he was too strict. In response, Mr. Joseph said, "Numbers don't lie. The student's didn't meet the standards the state mandates."

Mrs. Mathes, knowing that math is a subject many students either love or hate, decides to evaluate students in a variety of ways. She has objective tests every Friday on content knowledge. She also grades homework on neatness, clarity, completion of problems, and timeliness. During the week, Mrs. Mathes has individual on-the-board pop quizzes, asking students to rise and solve problems on the board. She even has students write a take-home essay on algebra in everyday life as part of their grade. Mrs. Markham is getting complaints from parents because Mrs. Mathes is in their words "asking too much of their students." Although Mrs. Mathes's students are doing quite well in algebra, their grades are suffering in other subjects. Teachers in other subjects are complaining of the "excessive" work in math.

Mrs. Markham begins to think that introductory algebra is getting a bad reputation. Parents, incensed about the differences among teachers' grading systems, complain that students' grades are based on what teacher they get, and not on their knowledge of math. Each teacher is criticized for being too lenient, too strict, too demanding, or too structured. Mrs. Markham decides to standardize the curriculum for all the introductory algebra courses and mandates a specific test to be given at the end of the year. She takes it on herself to write the curriculum and make up the test. The test scores are to be used to determine the final grades of all the students.

How would you evaluate the grading system of each teacher? Is it fair to mandate a standardized grading system, but not give teachers voice in either the curriculum or the test construction? Is Mrs. Markham overstepping her bounds of responsibility? What would you do if you were Mrs. Mathes? Should she lower her expectations because other teachers, students, and parents complain about her assignments? Is it wrong for her to look for other methods of evaluation? Are some forms of evaluation fairer than others? Is there a moral issue about academic freedom? How does a teacher exercise fairness and good judgment about grading? Who should be the final authority on what an individual teacher believes are appropriate standards for evaluating student success? Justify your answer to teachers, students, and parents.

Case #5: Possible Cheating

Ms. Wright is a fourth-grade teacher at Central Elementary School, in a large suburban area near Metropolis. Some of Ms. Wright's children are having trouble in their subjects, but no more than usual. Until a few weeks ago, Jill had been having a lot of trouble in science. She had even told Ms. Wright she "hated" it. Over the past few weeks, however, Jill has improved in her science tests and experiments. Her science partner, Washington, a boy from a nearby town, has been helping her in the classroom experiments and seems to be turning Jill's interest around. After grading the latest test in science, Ms. Wright notices that Washington got the same answers right and the same answers wrong as Jill. Some of the essay answers were almost exactly the same in the use of words! They both got the same grade on the test.

The children sit next to each other in class. The possibility of cheating does exist. If you were Ms. Wright, what would you do? Should you watch these two more closely than other students? Should you separate them and thereby risk losing the interest in science Washington has inspired in Jill? Is it possible they prepared for the test together? Should you confront them about possible cheating? Should you give them a similar test to see how they do the next time? Should you make an announcement to the class that you suspect cheating, and give the class a whole new test? Defend your conclusions to your colleagues.

Case #6: Equal Justice

Mrs. Rodriguez, a junior high teacher at Oakdale, has a problem. Two boys in her English class, Jimmy and Ramon, are very close friends. They seem to disrupt the class whenever they get near each other. They talk, joke, and just clown around the way good friends often do. She has tried to separate them in class. That seems to work most of the time, but at other times they disrupt the demeanor of the class with their antics. Mrs. Rodriguez asks Mr. Davis, the principal, if she can switch one of the boys out of the class. Mr. Davis agrees, but only on the condition that Mrs. Rodriguez move the boy to one of her other classes. Mr. Davis explains that since every teacher already has more children in each class than the state board recommends, he cannot ask another teacher to take one more student.

Which child should Mrs. Rodriguez move? Both boys are at the same level when it comes to English. The other English classes Mrs. Rodriguez teaches either are honors classes or are less advanced than the class the boys are in currently. Whatever she does, Mrs. Rodriguez fears being accused of racism, since she and Ramon are both Hispanic. Mrs. Rodriguez decides to move Jimmy into the honors class. Within a week he is frustrated by the pace of the class. The other students don't like having an "undeserving" student in the class. They treat Jimmy like an outsider. Mrs. Rodriguez then places Jimmy in a lower class. Jimmy is quickly bored by the pace of that class and causes even more trouble for the other students than when he was with Ramon. Jimmy's academic performance begins to slip as well. Jimmy is now in danger of failing English.

What should Mrs. Rodriguez do? Should she forsake the needs of the larger group and leave the boys in the same class? Should she switch them again, placing Ramon in the lower class and Jimmy in the original class? Is it fair to sacrifice Ramon for Jimmy or even for the rest of the class? Is it fair to the other classes to overburden one of them with another student? Is it fair to make decisions about individual students in light of the teacher's ethnic affiliation? If she again insists one be moved out of her classes altogether, who should it be? On what criteria should such decisions be made? Make a judgment about what to do and present it to the class for discussion.

Case #7:   Equal Punishment

Ms. Palermo, a fourth-grade teacher at Springfield Elementary, has been a teacher for only one year. She loves teaching and the children and finds the challenge rewarding. She is shocked, however, when the other fourth-grade teachers chide her for being too lenient on matters of student punishment. The other three fourth-grade teachers agreed last year to spank children for severe offenses and make them write one hundred times on the board for lesser offenses. The teachers have come to Ms. Palermo because they think it is in the best interest of the school and the children to take a united front for punishment. They argue, "Fourth graders need to know where they stand. We can't always reason with them, so corporal punishment is needed sometimes. We must be consistent with them."

Ms. Palermo agrees about consistency but does not agree with corporal punishment. She feels there is no reason for such discipline in the modern classroom. She reluctantly agrees to the board writing and suggests a few disciplinary measures of her own (detention, extra work, separating the child from others, etc.). Although the other teachers are not happy with her suggestions, they agree to consider these alternatives.

Before she has time to meet with the other teachers again, Ms. Palermo notices Tommy, a fourth grader not in her class, in the lunchroom eating his lunch standing up. When she asks why, Tommy doesn't answer. Ms. Palermo persists. She learns Tommy has been spanked by Mr. Wang, his teacher. Ms. Palermo takes Tommy to the nurse and finds he has huge welts on the backs of his legs and on his buttocks. When Ms. Palermo confronts Mr. Wang about the welts, he says Tommy squirmed. This, Mr. Wang says, caused him to miss Tommy's buttocks and hit his legs instead. At this point Mr. Wang reminds Ms. Palermo that he doles out equal punishment to all children, without prejudice and with the greatest of care. He asks her and the nurse to forget the incident. He assures everyone that there will be no permanent damage to Tommy and notes that even the Bible teaches not to spare the rod and spoil the child.

What should Ms. Palermo do? Should she report this to the principal as suspected cruel punishment? Mr. Wang has been teaching a long time and is her department head. She doesn't have tenure yet. Does that matter? Did Tommy deserve the punishment? Did Mr. Wang just miss his mark when Tommy moved? What counts as "abuse"? Teachers do have to report suspected abuse, but what are the grounds for suspected abuse? Is it desirable to have consistency in punishment? Should teachers be different in how they punish? By what criteria should a teacher decide that a punishment "fits" the crime? Is Mr. Wang's action *punishment* or something else? What are the elements of legitimate punishment? Explain the reasons you relied on to arrive at your decision.

Case #8:   Cheerleading and Affirmative Action

Mrs. Arceneaux has been assigned the job of sponsor for the cheerleading squad at Montgomery High School. Minorities make up approximately 40 percent of the student body and 60 percent of the athletes on various sports teams. For years the eight-person cheerleading squad has never had more than one minority member.

Candidates for the cheerleading squad are judged on appearance, skill, and school spirit by a panel of three faculty, the student council president, the school newspaper editor, the co-captains of the cheerleading squad, and the captains of the football, basketball, and track teams. After the judging, a list of twenty qualified candidates is given to the sponsor. She is to choose twelve to be on the ballot for schoolwide election.

Mrs. Arceneaux has long been a believer in affirmative action. In fact, she has advocated the maintenance of quotas and sincerely believes it is a travesty of justice that the courts have not allowed the use of quotas in hiring and admissions policies.

Mrs. Arceneaux has also made up her mind that as long as she is sponsor of the cheerleaders, at least half of the team candidates will be from minorities, assuming there is a sufficient number of minorities on the list of twenty finalists.

Mrs. Arceneaux tells some friends of her decision. As the word gets out, teachers and community members alike complain to Mrs. Abdul, the principal, asking her to intervene. After all, the critics point out, in business, government, and higher education the use of quotas is illegal. What gives Mrs. Arceneaux the right to buck the moral sentiments expressed in the courts' no-quota rule?

What should Mrs. Abdul do? Does Mrs. Arceneaux have the right to use race or ethnic affiliation as a criterion for judging among the finalists? The no-quota rule is not about the issue at hand, but should it be a consideration, as Mrs. Arceneaux's critics suggest? How important is the composition of the cheerleading team? Is this a matter people should take seriously? Under the current practice is anyone being victimized? Under Mrs. Arceneaux's proposal will anyone be victimized? What should Mrs. Abdul be thinking about?

Case #9:   Punishing Good Kids: The Reluctant Drug Dealer

Steven Rosenstein is a senior. He is one month from graduation. Mrs. Walsh is his physics teacher. Steven's mother is Mrs. Walsh's gynecologist. Dr. Rosenstein once performed major surgery on Mrs. Walsh that may well have saved her life. Because Dr. Rosenstein believes Mrs. Walsh is such a fine teacher, she waived the part of Mrs. Walsh's fee not covered by insurance.

Mrs. Walsh overhears a conversation among several boys, each of whom is negotiating with Steven to buy amphetamines. Mrs. Walsh pulls Steven aside and warns him that he could ruin his whole life if he continues selling drugs. She tells him if he is arrested he will lose his scholarship to Yale and that will break his mother's heart. Since Steven's mother is divorced and Steven is an only child, Mrs. Walsh knows she is not exaggerating.

Steven acknowledges the truth in Mrs. Walsh's observations. His eyes well up with tears as he explains he has only used speed once or twice before. The other boys are his best friends, all top students, and all are unlikely to become regular or recreational drug users. They tell him they only use speed to help them study. Steven asks Mrs. Walsh what she intends to do.

Mrs. Walsh is genuinely distraught. After a few moments of thought she says, "I should take you to the principal's office. But I just can't risk hurting your mother needlessly. I'm going to believe you, Steven, but this had better be the end. I never want to hear about or see you with drugs ever again. I want you to give up drugs for any purpose. Do I have your word on that?"

Steven tearfully agrees. He pulls out a small packet of white pills and gives it to Mrs. Walsh. Mrs. Walsh puts her arm around Steven—both seem pleased that a big change has been made in each of their lives. Mrs. Walsh believes she has done the right thing. Steven seems to have learned a valuable lesson.

Six days before graduation, during finals week, Mrs. Walsh overhears Steven say to another boy, "This is the last time, Jay. Walsh caught me with this stuff once before and I can't risk getting caught again." Jay replies, "Thanks, Steven, you're a pal. These will be enough to get me through." Mrs. Walsh then peeks around the corner and sees Steven giving Jay a clear plastic bag of the familiar white pills and Jay giving Steven some folded paper money.

What should Mrs. Walsh do? Does the fact that Mrs. Walsh caught Steven once before matter in deciding what should be done now? Should Dr. Rosenstein's previous kindness to Mrs. Walsh matter at all in Mrs. Walsh's current consideration? Did she err in considering Dr. Rosenstein's previous kindness to her after the operation, or her status as a divorced mother of one when she caught Steven the first time? Given the facts, does Steven seem like a bad kid? Is punishment only for bad kids? If Steven loses his scholarship as a result of being caught this time, would that be excessive punishment? Who should decide whether or not a punishment is excessive? Is this a matter Mrs. Walsh should consider? Seventeen years ago Mrs. Walsh used amphetamines to study for her examinations. After college she never again used drugs—not even alcohol. Should that fact matter to her now as she tries to decide what to do? There is a school rule against possessing and selling drugs. There are laws against such behavior. How should these facts weigh in Mrs. Walsh's considerations? Steven is one of Mrs. Walsh's favorite students. Should that matter to her now? Explain your thinking.

Case #10:   Being Hassled

Mrs. Blake has taught family relations for fourteen years at Lyndon B. Johnson High School. She has often seen students act in unusual ways. When Ning Fong runs past Mrs. Blake and into the restroom, Mrs. Blake knows immediately that something is wrong. Ning Fong seems to be crying and her clothes are in disarray. Mrs. Blake follows her into the restroom and asks two other girls in the restroom to leave them alone. Ning does not speak English very well and is also very shy. She doesn't want to answer Mrs. Blake's questions. Mrs. Blake persists. Finally, the story she gets from Ning Fong runs something like this:

The Devils Disciples, a local gang, started teasing her as she went outside to join her friends for lunch. They said mean things about her race and her body. Frightened, she said nothing in return but tried to hurry away. Provoked by this show of fear, the gang members began describing things they would like to do to her sexually. Finally, the boys started reaching out and grabbing at her body parts and tearing at her blouse. Most of the Devil's Disciples are black.

In this inner-city school, 63 percent of the students are black, 21 percent are Hispanic, 11 percent are Asian, 4 percent are white and 1 percent is Native American. The vast majority of students come from families in the lowest socioeconomic categories. Among the teachers and professional staff 46 percent are black, 36 percent are white, 12 percent are Hispanic, and 6 percent are other. All of the administrators are minorities. Mrs. Blake is white.

Ning has made it unequivocally clear that she will not tell anyone else about this event. After all, she says, no real harm was done. Ning told Mrs. Blake three of the gang members' names. Mrs. Blake recalls seeing them at the door of the school yelling at Ning as she came running in. All three are in Mrs. Blake's family relations class—a class most students take because they think it will be fun and an easy grade.

Mrs. Blake, a feminist, believes deep in her heart that Ning Fong is wrong when she says no real harm was done. Mrs. Blake is adamant in her beliefs that females should never be made to suffer at the hands of bullying, insensitive males. She is deeply incensed and thinks something should be done. Without Ning's cooperation there is no possibility of pressing charges against the boys. Even with Ning's support, her shyness and broken English may keep her from being a convincing witness.

The school authorities are concerned about issues of campus security, but, for the most part, they are content to "just keep the lid on things." As long as there are no riots or serious injuries on school property—the sort of thing that attracts public criticism—the administration tries to keep a low profile.

Mrs. Blake considers three courses of action. First, she could confront the school officials and try to force them into action. Second, she could confront the boys in class risking personal injury to herself and perhaps endangering Ning. Third, she could appeal to the media to do an exposè. Before deciding, Mrs. Blake reflects on her own motivations. She wants to be fair to all involved: the gang members, Ning Fong, and the school authorities. Mrs. Blake begins searching her conscience to ascertain the full extent of her motivations.

Mrs. Blake, who is from a well-to-do family, attended a prestigious women's college in the East. Her husband is a successful lawyer. Mrs. Blake works in the inner city because she is a crusader for the underdog. She always has been. She particularly finds herself quick to anger when confronted with acts of male oppressiveness, violence, or vindictiveness. Mrs. Blake thinks women have been made to suffer long enough under male dominance. Knowing her persistent concern with such feminist issues has sometimes biased her judgments of the actions of men, she tries very hard to guard against this. She is a feminist because she believes in justice and fair play for all. She is not a female chauvinist. Since the neighborhood where she grew up was free of gangs and was inhabited by few minorities, Mrs. Blake does not feel right about forcing her cultural imperatives on others. Still, she knows people cannot learn to live together if they are at war with one another or busy victimizing one another. Respect for personhood and a desire for interdependent cooperation are the only ways people can find security and optimize their opportunities for individual happiness.

After much reflection, Mrs. Blake concludes that a subculture dominated by gangs harboring little respect for women is morally corrupt. Good people must act to change such attitudes within that subculture. Good people must possess the virtue of moral courage because any action undertaken in such circumstances is liable to place the actor at risk.

Remembering the Supreme Court case of *Pickering*, Mrs. Blake concludes that she has the general approval of society to speak her mind publicly regarding the conditions of her school. Furthermore, she concludes that in a class on family relations, male class members must be confronted with any demeaning attitudes they may have regarding women. They must be told straight out that such attitudes are wrong. Mrs. Blake begins developing a plan of action to implement each of these conclusions.

Is Mrs. Blake doing the right thing? How does Mrs. Blake know she is acting on morally right motivations and not just on the basis of her elitist education and family upbringing? What right does Mrs. Blake have to try to change the attitudes of the gang members? What right did Mrs. Blake have to interrogate Ning and coax her to tell things she obviously wanted to keep to herself? Is Mrs. Blake, an acknowledged crusader for causes, naive in risking the wrath of both administrators and gang members? Should the potential threat to her job and to her personal safety deter Mrs. Blake from moving ahead on this issue? Should the Supreme Court's decision in *Pickering* matter to Mrs. Blake? Does Mrs. Blake have a right to act as Ning's champion? Is it an *obligation* to act in her behalf? If all the teachers in Mrs. Blake's school started thinking and acting as Mrs. Blake does, what do you think would happen to the school and neighborhood? Would you want Mrs. Blake for a friend? Would you hire Mrs. Blake as a teacher? Would you want Mrs. Blake teaching your children? Would you like to role-model Mrs. Blake in your career? Do you think Mrs. Blake is racially and ethnically tolerant and has a *transcultural* perspective on her job? Outline the steps you think Mrs. Blake should follow at this point.

Case #11: Religious Conscience

Mr. Barrett teaches sixth grade at St. Elizabeth's parochial school. He is offended by the religion lessons given to his students once a week by Ms. Primm, the school's director of religious education. Mr. Barrett approaches Ms. Winsome, the school principal, and complains that when Ms. Primm teaches she makes demeaning remarks about the cruelty of Arabic Muslims in centuries past. Mr. Barrett explains that he has a student, Ishmael, who is a native-born Iraqi. Mr. Barrett feels that Ms. Primm's comments hurt Ishmael's feelings and make him so depressed he seems wholly distracted the rest of each day. Ishmael's parents have even spoken to Mr. Barrett and asked if Ishmael could be sent to the library or assigned other work in lieu of attending Ms. Primm's weekly class. Mr. Barrett tells Ms. Winsome that he was very appreciative of the respectful and almost timid way Ishmael's parents broached the subject.

Ms. Winsome informs Mr. Barrett that no allowances can be made in Ishmael's case. She points out that St. Elizabeth's is a private, religious school. This is the one place parents can bring their children to get a good education along with religious instruction. When they enrolled their children at St. Elizabeth's, Ishmael's parents and the parents of several other children knew that religious instruction was part of the curriculum. Families are free to send their children to the public schools or to another private school if they object to the curriculum at St. Elizabeth's.

Mr. Barrett protests that people from other religions work hard to enroll their children at St. Elizabeth's because it has such an outstanding academic reputation. These families always pay the full tuition unlike many families who are members of St. Elizabeth's congregation. Since they pay their way, aren't their children entitled to a classroom experience free of such blatant prejudice? Mrs. Winsome brings the conversation to an end by announcing, "That's not for either you or me to decide. Ms. Primm is the director of religious education, and it is up to her to decide on the proper content of her classes."

Mr. Barrett had previously spoken to Ms. Primm about her teaching. He found her very dogmatic and concluded there was no point in going back to her. Still, he feels uncomfortable about doing nothing. Ishmael is polite and earnest and a serious student. He doesn't deserve such insensitivity on the part of school officials. Mr. Barrett considers ignoring Ms. Winsome's decision and on his own authority send Ishmael to the library. Ishmael could spend his time in the library studying his own religion and comparing it with that of other students at St. Elizabeth's. In making that decision, would Mr. Barrett be guilty of insubordination? The church and its parishioners are paying the majority of his salary. If he is insubordinate, is he betraying their confidence in him? Perhaps Mr. Barrett should consider resigning from St. Elizabeth's. Perhaps he should advise Ishmael's parents to take their child to another school. That decision doesn't feel quite right to Mr. Barrett either. Should he go to the local media and complain about St. Elizabeth's callousness? That, too, seems wrong. What should Mr. Barrett *do?*

Is prejudice all right if clothed in religious rhetoric? Is religious education to be subjected to the implicit approval of mainstream society? How important is it to protect religious or private education? How important is it to protect Ishmael? Who should act in Ishmael's behalf? What should Mr. Barrett identify as his principal duty? What should Ms. Winsome identify as her principal duty? What should Mrs. Primm identify as her principal duty? What should Ishmael's parents identify as their principal duty?

IV.   Professional Planning

Throughout this book much has been said about teachers' duties regarding concepts such as respect for persons; disciplinary rigor; cultural, gender, and socioeconomic studies; mutual interdependence; the moral community of the teaching profession; acting in accord with individual conscience; and much more. In this chapter you have been given two exercises to advance your understanding and respect for other cultures. In addition, you have been provided with several provocative cases to focus your attention on the subtlety of the challenges that confront the professionally conscientious teacher. Now, a final activity will help you prepare a plan that should advance your achievements as a professional.

Figure 7.3 is a Moral Self-Assessment Protocol (MSP). Copy this form in a notebook for as many goals as you think should direct your professional life. Be careful to keep your goals simple. Goals that are too specific are not goals, but objectives. Goals that are too numerous are difficult to track. Goals should be universal-like statements

GOAL: Statement of Ideal.	Objective related to goal: An "ought" statement prescribing something you should do or not do.	Assessment: Note how often you have been deficient in each objective.	Evaluation: Construct a hypothesis explaining your deficiencies for each objective.	Plan: Changes to be made and protocols to be maintained to further the achievement of this objective in your professional life.

You will need to complete one of these protocols for each goal that frames your professional life. Limit the number of objectives associated with each goal to six. More than that and your protocol will appear unwieldy.

Figure 7.3 **Wagner-Kierstead Moral Self-Assessment Protocol**

---

of ideals that are easily agreed-to by the teaching profession. In this first attempt, your instructor may want you to start with no more than ten clearly stated goals.

With each goal, you will identify one to six objectives. Objectives are specific moral rules you intend to follow as you incorporate your ideals into your classroom practice. Periodically, you should assess your success in following each rule. The assessment portion of the protocol is a record of the extent of your success as well as the frequency and intensity of your failures after a determined period of time. (For beginning teachers, this may be every six to ten weeks. For more experienced teachers, it might be once a semester.) After assessment, must come evaluation. The evaluation should identify both the causes and effects of any transgression. In particular, the effects your transgressions have had on other people should be noted. Finally, when your evaluation is complete, you must articulate a plan for the future. This plan will ordinarily consist of initiatives that can bring you closer to fulfillment of each articulated objective. On rare occasions, the plan may call for a revision of your original objective—or rarer yet, a revision of your goal. Any changes in behavior recommended by your plan ought to be subsequently reflected in your next Moral

Self-Assessment Protocol, which you will immediately construct. After the allotted time, your new objectives with all of those you retain will again be assessed and evaluated and will lead to a new plan, just as this review did.

This technique, common to evaluation theory, is designed to help you ascertain *your duties* in concert with the rest of *your profession*. Figure 7.4 provides an example of how an actual teacher used the Moral Self-Assessment Protocol to address one goal. As you can see from the example, the teacher tried to keep the goal statement and objectives simple. Remember, this protocol is for his personal use, and not for review by anyone else. The assessment was made six weeks after the teacher had constructed his original goal and set of objectives. His assessment notes the number of lapses associated with his attempt to implement each objective into his professional repertoire. His evaluation of the assessment data reveals what he takes to be the causes of these lapses, as well as the effects they had on students. (Although he mentions no positive benefits for the objectives he met, the evaluation helps him further plan for his next protocol.)

Once the evaluation was complete, the teacher was able to plan in an informed and a systematic way. In this case, the teacher saw no need to modify either his goal or his objectives. His decision to assign time each week for students to explain the relation of current studies to their own cultural background should be included either in parentheses or as item a under objective 5 in the subsequent self-assessment protocol he prepares for the next review process.

The MSP concludes this book's efforts to move you from the protected environment of the university classroom to a more professional approach to your teaching career. The attempt has not been to make bad people good or good people better. Rather, the task has been to draw attention to the subtlety and the challenge of teaching professionally and morally in the multicultural world in which we live.

In summary, this chapter is designed to give you practice in making responsible moral choices. Adequate solutions require you to be both detailed and subtle in your thinking. It is important that you recognize the complications and contributions of various cultures to the school's social milieu. Probably the next time you engage in such deliberation, it will be for real. Teachers make mistakes, but the mark of a professional is to minimize them. Furthermore, when the inevitable error occurs, the professional learns from it and does not repeat it. Remember, professional teachers are first and foremost moral agents who must live with high standards. Moral agents live in a world of uncertainty. They must *act* as if their decisions are fully informed by TRUTH, knowing all the while how elusive TRUTH really is. While our moral actions must be based on reasoning that is forever tentative, there is a big difference between an individual who acts with such cautions in mind and an individual who concludes that all is relative and subjective. The former is characteristic of morally mature people, while the latter represents those seeking license for the most capricious and whimsical moral behavior. Teachers must ensure that they and their colleagues are people of the first sort. We must act in ways that show we genuinely CARE about getting it right. We must act to make for a better world. We must act in such a way that role-models our high regard for the moral domain of human experience.

GOAL: Statement of Ideal.	Objective related to goal: An "ought" statement prescribing something you should do or not do.	Assessment: Describe how successful you have been in following the objective.	Evaluation: Describe how your efforts have succeeded in making you an appropriate role model for students.	Plan: Changes to be made and protocols to be maintained to further the achievement of this objective in your professional life.
A: *Respect all students equally*	1. I should never single out a student for public ridicule. 2. I should never knowingly punish an innocent student, no matter how much good might result. 3. I ought to listen attentively to every subject-matter observation a student makes. 4. I ought to evaluate students' work as objectively as possible. 5. I should show interest in the cultural background of every student.	1. *During the past six weeks I* made sarcastic comments to three students because I was frustrated with their performance. 2. Punishments successfully directed toward offending parties only. 3. Except during periods of frustration, attentiveness to student comments has been optimal. 4. Evaluation of student work is consistently objective. 5. Have not had time to discuss such matters with students.	1. Objectives 2 and 4 are met. These are strengths in my professional behavior. 2. Objectives 1 and 3 are generally successful though I seem to lose control when frustrated. This distracts from the ideal I am trying to role-model. 3. Objective 5 has not been met during the past six weeks.	1. Continue as currently proceeding. 2. Reflect on the causes of frustration and then implement ways either to avoid the situation or to manage frustration better (e.g., through exercise extending my sense of self-control). 3. Take time at least once a week to ask at least three students to show something from their own cultural background that gives them a special angle or insight on the subject currently being studied.

Figure 7.4 Sample Wagner-Kierstead Moral Self-Assessment Protocol

NOTES

1. For example, see Lawrence Kohlberg, "Stage and Sequence: The Cognitive Developmental Approach to Socialization," in *Handbook of Socialization Theory and Research*, D. A. Goslin, ed. (New York: Rand McNally, 1969); Richard Dawkins, *The Selfish Gene,* (New York: Oxford University Press, 1976); Philip Kitcher, *Vaulting Ambition* (Cambridge: MIT Press, 1985); and Trivers, "The Evolution of Reciprocal Altruism," *Quarterly Review of Biology* 46 (Spring 1971): 35–39, 45–47.

2. For further elaboration of this point from an economist's viewpoint, see Robert Axelrod, *The Evolution of Cooperation* (New York: Basic Books, 1984).

3. As this pertains to college campuses, see Richard D. Alba, *Ethnic Identity: The Transformation of White America* (New Haven: Yale University Press, 1991). The author cites over two hundred incidents of bigotry on college campuses directed at race, gender, and groups exhibiting a minority sexual preference. See also Howard J. Ehrlich, *Campus Ethnoviolence and the Policy Options* (Washington, D.C.: National Institute Against Prejudice and Violence, 1991).

4. New York State Department of Education, A *Curriculum of Inclusion: A Report of the Commissioner's Taskforce on Minorities* (Albany, N.Y.: State Printing Office, 1991).

5. See Diane Ravitch, Arthur Schlesinger, et al., "A Reply to the New York Report of the Commissioner's Taskforce on Minorities," *Newsday,* June 29, 1990. The authors claim the report "contemptuously dismisses the Western Tradition" . . . and declare further that "the Western Tradition is the source of individual freedom and democracy to which other cultures aspire."

6. For an excellent discussion of lying, see Sissela Bok, *Lying: a Moral Choice in Public & Private Life* (New York: Pantheon Books, 1978). See also Sissela Bok, *Secrets* (New York: Pantheon Books, 1983).

Glossary of Terms Common to Moral Philosophy

Action An *intentional* effort to engage the world in particular fashion. The word *action* avoids the sterility of the term *behavior*.

Duty The consequence of the creation and assignment of rights. In the domain of morality, a duty exists when a moral agent recognizes a compelling obligation to act or forego acting, in behalf of another.

Equality Treating everyone the same. When this is done *without* regard to relevant differences, considerable unfairness can result. For example, it costs more money to ensure equal education for the physically disabled. To spend the same number of dollars on all students alike would cause serious harm to the disabled.

Fair To assign to no one a disadvantage prior to an activity's commencing. This does not prohibit differential treatment of persons—only the assignment of disadvantages (events inhibitory of self-fulfilling actions). In more rough-and-ready fashion we might say that as a rule of thumb, fairness is a matter of treating equals equally and unequals unequally.

Freedom Absence of restraint.

Guilt The natural emotional response to wrongdoing.

Justice Following the rules of fair. Justice involves such things as distributing the goods and risks of communal life without prejudice.

License No community social norms prohibiting or inhibiting a behavior, thus freeing the individual to pursue a plan of action.

Morals Statements that prescribe or prohibit action. The key moral term in such sentences is the self-revealing *should* or *ought*.

Moral discourse The realm of language use in which people try to figure out what they ought and ought not to do.

Obligation An intellectual awakening to the fact that if individuals do not act as they ought, they will suffer guilt. Failure to suffer guilt when knowingly engaged in wrongdoing is central to the psychiatric diagnosis of a sociopath. For all others, guilt is educative. It serves to inform people of their obligations.

Pathologic guilt An unnatural emotional response to wrongdoing or alleged wrongdoing. If a person feels guilt when no wrong is done, the feeling is pathologic. Similarly, if a person feels excessive guilt for minor infractions or minimal guilt for grave infractions, the response may again be pathologic.

Respect   A decision to regard persons, objects, or rules as meriting special consideration when creating a plan of action. This is not just an expression of preference or valuing. It is an intellectual event, as opposed to an emotional event.

Right   A human artifact. Rights are prescribed specific protections for the purpose of managing social relations. Rights create license for one or more persons simultaneous with the creation of duties on the part of others. In this sense, rights and duties are properly understood as two sides of a single concept. Whenever a right is created, a duty is created that thereafter obligates one or more other individuals. No right was ever created that did not simultaneously create one or more duties obligating others.

Value   An intentional preference, showing desire for one thing, person, gesthetic quality or plan of action over another. Value is simply a morally neutral report of desire. It suggests nothing about the moral merit of what is desired.

Court Cases

Beeze v. Smith (501 P 2d, 159, Alaska, 1972)

Board of Education v. Rowley (458 U.S. 176, 1982)

Brown v. Board of Education of Topeka (349 U.S. 249, 75 S. Ct. 753, 1953)

Brown v. Board of Education of Topeka (347 U.S. D.C. 483, 1954)

Chiaramine v. Immigration and Naturalization Service (626 F 2d 1093 2d Cir., 1980)

Cisneros v. Corpus Christi ISD (324 F. Sup. 599, 1970)

Davenport v. Randolph Co. School Board of Education (730 F 2d 1395, 1984)

Desedare v. Schweiker (683 F. 2d. 1138 5th Cir., 1982)

District #8 Seiling v. Swanson (551, P 2d, OK 496, 1973)

East Hartford Education Association v. Board of Education of Town of East Hartford (562 F. 2d 838 U.S. 2d Cir., 1977)

Edgewood ISD v. Kirby (No. 362 516, Travis Co. D. C., 1987)

Elrod v. Burns (96 S. Ct. 2673 U.S., 1976)

Garrison v. State of Louisiana (379 U.S. 64, 85 S. Ct. 209, 13 L. Ed. 2nd 125 [125], 1965)

Gaylord v. Tacoma School District No. 10 (88 Wash. 2d 286, 559 p.2d 286 1340, cert. denied, 434 U.S. 879, 1977)

Gillett v. Unified School District No. 276 (605 Kans. p. 2d. 105, 1980)

Green v. County School Board (391 U.S. 430, 442, 1968)

Griffin v. County School Board of Prince Edward County (377 U.S. 198, 86 S. Ct. 1226, 1964)

Grove v. Mead School District No. 354 (753, F 2nd, 1528, 1985)

Hobson v. Hansen (393 U.S. 801, 89, 1985)

Ingraham v. Wright (430 U.S. 651, 662, 97 S. Ct. 1401, 1407, 51 L. Ed. 2d 711, 1977)

In Re Gault (387 U.S. 1, 1966)

Irby v. State of Texas (751 S. W. 2d. 670 [Tex. app.-Eastland], 1988) .

Island Schools v. Grove (393, U.S. 757, 88, 1980)

Island Schools Free School District No. 26 v. Pico (1982)

Keyishian v. Board of Regents (385 U.S. 589, 87 S. Ct. 675, 1967)

Keyes v. School District No. 1, Denver, Colorado (93 S. Ct. 2686, 1973)

Kirby v. Edgewood Independent School District (804 S. W. 2d 491, 1989)

Lau v. Nichols (414 U.S. 563, 39 L. Ed. 2d, 1974)

Lead Industries Ass'n. Inc. v. Environmental Protection Agency (647 F. 2d 1130, D. C. Cir., 1980)

Martin Luther King Elementary School Children v. Ann Arbor School District (U.S. Dist. Mich. Civ. Action #7-71876, 1979)

Mercer v. North Forest School District (538, S. W. App., Texas, 1976)

Milliken v. Brandley (402 U.S. 717, 94 S. Ct. 3112, 1974)

Mozert v. Hawkins County Public Schools (827 F 2nd, 1058, 1985)

Neuhaus v. Federico (12 Or. App. 314, 505, 1973)

New Jersey v. T.L.O. (469 U.S. 325, 1985)

New York Times Co. v. Sullivan (376 U.S. 254, 280, 84 S. Ct. 710, 726, 11 L.Ed. 2d 686, 1964)

Pickering v. Board of Education of Township High School District 205, Will County, Illinois (391 U.S. 563, 1968)

Pierce v. Society of Sisters (268 U.S. 510, 1925)

Plessy v. Ferguson (163 U.S. Dis. Ct. 537, 1896)

Plyler v. Doe (457 U.S. 202, reh'g denied, 458 U.S. 1131, 1982)

Quinlan v. University Place, South Dakota (660P. 2d 329 [Wash. App. 1983])

Rogers v. Paul (382 U.S. 198, 86 S. Ct. 1226, 1964)

San Antonio ISD v. Rodriguez (411 U.S., S. Ct. 1, 1973)

Shelton v. Tucker (364 U.S. 479, 81 S. Ct. 247, 1960)

Stuart v. School District No. 1 ([of Kalamazoo], 30 Mich. 69, 1874)

Swann v. Charlotte-Mecklenburg Board of Education (402 U.S. 1, 911 S. Ct. 1267, 1967)

Texas v. Certain Named and Unnamed Undocumented Alien Children (1980)

Tinker v. Des Moines Community I.C.S.D. (939 U.S. 505, 1969)

Trent v. Perritt (391 F. Supp, 171 Miss., 1975)

Weiman v. Updegraff (344 U.S. 183, 73 S. Ct. 215, 97 L. Ed. 216, 1952)

About the Authors

Fred D. Kierstead, Ph.D., is professor of educational foundations and studies of the future at the University of Houston-Clear Lake. He has served as president of the Education Section, World Future Society, and as president of the Southwest Philosophy of Education Society. Dr. Kierstead is review editor for *Vitae Scholasticae* and the *Journal of Thought* and coauthor of *The Far Side of the Future, Educational Futures: Sourcebook I,* and *The Future in Education: Problems, Possibilities and Promise.* He is a member of the Long-range Planning Committee, Texas Education Agency, and has been active in national and state-level planning for public education. Dr. Kierstead has been a Fulbright Scholar in Egypt; taught in Nigeria, South Vietnam, and the Philippines; and written numerous articles and chapters in books pertaining to comparative education, multicultural education, and the future of education.

Paul A. Wagner, Ph.D., is professor of philosophy and educational foundations, University of Houston-Clear Lake. He is director of the Institute for Logic and Cognitive Studies and director of the university's self-study. Dr. Wagner has also served as a leader in the university's strategic planning efforts, student and program outcomes assessment and the design of a management information system. Dr. Wagner is currently secretary/treasurer of the Philosophy of Education Society, vice-president of the Association of Philosophers in Education, and president of the Texas Education Foundation Society. He is also a member of the American Philosophical Association, the Philosophy of Science Association, and the American Educational Studies Association. Dr. Wagner is the author of over seventy articles, book chapters, and reviews. He is an editorial associate of *Brain and Behavioral Sciences,* served on the editorial boards of *Focus on Learning* and the *Journal of Thought* and served as an editorial consultant to *Instructional Sciences.*

Index

Environment
    formation of social structures, 25–30
    influence on potential for learning, 120–21
Equal opportunity, educational
    consensus and role of schools, 100–101
    educational policies and economics, 119
    expulsion and suspension as punishments, 66
    theory and practice in multicultural
        teaching, 135
Escalante, Jaime, 34–35
Escuelitas, 139
ESL (English as a Second Language) education,
    126–30
Establishment, 31–38
Ethical egoism, 3
Ethical egotism, 3
Ethical nihilism, 3
Ethical relativism, 3–4
Ethics, codes of. *See* Codes of ethics
Ethnic groups
    definitions, 87
    need for diversity and cultural pluralism,
        96–102, 104–6
Ethnic studies, 99–100, 111
Ethnism, 87
Ethnocentrism, 104
European Economic Community (EEC), 166
Expulsion, as punishment, 65–67

F

Family, 87–88
Family Educational Rights and Privacy Act of
    1974, 101
Feminism, 189
Freedmen's Bureau, 90
Freedom, 53, *54*
Free speech, 73–74

G

Gangs, 188–90
Garrison v. State of Louisiana (1964), 73
Genocide, 92
Gestalt psychology, 44–45
Ghettos, 89–90
Goals, professional planning, 191–92
Grading, 183–84
Green v. County School Board (1968), 91
*Griffin v. County School Board of Prince Edward
    County* (1964), 106
Grooming, 182
Grove v. Mead School District No. 354 (1985),
    108–9

H

Hairstyles, 182
Handicapped students, 78, 108
Happiness, 59–61
Hedonism, 6
Hegel, Georg, 27
High culture, 31, 33
Hispanics. *See also* Mexican-Americans
    American history and cultural experience,
        93–94
    community and multicultural education, 139
    segregation and discrimination, 107
History
    American experience of enculturation,
        83–84, 87–96
    Horatio Alger myth in educational, 152–53
    multicultural teaching, 119–20
    mutual dependence in real world, 56–57
    mythology and moral courage, 42
    teaching and professionalism, 151–52
Hitler, Adolf, 20, 30
Hobbes, Thomas, 52–59
Hobson v. Hansen (1985), 109
Holocaust, 29
Hume, David, 17, 18

I

Illinois, 70–74
Illiteracy. *See* Literacy
Immigration, 83, 95–96
Immigration Act of 1965, 95
Immigration Acts of 1917 and 1924, 97
Individualization, 163. *See also* Site-based
        management
Ingraham v. Wright (1977), 65
Inheritance, 120–21
In Re Gault (1966), 75
Intellectual disposition, 12
Intelligence, 121. *See also* IQ tests
Intentions
    nonconsequentialism, 8
    rule utilitarianism, 12
Interdependency
    as central theme, 165–66
    group competition, 56
    history of mutual in real world, 56–57
    teachers and professional responsibility, 172
Internment, Japanese-Americans, 69, 95
Intersubjective agreement, 4–5
Intuitions, moral, 39
IQ tests, 34, 120–21
Irby v. State of Texas (1988), 76

Public policy
    moral debate, 18
    utilitarianism, 6
Punishment. *See also* Corporal punishment
    case studies, 186, 187–88
    law and morality of in schools, 63–67

Q

Quinlan v. University Place, South Dakota (1983), 65

R

Racism
    apathy and moral challenge, 41–42
    in curricula, teaching, and educational institutions, 131–34
    definition, 130–31
    influence of heredity and environment on learning potential, 121
Rawls, John, 17–18
Reagan, Ronald, 94
Reflective equilibrium. *See* Rule utilitarianism
Reform, legal, 62–63
Religion
    case study, 190–91
    consequentialist thinking, 6
    nonconsequentialism, 8
Remedial education, 107
Reservations, Native-American, 92
Respect
    culture and moral universals, 16
    intellectual disposition, 12
    rule utilitarianism, 10
Review panels, 109
Right, concept of, 3–4
Rights. *See also* Constitution; Supreme Court
    court cases describing student, 75–77
    court cases describing teacher, 77–78
    moral elements of punishment, 64
Rogers v. Paul (1964), 106
Role models, 151
Roosevelt, Franklin, 95
Rousseau, Jean Jacques, 27
Rule utilitarianism, 10, *11*, *12*, *13*

S

San Antonio ISD v. Rodriguez (1973), 107
Schools. *See also* Education; Teaching
    common sense and order, 75–78
    consensus and role of in multicultural education, 100–102, 104–6
    cultural diversity, 30–32

law and morality of punishment, 63–67
    mandatory attendance laws, 91
Science, 105, 124–25
Search
    case studies, 181–82
    court cases and student rights, 75–78
Segregation, 106–8. *See also* Civil rights movement; Racism
Seizure
    case studies, 181–82
    court cases and student rights, 75–78
Selective inclusion, 132
Self-interest, 44
Selfish-gene theory, 14–15
Semiprofession, 153–54
Separatism, 99–100, 111
Sexism, 41, 43
Sexual harassment, 188–90
Simulation games, 8–10, 12
Site-based management, 140, 162–63
Skinner, B. F., 28
Slavery
    African-Americans and cultural experience, 90
    culture and societal reforms, 29
    intersubjective agreement, 4–5
    moral courage, 40
Slogans, 102
Social competition, 52–53
Social contract, 53–54, 59, 172
Social forum, school as, *103*, 105–6
Social justice, 60
Social movements, 2. *See also* Civil rights movement
Social psychology, 44–47
Social responsibility, 138–39
Social structures, 25–30
Social sympathy, 17–18
Society. *See also* Culture
    elements of ethical analysis, 39
    trends and prospects in education, *161*
Sociobiology, 14–15
South Africa, 29
Sovereignty, 74
Standardized tests, 109–10
Stereotyping, 131
Student rights, 75–77
Success, educational, 135–36
Suffrage movement, 57
Supreme Court
    African-American cultural experience and education, 91
    censorship and minority inclusion, 108
    de jure and *de facto* segregation, 106–7
    education equality and constitutional rights, 66